Marcello Mollica (Ed.)

# Fundamentalism

# Freiburger Sozialanthropologische Studien
# Fribourg Studies in Social Anthropology
# Etudes d'Anthropologie Sociale de l'Université de Fribourg

herausgegeben von/edited by/édité par

Christian Giordano (Universität Fribourg, Schweiz)

in Verbindung mit/in cooperation with/avec la collaboration de

Edouard Conte (Universität Bern),
Mondher Kilani (Universität Lausanne),
Véronique Pache Huber (Universität Fribourg, Schweiz),
Klaus Roth (Universität München),
François Ruegg (Universität Fribourg, Schweiz)

Band 44

LIT

# FUNDAMENTALISM

## Ethnographies on Minorities, Discrimination and Transnationalism

edited by

Marcello Mollica

LIT

Cover image: Refugees on the Turkish-Syrian Border;
Photo by Selmet Güler

This book is printed on acid-free paper.

**Bibliographic information published by the Deutsche Nationalbibliothek**
The Deutsche Nationalbibliothek lists this publication in the Deutsche Nationalbibliografie; detailed bibliographic data are available on the Internet at http://dnb.d-nb.de.

ISBN 978-3-643-80201-9

**A catalogue record for this book is available from the British Library**


Klosbachstr. 107
CH-8032 Zürich
Tel. +41 (0) 44-251 75 05
E-Mail: zuerich@lit-verlag.ch http://www.lit-verlag.ch
**Distribution:**
In the UK: Global Book Marketing, e-mail: mo@centralbooks.com
In North America: International Specialized Book Services, e-mail: orders@isbs.com
In Germany: LIT Verlag Fresnostr. 2, D-48159 Münster
Tel. +49 (0) 2 51-620 32 22, Fax +49 (0) 2 51-922 60 99, e-mail: vertrieb@lit-verlag.de
In Austria: Medienlogistik Pichler-ÖBZ, e-mail: mlo@medien-logistik.at
e-books are available at www.litwebshop.de

# Contents

# Acknowledgments

We wish to thank Professor Nicolas Hayoz for his support and assistance and Ms. Lura Ann Munsel for her English language revision of the chapters.

We also wish to thank the Marie Curie International Research Staff Exchange Scheme Fellowship within the 7th European Community Framework Programme (grant no: PIRSES-GA-2012-318961) for supporting a number of seminars that later developed into some of the chapters included in this volume.

This publication was made possible through funds from the Academic Swiss Caucasus Net (ASCN) program, supported by the Gebert Rüf Stiftung, coordinated and operated by the Interfaculty Institute for Central and Eastern Europe (IICEE) at the University of Fribourg and the Department of Social Anthropology, University of Fribourg.

# Introduction

*Marcello Mollica*

The lady had serious foot problems and a bag with food rations for three days for her husband, her son and herself. Although she was proudly trying to hold back her tears, they streamed down her face as if down well-ploughed furrows. It was my last interview, the third of the day. I had asked to speak with Armenian refugees who fled Aleppo in 2016. However, all families contacted the day before and that morning denied the request. The group contacting potential interviewees was an NGO based in a narrow alley on the second floor of a new building on the right side of Marash Street, in Beirut's Armenian quarter of Bourj Hammoud. The social workers asked me whether I wanted to continue to interview people who escaped from 2012 to 2015, and I agreed.

I conducted this interview when a good portion of this introduction had already been written, but what the lady told me in that quarter of an hour deeply affected its content, making it cogently alive. Hers was a middle-class Armenian family, owning a home and a shop; her son was employed at a nearby church. However, six months after the war reached Aleppo, the family's home, shop and church suddenly found themselves too close to the front line. First, the shop was bombed; next, the house was hit by a rocket; finally, members of a jihadist faction allied with the Western-supported so-called Free Syrian Army visited the church, warning the priest that they would return in a few days and kill all employees.

In less than a week, the three of them had lost virtually everything they owned. A few days later, they left for Yerevan via the still-functioning Aleppo Airport, which they reached by paying twenty times the normal rate on a taxi ride that took about two hours since many roads were controlled by the Free Syrian Army or jihadist factions. Once in Yerevan, they were relocated in a town about an hour from the capital and enrolled in an assistance program. However, one evening, about two months later, a drug addict looking for money repeatedly stabbed the woman's son outside their rented apartment. Taken to the hospital in critical condition, he was discharged after numerous operations, while remaining disabled. After a month, her husband suffered a stroke that rendered him partially disabled as well.

The three decided to leave the Republic of Armenia for Lebanon, where they found accommodations in Bourj Hammoud and could survive with community support. However, when transnational Armenian agencies began to help refugees by relocating them abroad (at the time of my fieldwork there were opportunities in Canada), the three began coming on a daily basis hoping to be selected (which is why I met the lady).

Yet, in the end, the interview took an unexpected turn. Although she had been told the aim of my research, the woman asked the social worker who was facilitating the interview, translating from Armenian to French, whether I could take them to Europe. I replied that I did not have that power, adding that, if nothing else, as Armenians, unlike others, they had a second passport. Although the social workers kept trying to dissuade her, she suddenly removed a transparent folder from her bag where she kept their documents. These included temporary Armenian passports valid for two years that she wanted to show in a desperate attempt to convince me. Told again by the social worker that I could not help, she left without saying goodbye, leaving us stunned.

Were they wrong to ask her to tell me her story? Was I mistaken in asking them to ask her? Could she, from the beginning, have hidden objectives or expectations that we, unwittingly, fed? Whatever the truth may be, in that woman's tears were all the themes I had wanted to touch upon in this introduction: from fundamentalism to transnationalism, from religiously driven deviations to challenges in data collection, from researcher's mistakes to interviewee's expectations.

* * *

If the ongoing *Lebanisation* of the conflicts in what were once Syria and Iraq produced an immediate victim it was "language". This created an absolute confusion that subsumed the Syrian victims trapped in events already incomprehensible to them and made even more so by both local and international rhetoric. In turn, local and international audiences mirror the inability of politicians, practitioners, and policy makers – as well as academics who are experts (often self-defined) in theoretical conflict-related *foci* and Middle-Eastern, Anatolian and South Caucasian *loci* – to define the context and locate the agents. In this framework, for instance, an ethno(-religious) group can be called a majority in a kin-state (Syrian Armenians in the Republic of Armenia) and a minority when dwelling on foreign soil (Syrian Armenians in the Arab Republic of Syria). Others are considered minorities in their own countries (Alevi in the Republic of Turkey) or minorities in their own countries as well as in foreign countries (Ezidi in the Caucasus and in the Republic of Iraq).

This semantic trap often builds upon religiously or politically motivated (forced) migration. In this case, the representation (or self-representation) of perpetrators (or victims), pace Riche (1986), changes in accordance with the migrants' transnational sponsors (or enemies), as is happening in Syria or Iraq and in their neighbouring countries. Alternately, it may take peculiar forms in countries represented as stable but in reality facing huge structural problems.

With the aim of shedding some light on the many ambiguities that contemporary dramatic events are bringing to the fore, this volume collects eight ethnographic contributions, the product of fieldwork conducted in the last two years in geographical problem areas. It aims to provide a slightly different contribution from the dominant academic rhetoric, with chapters that cut across established historical "academic" regions while intersecting anthropological or cultural areas (Gilmore 1982, Giordano 2001), thus deliberately connecting the Caucasus to the Eastern Mediterranean shores through the Anatolian peninsula and the northern Mesopotamia region.

This volume is primarily the result of a workshop I organised with Ketevan Khutsishvili while working as a visiting staff member at the Institute of Ethnology, Faculty of Humanities, of the Ivane Javakhishvili Tbilisi State University[1]. This workshop was held on January 30, 2015, and its topic was *Fundamentalism: Transnationalism and Religious Minorities*. Khutsishvili, Arsen Hakobyan, Tamar Antadze, Rozeta Gujejiani and I presented papers that later developed into some of the chapters contained in this volume. Three additional contributions were produced by authors who could not make it to Tbilisi (Nurdan Z. Atalay Günes, Kayhan Delibaş and Benedetta Panchetti). Additional input also emerged from two seminars I held at Tbilisi State University: on November 14, 2014, on *Methodological Problems of Anthropological Research in Conflict Zones* and on September 10, 2015, on *Ethical Issues in Ethnography*, and from two subsequent academic trips at the Yerevan State University and Yerevan Institute of Archaeology and Ethnography, and at Ilia State University in Tbilisi[2].

However, since these workshops, lectures and visits took place, a number of events have unfolded, shaking both Western and non-Western audiences. Those events have been categorised based on inveterate academic divisions that stem from the inability of the Middle East to adapt to the collapse of Cold War ideological paradigms and to a reading of ongoing religious troubles (mostly Middle Eastern) as the result of the inherent instability left by colonial powers following the collapse of the Ottoman Empire.

* * *

The issue of contextualisation when gathering data on minorities with transnational loyalties in conflictual environments is critical (Smyth and Robinson 2001, Mollica 2006). This is especially the case when minorities are highly diversified in ethno-religious terms (Giordano 2013) or compete over the symbolic role of identity in identity construction (Laitin 1998, Isaacs and Polese 2016). Taking those challenges into consideration, the trajectory of data analysis in our ethnographies is threefold, focusing on locations, informants and researchers. Let's locate these three factors with reference to the chapters.

Threatened ethno-religious minorities may be (subliminally) forced to change their religion, or the minority group may even accept the change if they perceive it as guaranteeing higher security, e. g., Molokans (Antadze) and Ezidis (Mollica) in the Southern Caucasus. Nevertheless, religious motivations may be a camouflage for personal interests, e. g., intra-Christian conversions in Lebanon

---

[1] Marie Curie International Research Staff Exchange Scheme Fellowship within the 7th European Community Framework Programme.

[2] Academic Swiss Caucasus Net (ASCN).

(Panchetti) or kidnappings by terrorist and paramilitary groups in Syria (Hakobyan). Thus, personal beliefs can simply become irrelevant if the aim is to defend a new life choice, e. g., divorces in Lebanon (Panchetti). Paradoxically, this can lead to even deeper confusion, which may mirror deeper identity problems, e. g., inter-Alevi communities' tensions in Turkey (Delibaş), within which assimilationist policies easily prosper. On a communal level, minorities may require respect for their *loci* or events, e. g., Assyrians (Khutsishvili) and Molokans (Antadze) in Georgia, above all when those *loci* or events intersect with ongoing political happenings, e. g., Ezidi in the Caucasus (Mollica) or Alevi in the Anatolian peninsula (Delibaş). Here respondents may even prove to not have academic interests or feel entitled to control data, e. g., Ezidi in Georgia (Mollica). They may even ask for money in exchange for information, e. g., Molokans in Georgia (Antadze). This process touches upon the longstanding and sensitive methodological debate regarding not only who has the power of representation and consequential access to knowledge, e. g., political hierarchies in Turkey (Atalay Günes), but also the very realities of data gathering in contested environments.

First, the topographical dimension poses multilevel academic challenges, i.e., a quarter in a conflictual city such as Beirut (Panchetti) or even a safe area contaminated by the reverberations of a (geographically) remote conflict, as in Tbilisi with reference to Mount Sinjar in the Kurdish region of North Iraq (Mollica).

Second, given the sensitive nature of interviews (Hakobyan) and the problems inherent to fieldwork, informants must remain anonymous. Informants often request anonymity for fear of retaliation (Panchetti) or because they still retain a certain degree of suspicion (Mollica). However, fieldwork also allows informants a sense of freedom connected to the ability to discuss such sensitive issues (Hakobyan), to express hidden feelings (Atalay Güneş), or, paradoxically, to view the researcher as a means to transmit their history (Antadze).

Third, researchers encounter problems with unclear numbers and must thus rely on long-term observations (Delibaş). Widespread rumours may help, as the researcher "like the others" heard about "something" concerning the "informant" (Khutsishvili). On the other hand, the researcher may be directly involved with the object or the actors of the research, which facilitates data collection (Atalay Güneş). The researcher may even become a subject of study, being the first kin-group member performing research on that specific unit (Gujejiani). Nevertheless, for the researcher, the field can still change while he is conducting his research, which can lead him to misjudge informants' data (Mollica). For Hakobyan, for instance, despite his (difficult) position as a researcher, it was easy to work with Armenian refugees because he is Armenian himself; he experienced the same trust refugees felt towards Armenian drivers who helped them get out of a devastated Aleppo (Hakobyan). Obtaining data from authorities or registrars is not always easy either, and data can be limited to confrontations of trends (Panchetti), or jeopardized by lack of material (Gujejiani), delays (Mollica), lack of security or trust (Panchetti, Antadze, Gujejiani), or structural problems of power-relations that do not allow empirically reliable comparative analysis (Gujejiani). In addition, issues such as demography can be highly sensitive since they can unbalance power-sharing systems, as in Lebanon (Panchetti), or disclose ethno-religious affiliations, as in Turkey (Atalay Güneş). Needless to say, the contributions of at least two authors must be read between the lines as well since their ethnographies are critical of those in power and of their abuses, including abuses against academia.

* * *

Fear and its ramifications (Mollica) are immediate products of fundamentalism. Fear can be part of everyday life (Hakobyan) and it take different shapes.

From the ethnographies collected in this volume, the issue of assimilation emerges first. Prejudices may proliferate in both public and private sectors, while another religion is often seen as representing the religion of *the* "nation" (Delibaş). Moreover, integration dynamics may affect the religious sphere (Mollica) to the point of slowly destroying group composition (Gujejiani). Ethno-religious traditional names are no longer given, having been replaced by new names imported from majoritarian cultures (Khutsishvili). Meanwhile, festivities are re-framed to meet the requirements of the dominant cultures (Antadze, Mollica, Khutsishvili, Gujejiani), thus losing not only their original names but also their meanings.

Memory plays a major role here. Conflicts are constructed upon previous occurrences (Hakobyan), and old tragedies manifestly influence perceptions in contemporary conflicts both at home and abroad (Delibaş). For their part, informants may characterise people according to contemporary events or by attributing to them different degrees of danger, e.g., according to their aspect or clothes (Hakobyan). Codes may even sediment or be in need of continuous renegotiation (Delibaş).

Conflicts often bring about changes of *loci*. Some *loci* are perceived as safer than others because they are in kin-ethnic areas or because war morphology is expressed differently according to which quarter or room it penetrates, thus maintaining the context fluid. Hakobyan demonstrates this with reference to Syrian Armenian refugees' routes, regardless of the way they define their departure or the "normality of violence" they encounter at checkpoints.

Yet, we would be adding almost nothing to the ongoing academic debate by presenting fundamentalism and its relation to minorities in a framework that would simply depend upon the terrorist actions of some terrorist organisations attracting worldwide attention. Nevertheless, though I do believe religion plays a major role in the ongoing destabilizing processes (Mollica 2015), its role is not exclusive. Some ethno-religious minorities investigated in this volume (e. g., Alevi, Ezidis, Armenians) are the patent victims of some fanatic groups, but the shapes fundamentalism can take, the domains it can enter, or even the religions it can penetrate are much larger than anything a reductionist and simplistic Islamophobic reading may suggest. What is now known as *religious revival,* is not simply entering multilevel domains while affecting inter- and intra-sectarian dynamics. Instead, the actions of peoples or groups (violent or not) are defined as religiously driven even if they are not religiously motivated, or even paradoxically, vice versa.

For instance, despite the fact that remaining in the Christian faith is crucial to choosing to change one's denomination in Lebanon, the inter-Christian tensions along with Uniatism and the installation of the Latin Roman Church in the Middle-East region have clearly hindered peaceful relationships between churches, as Panchetti proves by reference to contemporary divorce-motivated inter-Christian conversions. Mixed marriage is an issue addressed in other contributions – e. g., Ezidi with Christian Orthodox in Southern Caucasus urban areas (Mollica) or Molokans with Muslims in rural Georgian areas (Antadze). In the same country, intra-Christian tension nearly turned violent over the establishment of a contested religious structure (Khutsishvili).

Inter-group tensions are also evident within Ezidi communities in both Georgia and Armenia (Mollica) and in the entire Anatolian peninsula, where their struggles lead some Alevi to see their religion as a tradition within Islam, while others view it as an alternative lifestyle (Delibaş). Nevertheless, all Alevi were viewed as a homogeneous group and as such were attacked: an event that helped them forge a new Alevi identity (Delibaş). At the same time, the Alevi were mirroring tensions with the very meaning of their native state (here Turkey), perceived as discriminating against them (in this context, Alevi of all affiliations). On the other hand, in *confessional* Lebanon, national legislation clashes with religious injunctions (Panchetti) to the point of creating serious blackouts within constitutional segments of the state.

* * *

The minority movements investigated in this volume were the result of (often forced) migration policies (Delibaş, Hakobyan, Antadze, Mollica). Once minorities relocate, their resistance strategies adapt to keep their customs alive. These strategies occasionally take shape in a reorganisation in the form of cultural associations (Delibaş) or in fighting (at times invisible) wars to preserve their cultures (Gujejiani). The religious ideas of post-Soviet Caucasus ethno-religious minorities spread due to the collapse of a former ideological system of values (Mollica, Antadze), consequently bringing about an identity crisis that slowly allowed (hidden) problems to emerge (Khutsishvili). However, any resistance lacking an organised diaspora left minorities unprotected (Mollica) or forced them towards dramatic changes, even to the point of changing their "identity defining factor" from "religion" to "nationality", as Antadze argues about Molokans in the Southern Caucasus.

In a Muslim-dominated majority context (here North Iraq), a minority (here the Ezidis) perceived itself as persecuted before the ongoing conflict or the massacres they endured in August 2014. On a transnational level (here in Georgia), they were continually affected by the developments in their traditional homeland, as Mollica argues. In terms of policies (here in Turkey), the increase of the democratic deficit, the government's refusal to acknowledge religious institutions and the insecurity generated by political rhetoric and ambiguous agendas created fear for the Alevi, as Delibaş postulates. Nationalism and discrimination may be responsible for the decline of minorities (Antadze, Mollica), but discrimination can take on a multilevel form, ranging from gender-related issues to national policies, as Atalay Güneş sets forth.

In Gujejiani's ethnography on ethnic Georgians in Turkey, she submits that political control of minorities' events can be considered responsible for weakening minorities' identity. This may take a dramatic turn when rulers force minorities into exile fearing they may spread "heretic ideas". A case in point is Soviet ideological pressure on minorities manifested when Molokans refused to serve in the armed forces for religious reasons, as argued by Antadze, or when it altered the cohesion of the religious group, as submitted by Khutsishvili with reference to Assyrians.

Some minorities are more united by their cultural than their religious ethos (Antadze, Delibaş). However, minorities that feel threatened may conveniently resurrect some aspects that are culturally attributed to them in peculiar contexts to differentiate themselves (here, for instance, trustworthy Molokans) from others (here, for instance, Russian drunkards) (Antadze). After all, stereotypes and linguistic similarities between names were even mentioned in a 2008 UNHCR Report on the Ezidi in Georgia to explain how police officers' brutality was motivated by perceived impunity (Mollica). Derogatory characteristics or stereotypes attributed to minorities often do not disappear even when they are no longer part of the conflict (Mollica) or a secular ideology has been introduced in their country (Delibaş).

Old minority religious rituals can be maintained when reframed by the dominant culture (Gujejiani). In this case, fear acts on religion and its surrogates on a deeper level. Some minorities may even prefer to fight to the death simply because they would rather support an authoritarian non-religious government than a radical one (Hakobyan). Some experience how religion can become a disruptive force and can slowly penetrate even their most important religious events, simply by incorporating them (Gujejiani). In Turkey, secularism was never seen as a guarantee, as it has never been taken for granted that freedom would ensue (Delibaş). Thus, concealment is often the rule, despite any emphasis on multireligiosity, as Atalay Güneş argues in her ethnography on gender-mainstreaming NGOs in Mardin.

However, despite their weakness, if those gender-oriented projects (here carried out by some Turkish NGOs) were not implemented, there would be no possibility of bringing women (either as informants or researchers) to reflect on sensitive topics (here gender inequality) (Atalay Güneş). On the contrary, gender equality is institutionalised within some ethno-religious groups (Delibaş) or simply becomes a dramatic necessity in others, as there are no men left (Antadze).

* * *

Ethno-religious groups analysed in this volume often have transnational religious and political loyalties. The fact that they place their affiliations outside the states where the fieldwork was conducted invariably affects the research. Armenians, Ezidis, Molokans and Assyrians lack strong inner support and must rely on external links for their religious and social activities (for instance, when Ezidi and Assyrians recently built new temples in Tbilisi, as documented by Mollica and Khutsishvili). This topographical and cultural liminal terrain displays a major weakness both in terms of their (foreign) kin-groups and of their communal cohesion dynamic. Collective memory again plays a significant role in how foreign conflicts are perceived and how sectarian violence is viewed as a cultural threat to their groups. Nevertheless, the issue of cultural threat affects other groups as well. Foreign events also have an impact in this area, e. g., Alevi in the Anatolian peninsula (Delibaş), Syrian Armenians in the Republic of Armenia (Hakobyan) and Ezidi in the Southern Caucasus (Mollica). However, in wartimes, kin-states may support their kin-citizens (Hakobyan), and family relations may be re-activated (Mollica). On the other hand, however, religious memory may structure the ethno-cultural identity when communities are not originally from the areas where they dwell (Khutsishvili), even more so when similar cultural-religious events still take place, unchanged, in their original ethnic land (Gujejiani). Informants frequently point to a dominant culture's assimilation polities, which often entail a radicalisation or forced enculturation.

When under (real or perceived) attack, minorities highlight some aspects of their identity to better represent themselves (Antadze) or new organisational structures are formed to face new needs and topographies if dictated by migratory patterns (Delibaş). These are stronger when the changes affect the relationship between leaders and congregations (Delibaş, Mollica, Antadze), even more so when the movement of a population is perceived as linked to persecution (Mollica). Self-representation took an extraordinarily cogent path in conflictual scenarios. At the beginning of the ongoing Syrian war, outsiders perceived Aleppo inhabitants (including Armenians) as loyal to the government, while for Aleppo inhabitants (including Armenians) the conflict was *somewhere else* (Hakobyan). Once the war changed (and contingently the way Aleppo inhabitants were represented or represented themselves changed too), the conflict slowly formed new borders and shaped new words, re-framing the categories of "us" and "them" (Hakobyan).

* * *

Keeping this in mind and framing the transnational field by considering the variables of religion (or *other* religions) and minorities, the structure of this volume follows both a thematic and a geographical path. Islamic–Christian and Abrahamic religions' tensions towards groups considered heretics run parallel to intra-Christian denominational struggles and inter-Islamic sectarian problems. The forms taken by those religiously-driven (or as such represented) frictions range from ethno-religious conflicts, ideological persecution and ethno-religious persecution (as portrayed in the first six chapters) to diverse (both positive and negative) forms of discrimination (These are expounded in the last two chapters, where deeds are seen simply as surrogates for religiously-motivated actions or, better still, are camouflaged as being justified by religiously-driven beliefs.)

In the first chapter, Hakobyan investigates how longstanding traditional routes from Aleppo (Syria) to Yerevan (Armenia) became a survival strategy, part of everyday life for Syrian Armenians. Mapping the geography of checkpoints controlled by various groups (military, paramilitary, terrorist), he examines expectations and reactions as well as different negotiation strategies set by the new religio-communal boundaries dictated by the war. Here, the way the conflict is expressed demonstrates diversity and discloses danger, above all for Christians, regardless of the fact that their migration was never represented as a community's collective decision.

Mollica's ethnography examines the encounter between a migrant and an established Ezidi community in Georgia. The former was escaping Daesh terrorist persecution in Iraq whereas the latter was involved in a revitalisation attempt (mostly via the building of a religious structure). Migration is a dominant theme, overshadowing all intra-communal tensions and paradoxically seen as an opportunity for cultural survival. However, on Caucasian soil, firstly the Ezidi leaders reduced their ability to interact with indigenous civil society, secondly the religious structural and economic problems deprived them of spaces to keep endogamous marriage practices alive, and thirdly, a longstanding religio-ideological split within the group was reproduced in contemporary debates.

Khutsishvili's ethnography concentrates on how Assyrian culture in Georgia is determined by religion and how Assyrians' religious idiom (Aramaic) became a source of communal pride and a unifying symbol. This phenomenon stemmed from a religio-educational revival fostered by wealthy Assyrians, which helped them resist assimilation. Nevertheless, intra-Assyrian (Catholic and Orthodox) relations are tense. One group chose "integration" into the dominant culture whereas the other struggled to resist. Although both groups share a liturgical language that acts as an ethnocultural marker, their conflict reached its peak at the opening of a religious structure contested by one of the two groups.

Antadze examines the transformation of Soviet-era agricultural Molokan communities in Georgia. Besides changing their settlements into collective farms and then losing ownership of them, they slowly turned secular celebrations (e. g., World War II Victory Day) into religious ones (e. g., All Souls' Day). Building upon the old connection between Soviet ideology and Molokans' beliefs, she argues that, in order to survive and maintain their confessional unity, Molokans "naturally" melded together secular and religious ethics. However, adaptation to economic changes led to a struggle to defend culture and unity. These were threatened first by the exile and then by the collapse of the Soviet economic organisation (kolkhoz) upon which their farming system was based.

Based on her fieldwork on surviving ethno-religious Georgian celebrations conducted in the Turkish Tao-Klarjeti region, Gujejiani argues in her chapter that a defining factor of Georgian identity in Turkey was folk festivals. However, festivals were transformed in the 1960s and are now organised by local administrations. Discussing the way in which contemporary rituals of traditional bull fights have been adapted to the modern (Turkish) festival system, she submits that a portion of the population of ethnic (now Sunni) Georgians continues to struggle to keep those events a distinct feature, using them as an attempt to maintain their identity and resist assimilation. However, another portion of the community no longer shows an interest in this goal.

Delibaş focuses on how the rise of pro-Islamic parties (1990s) and the subsequent authoritarian attitudes of the government (since 2002) have been crucial to the Alevi identity movement in Turkey. Based on surveys conducted in several Alevi organisations in Izmir, he submits that the Alevis want their children to keep their culture alive and develop solidarity. New Alevi centres are seen as central for cultural survival and as capable of playing a major role in re-creating Alevi structures in urban areas. Indeed, following the crisis of massive, rapid urbanisation, Alevis became an even larger target of traditional prejudices. The violence Alevi communities endured (and still endure), has left a mark on their collective memory.

By reference to two gender-mainstreaming projects, Atalay Güneş focuses on inequalities in the multiethnic and pluri-religious border city of Mardin in southeast Turkey. Addressing the discussion from different perspectives (including that of religion), she illustrates conceptual limits of those projects' application to field experiences. The city's position affects its socioeconomic composition, while unemployment and a turbulent political environment are reasons for migration. This runs parallel to the rise of identity politics, which brought women's positions and gender inequality to the fore. However, despite various pieces of legislation passed to prevent violence against women and early marriages, violence against women is still widespread.

Finally, Panchetti analyses problems among Christian Lebanese communities with reference to marriage. Catholic couples convert to Orthodoxy since the latter church's canonical laws grant easier dissolution processes. Those conversions shake Lebanon's *confessionalism*, as they expose it to contradictions inherent to a system that not only allows intermediary bodies between the citizen and the State, but also freedom of conversion, even if this is prohibited by some (religious) community rules. Moreover, in the event of a request to dissolve a marriage, the divorce remains under the laws of the sect whose authorities celebrated the marriage, even if one of the spouses has converted.

## Bibliography

Gilmore, D. David (1982): Anthropology of the Mediterranean Area. In: *Annual Review of Anthropology,* 11: 175–205.

Giordano, Christian (2001): Europe: Sociocultural Overview. In: *International Encyclopaedia of the Social and Behavioural Sciences*, vol. 7. Oxford: Pergamon Press, 4917–4923.

Giordano, Christian (2013): Corporate Groups, Factions and Networks: Social Organization of the Chinese Diaspora in the Straits of Malacca – the Case of Penang. In: Waltraud Kokot, Christian Giordano, Mijal Gandelsman-Trier (eds.): *Diaspora as a Resource. Comparative Studies in Strategies, Networks and Urban Spaces*. Fribourg Studies in Social Anthropology 36. Münster: Lit Verlag, 199–221.

Isaacs, Rico and Polese, Abel (eds.) (2016): *Nation Building and Identity in the Post-Soviet Space: New Tools and Approaches*. London: Routledge.

Laitin, David (1998): *Identity in Formation: The Russian-Speaking Populations in the Near Abroad,* vol. 22. Ithaca: Cornell University Press.

Mollica, Marcello (2006): Challenges in Data Collection in a Violently Divided Society. In: Alex. I. Gray and Ibrahim Al-Marashi (eds.): *Peace and Conflict: Europe and Beyond*. Bilbao: University of Deusto Press, 21–31.

Mollica, Marcello (2015): Introduction. In: Marcello Mollica (ed.): *Bridging Religiously Divided Societies in the Contemporary World*. Pisa: University of Pisa Press, 7–16.

Riches, David (1986): The Phenomenon of Violence. In: David Riches (ed.): *The Anthropology of Violence*. Oxford: Blackwell, 1–27.

Smyth, Marie and Robinson, Gillian (2001): *Researching Violently Divided Societies*. Tokyo: United Nations University Press.

# From Aleppo to Yerevan: The War and Migration from the Window of the Bus

*Arsen Hakobyan*

## Introduction

> I saw the war for the first time on my way to Aleppo Airport, when ruined buildings were visible along the road from the bus window (Informant 1, male, 57, April 2015).

A noteworthy occurrence of war's everydayness emerges in the stories of Syrian Armenians established in Yerevan regarding the conflict, war and migration to Yerevan.[1] This occurrence was determined by migration to Armenia via bus routes leaving from Aleppo. Bus routes were a way of migration, and at the same time a part of everyday wartime life, where conflict and its various perceptions were interlinked, war and peaceful life collided, confronting «parties» emerged and various strategies of survival and salvation were formed.

We have a chance to understand some specifics of social transformations conditioned by wartime everyday life by following the migration routes through these stories, as the refugees' "stories are part of everyday life and constitute a means for actors to express and negotiate experience [...], they provide a site to examine the meanings people, individually or collectively, ascribed to lived experience" (Eastmond 2007: 248).

Thus, my objective in this chapter is to illustrate some aspects and manifestations of the everydayness of conflict and war among Armenians from Aleppo: how it is represented and how surviving strategies formed new practices of everydayness during the war.

Migration to Armenia was accomplished on buses through the Aleppo-Yerevan or Aleppo-Beirut (Lebanon) routes and from Beirut by plane to Yerevan.

---

[1] Given the nature of the interviews, all interviewers will remain anonymous. All interviews are in Armenian. The Syrian Armenians speak in Armenian (Western Armenian). The informants' age ranged from 25 to 72. They represent various social groups: students, workers, businessmen, intellectuals etc. Represented materials are related to the Armenians of Aleppo. Field material is the result of two research projects: *Syrian Armenians in Armenia: Repatriates or Refugees?* (Open Society Institute Assistance Foundation – Armenia. Head of project – Arsen Hakobyan, 2013–2014) and *Migrant Groups in the Republic of Armenia (1940–2012): Parameters of Complex Identities* (Joint project: Institute of Archaeology and Ethnography – Armenia and INALCO/CNRS – France: 2014–2015). According to data from May 2014, there were 11 000 Syrian Armenians established in Armenia (A short reference ... 2014).

When the Aleppo Airport stopped functioning or was closed due to the war, the bus routes became the main way of migration. The Aleppo-Yerevan bus route had existed before the war and was in operation until 2013. People also migrated on their private cars, alone or joining other cars to form a small caravan.

This chapter is based on field material I have collected mostly in Yerevan and partly in Beirut from 2013 to 2015, and includes the events of 2011–2013. This material relates to the current war, conflict, violence, events and people's own life experiences in this context.

Fieldwork became problematic, however, as it was related to specific sensitive and traumatic situations, events and phenomena. Actually, we have to take into consideration the socio-political conditions and the current war situation in which Syrian Armenians have lived or are still living with relatives. The people who tell these stories are *de facto* refugees and the victims of situation. Their future prospects are still not clear and the future is uncertain.

The fieldwork itself gave them a sense of freedom because they had never before experienced the liberty to discuss such highly sensitive issues. On the one hand, the current situation allowed them to speak more openly, but on the other hand, they might be wary as they used to be in Syria's restrictive social-political life.

I should mention that it was easy for me to work with Syrian Armenians because as a researcher from Armenia they trust me and I had no problems of access to the field. From their perspective I was both an "insider" and an "alien".

I seemed an "insider" because I came from Armenia, but I was "alien" because I was not from their same environment and did not endure the war situation they had experienced.

## The Beginning: "Everything began in lower Syria [...] we hadn't thought it would reach Aleppo"

The Armenian population in Syria numbered several tens of thousands before the war. Armenians lived mainly in the cities – Aleppo, Damascus, Latakia and other places[2] – but were mainly concentrated in Aleppo. During the 2000s, the number of Armenians was around 50000 in Aleppo (Ayvazyan 2003: 518). Though they had inhabited Syria since ancient times, the present Syrian Armenian community was formed in 1915 after the Armenian genocide (Hovhannisyan

[2] According to the encyclopaedia *The Armenian Diaspora* published in 2003, the number of Armenians in Syria reached 65–70 thousand. The number of Armenians in Damascus was around 5000, in Latakia around 1600, in Kesab around 1500, in Kamishli around 12000 (Ayvazyan 2003: 509, 516–519). According to the data of the Armenian Apostolic Prelacy of Aleppo, the number of Armenians in Syria in 2003 was 90000 (Migliorino 2006: 14). On the eve of 2011, the Armenians formed 0.3 per cent of Syrian population (Sanjian 2015: 74).

1974: 25–26). The Armenians of Syria along with other local population groups suffered the consequences and impact of the conflict that began in 2011. At the same time, the conflict and continuing war caused new manifestations of individual and collective experience. These experiences are conditioned by the daily specifics of conflict, by the existence of the institutionalized Armenian community, forced migration, opportunities for individuals' further perspectives and collective survival during the war.

The perception of the Syrian conflict among Syrian Armenians includes some chronological and event trigger-points, around which the conflict or war narrative is built. In order to understand how the conflict is represented and perceived, we must bear in mind that "Narratives are not transparent renditions of 'truth' but reflect a dynamic interplay between life, experience and story. Placed in their wider sociopolitical and cultural contexts, these stories can provide insights into how forced migrants seek to make sense of displacement and violence, re-establish identity in ruptured life courses and communities, and/or bear witness to violence and repression" (Eastmond 2007: 248).

The stories of Syrian Armenians on conflict or war began with the occurrences in Tunisia, Egypt and Libya in 2011–2012, which, according to informants, caused anxiety among Syrian Armenians:

> It began in Tunis [...] after Tunis it continued in Libya. Libyan occurrences lasted for a while, and, since Libya was an usurper state, we thought they would not make a revolution. After it exploded, we thought that something could also happen here, but as our Internal Ministries and KGB[3] are very strong, we supposed nothing would happen. In the end when it [the revolution] moved to Egypt and continued for 15 days, we thought that it might happen (Informant 2, male, 43, November 2013).

At the same time, the revolution marked the beginning of the "disquieting period" in Syria, as well as defining that perception's "mental geography", outlining certain regional boundaries that were politically separated inside, but formed an imagined region of cultural mentality. The general important feature was also the existence of a "politically sustainable regime". In this case, the narrative demonstrates "the wider social-political and cultural context" of the perception of the conflict (Eastmond 2007: 248). Though these occurrences and events caused certain anxiety, this was neither expressed nor perceived as the onset of conflict or martial law among Syrian Armenians. In this case, conflict perception was directly connected with Syria and was considered or thought of as an axis of narrative description of the Syrian conflict. The events that took place in the city of Daraa[4] in southern Syria in 2011 were transformed into antagonism.

---

3 Russian acronym of the Committee of State Security in the USSR here used in reference to Syria's State Security Service.

4 Daraa, also known as Dera'a or Dera, is a city in southwest Syria just north of the border with Jordan. According to the 2004 census, Daraa had a population of 97969.

"Some problems had occurred in Daraa in southern Syria." It is important to note that although the Daraa events are considered the beginning of antagonism, these occurrences are described differently. For example:

> In Daraa city, southern Syria, the government had planned to lay a road on their land territories, although many of these were private lands. The Syrian television provided little information. We were aware that after *namaz*[5] on Friday, people went on strike for economic reasons. There was no question of the government resigning [...] people striked and demanded jobs. After the strikes, we saw on TV that weapons were being amassed in Daraa (Informant 3, male, 43, December 2013, Yerevan).

According to another description:

> Daraa started when young people wrote different things about the president on the wall [graffiti]. This was why they were arrested and thrown into prison. They called their parents as well [...] There are many stories told, but which ones were true we don't even know (Informant 2).

Though the event's descriptions differ, there is one recurring expression in the conflict narrative: "It began from Daraa", without main event descriptions. This expression could be determined by the circumstance that Daraa is quite distant from Aleppo and information about occurrences was not always available.

---

The inhabitants are predominantly Sunni Muslims. About the beginning of events in Daraa in 2011, BBC mentions "The demonstrations in Deraa – where the police have reacted most brutally – started on Friday. Several families had gathered to demand the release of 15 school children who – influenced by the protests in Tunisia and Egypt – wrote the popular revolution slogan on the wall: "The people want the fall of the regime" *(Lina Sinjab, "Middle East unrest: Silence broken in Syria" http://www.bbc.com/news/world-middle-east-12794882).* The report "The struggle for Syria in 2011" stated: "The incarceration of several youths in Dera'a triggered demonstrations on Friday, March 18, 2011 that escalated until the following Monday, when security forces fired live ammunition against a mob that had succeeded in burning down the Ba'ath Party headquarters and other public buildings. Unarmed but destructive demonstrations in Dera'a prompted the Syrian government to respond with violence" (Holliday 2011: 13–14). Damascus-based Al Watan newspaper reported. "Residents of two Syrian cities where protests broke out March 18 handed a list of demands to authorities to halt an escalation. In the southern Syrian city of Daraa near Jordan, protesters demanded the release of detainees recently jailed on political charges, the dismissal of some officials and permission to sell land on border territories without prior government approval. They also want those responsible for the killing of two during the March 18 clashes put on trial" *(Lina Ibrahim, "Syrians of Daraa, Baniyas Set Demands to End Protest, Watan Says" Bloomberg News,* March 20, 2011. *http://www.bloomberg.com/news/articles/2011-03-20/syrians-of-daraa-baniyas-set-demands-to-end-protest-watan-says).*

[5] Prescribed ritual prayer in Islam and obligatory religious duty for every Muslim.

"There are few things shown on the Syrian TV." On the other hand, mass media with an anti-Syrian orientation declared: "From Al Jazeera etc., media sources were under the influence of Qatar, Saudi Arabia." "Daraa", however, is considered the beginning of the conflict, from which it spread to other Syrian territories and settlements: Homs, Hama and the Turkish bordering territories, Latakia etc. As one informant from Latakia recalls after the occurrences in Daraa:

> Many people who studied with me clearly said that we are oppositionists [...] The friends who sat next to each other, who had lunch together after classes, started to keep some distance between each other. After the events in Daraa, they started to form small groups. Though they studied together [at the university] and greeted each other, they were cautious not to insult each other or to provoke a fight (Informant 4, male, 25, December 2013, Yerevan).

Conflict was expressed differently in various places, demonstrating diversity in the problems within the society. In Aleppo, people avoided talking about it, discussing it or having oppositionist standings,

> as it was unknown what would happen at that time. People were not showing their opposition, they were afraid of losing their jobs (Informant 3).

The strikes that began in Latakia demanded the liberation of the people arrested at Daraa.

> When these liberation demands started in Latakia, there were already prisoners in Daraa and [...] they demanded freedom for all imprisoned people (Informant 4).

The resulting conflict that exploded in the cities of Homs and Hama was conditioned by the memory of the occurrences of 1982, when the Syrian army harshly suppressed disorders among the local Muslim population (headed by the "Muslim Brothers" organization). Thousands of people were killed.[6] The local population was already "oppositionist" in its collective memory, and accordingly that "latent" conflict broke out again in 2011.

At the same time, outsiders perceived Aleppo and its inhabitants as being loyal to the government. According to an informant, outside Aleppo various groups violently attacked cars with Aleppo license plates along Syrian roads. They tried to rouse Aleppines against the regime, as Aleppo was considered loyal and had not protested against the government.

---

[6] In 1964 and 1981–82, the Islamist uprisings in Hama were brutally suppressed by the Syrian Army. According to different data, the number of casualties in 1982 in Hama is between 10000 and 30000 (Droz-Vincent 2014: 42).

Aleppo's Armenians initially perceived the conflict as a suburban, peripheral and frontier phenomenon chiefly because the involved settlements and towns (Daraa, Homs etc.) were in distant areas.

The conflict was perceived not only as peripheral in a geographical sense, but was also regarded as a transient and, to some extent, marginal social phenomenon in terms of its scale, depth and scope.

This is why they believed it could not "reach" Aleppo, as Aleppo was a government stronghold and the Syrian state and army were "strong".

> We thought that it would not reach Aleppo. A year after Daraa the conflict reached Aleppo[7] [...] we hadn't felt it before (Informant 2).

The perception of conflict revealed the connection between identity and country in a conflict situation. The country as a spatial feature of identity in the context of conflict was not fully and deeply perceived since the events at "Daraa", "Homs" or "Hama" were considered isolated and distant phenomena in spatial and social terms, not directly connected with Aleppo. In this case, the spatial feature of identity is mostly manifested at the local level as the main descriptor of local identity. The war itself becomes a narrative axis, beginning from Aleppo, in which the war and local identity are interconnected.

### War and Everyday Life: "When you are on the battlefield, you know your enemy is there. You will kill him, he will kill you. Here it is different"

If the "Daraa occurrences", the beginning of conflict perception, were not seen as dictating war's everydayness in Aleppo, the continuance and extension of antagonism gradually led to dangers and threats, creating conflict or war with its manifestations, thus new individual and collective experiences. The strikes in Aleppo did not cause anxiety at first. "Every day [...] after the mosque they

---

[7] Aleppo is Syria's largest city. According to the 2004 census, its official population is 2 132 100. More than 80 per cent of Aleppo's inhabitants are Sunni Muslims. These are mainly Arabs, followed by Kurds. Other Muslim groups include small numbers of ethnic Turkmens, Circassians etc. Aleppo is also one of largest centres of Christian communities in the Middle East comprising several denominations, mainly Armenians (Apostolic, Catholic and Evangelic), Assyrians/Syriacs, Melkite Greeks, Orthodox Greeks, Maronites, Latins and Chaldeans. Before the war, there were over 250 000 Christians in the city representing about 12 per cent of the total population. Several areas of Aleppo have a Christian and Armenian majority. Until July 2012, Aleppo had remained undisturbed. From March 2011 to July 2012, anti-government or pro-government demonstrations and rallies took place. Violence broke out in February 2012 when several terrorist actions were organized and some clashes occurred in the city. The opposition fighters from the neighbouring villages converged and entered into Aleppo on July 2012. The *Battle of Aleppo* between the Free Syrian Army and different Islamic units against the Syrian Arab Army still continues.

struck, still without weapons." These had not escalated into bloody collisions and war. There was also the opinion that everything might end with a peaceful "revolution" or changes. An informant recalls:

> The first year, in Aleppo the soldiers [state army] were not allowed to shoot the oppositionists. The army did not shoot demonstrators (Informant 2).

The development of successive events, however, caused various manifestations of violence, starting with terrorism and escalating to military operations.

The "collision" of violence, war and people is expressed in different ways, depending on specific situations and occurrences; it gradually or accidentally "enters" a quarter, a house, a street or a shop. In this case, there is no unified perception of martial law and its resulting manifestations. Everyone has his own occurrence, history or experience.

> We woke up cheerfully and happily on Monday, went and saw that a car bomb had exploded in front of my pharmacy: the shop was completely ruined. People were going to their shops for another week. After that, the war broke out again. I did not go to the pharmacy on September 25th, as the sniper was shot and the army prohibited entrance. These areas [four quarters] were not inhabited when I arrived in Armenia because it was dangerous there (Informant 3).

In other cases, people faced danger and anxiety on their way from Damascus to Aleppo. A group started to throw stones at their car; they were about to shoot them when the driver managed to escape at high speed from this trap, encircled by aggressors and burning tires.

In military occupied Aleppo, "many people set up curtains in their yards, often from the 4th floor, outlining boundaries from balcony to balcony; they covered the building so that snipers couldn't spot them".

As the war expanded, the situation became more indefinite and critical in Syria. The conflict exploded everywhere, also, affecting different layers of Syrian society, transforming old social actors and creating new social actors and roles. The war was described as:

> In the battlefield, you know your enemy is there: you will kill him and he will kill you. Here it is different (Informant 5, male, 72, April 2015).

In these conditions, the conflict's "parties" become fluid, changeable and amorphous. For example,

> There were differences among the Bashar[8] followers. Some people were ready to resort to weapons in survival fighting, due to their feelings about

8 Bashar Hafez al-Assad is the incumbent President of Syria, commander-in-chief of the Syrian Armed Forces, General Secretary of the ruling Ba'ath Party.

> the Islamists. They were not Alawis[9] but preferred a non-religious government. The Islamic government was viewed as not good for them. Some people said that our government had made many mistakes, but had attempted to improve the situation. This group was sure the government would not take any steps (Informant 4).

The opposite party was described as following,

> There was a new group every day. Change was continuous; this group was the "Free Army"[10] last week, then the head of the group died and a new one was elected. He changed the concept of the "Free Army", and turned it into a new group with a new name or joined another group (Informant 4).

Under these conditions, for example, your neighbour or colleague could be "an oppositionist". An informant recalls:

> I had a client who was an oppositionist; he went to fight, came back and said that if we did this, they [the government] would do that [...] One of my clients who could not read or write considered himself a rebel. He came to my house and abused the president every time. The president's portrait was on my wall. When I felt that it would lead to some problems, I took it down. I hung it in another place. That man [Bashar al-Assad] actually liked Armenians: we all had freedoms, and that man [...] contributed to Syria's development for ten years. Another man [a client] came and always complained about people's actions, about his son who went and killed someone. The army started to shoot and after a year, that man came and told me that his son had been shot (Informant 2).

Regardless of the war and the various political orientations, the conflict's consequences on individual and family life were worse, yet former social interrelations and connections were maintained under these war conditions. An interviewer stated:

---

[9] The Alawites, also known as Alawis, are a religious minority group in Syria. Representing 12 per cent of the Syrian population, they follow a branch of the Twelver school of Shia Islam with syncretistic elements. Alawis form the dominant religious group on the Syrian coast and towns near the coast. Since Hafez al-Assad (President of Syria from 1971 to 2000, Prime Minister from 1970 to 1971) came in power in 1970, the government has been dominated by a political elite led by the Alawite Al-Assad family.

[10] The Free Syrian Army is a military unit formed in 2011 by a group of defected Syrian Armed Forces officers and soldiers. Within the Syrian armed opposition, the Free Syrian Army is the largest group comprising small, ideologically moderate and uncoordinated militias and battalions operating at local levels. The Free Syrian Army is supported by Turkey and the Gulf States (Holliday 2012, O'Bagy 2013).

> He [the oppositionist client] escaped from Aleppo. I just called him and he is in the village on the Turkish border ... He thought there would be strikes like in Egypt ... I called him and he cried, telling me that he didn't expect an Armenian to call him since his Syrian friends and relatives were not calling him. As this type of clients came by every day, I would talk with them personally. They are kind [Syrians, Arabs], very kind, that is why they were fooled [betrayed]. If they hadn't been kind, they wouldn't have been ensnared. I said they wanted freedom, already two years before we separated. He answered that if he had known at the time [...] freedom, yeah, right [...] His children do not have a good job in Turkey, they are workers (Informant 2).

## Changing Society through Conflict and War: *"Neighbours turn into antagonists in one day"*

Before the Syrian conflict and war, as an informant recalled:

> We didn't know whether a person was Sunni or Alawi. The Kurd came and spoke Kurdish: Kurds we know, but I never asked them if they were Sunni or Alawi and nobody asked me whether I'm Armenian, Christian or Christian Arab. There are Christian Arabs also in Syria, Orthodox, Catholic, Assyrian, there are many who do not even know that [...] we did not have such discrimination (Informant 2).

But the conflict formed new borders and perceptions of "we" and "they", "opponents" and "insiders": this new differentiation of the groups was linked to direct involvement in the conflict, political-religious or confessional affiliation and political or religious orientation.

The conflicting sides became the main actor in this context. Which internal/external perceptions they had about themselves and which relationship experiences they had become the important part of wartime everyday life and conflict narrative. We should also mention that during the war or in similar situations the "sides" were characterized either by war-markers such as "army" or "militants" or by other characterizing elements, for instance, "oppositionist", which meant members of armed groups or "armed opposition". It reflects not only the current situation of the war, but also the people's experience and dealings with the sides.

It is interesting that one of the sides in conflict was named "state" or "government's army" or just "army" in people's imaginations and stories. Different words and names were used for opposite sides: "oppositionists", "insurgents", "militants". They did not mention the names of specific groups in the context, probably because "the Syrian armed opposition" was not a homogeneous unit, but consisted of various combinations (Holliday 2012, O'Bagy 2013). These were often variable and, contingent on circumstances and situations, they would also change their military-political affiliation.

> There was a new group every day. Change was continuous: this group was the “Free Army” last week, then the head of the group died and a new one was elected. He changed the concept of the “Free Army” [sometimes the word “Army” was also used in reference to the “Free Syrian Army”], and turned it into a new group with a new name or joined another group (Informant 4).

In parallel, to characterize marauding, violence or robberies they used “ragtag”, “terrorists” or “thieves”. These terms were used in both “armed opposition” contexts to indicate the groups’ senseless, political or criminal violence and, because of total anarchy, for the different criminal groups or individuals that surfaced: “They are thieves and bandits who just call themselves ‘Free army’.”

At the same time, people characterized the Islamist terrorists or terrorist groups involved in the conflict differently:

> There are real terrorists, the same al-Qaeda or other terrorists: we are all more afraid of being caught by them when we are out than by the Free Army (Informant 2).

At the same time the other groups’ names remained unchanged (for instance Al-Nusra[11]) and in particular “Free Army”. Their appearance was different: a member of the “Free army” wore a military uniform, whereas members of Al Nusra wore religious symbols, black bandanas with their group’s name, quotes from Quran. Worth mentioning is that when the Aleppo-Yerevan bus was stopped at a checkpoint by members of Al Nusra, the driver told the women to cover their hair because they would come in contact with members of radical Islamists. In another case, on the Lebanon-Syria border “armed opposition” “reminded” Armenian passengers that Syria is a Muslim country and that they should follow the rules or to leave the country.

Another feature differentiating Islamists was the form of address: they call their leaders *“amira”*[12]. As one of the informants mentioned, the Islamists of Al Nusra who stopped the bus on the Syrian-Turkish border, wore military uniforms bearing a “security” badge, but they addressed their leader as *“amira”*.

---

[11] The al-Nusra Front or Jabhat al-Nusra, sometimes called al-Qaeda in Syria, is a Sunni Islamic jihadist militia fighting against Syrian State forces in the Syrian war with the aim of establishing an Islamist state in the country. It is the Syrian branch of al-Qaeda. Jabhat al-Nusra is designated a terrorist organization by the United Nations Security Council (Cafarella 2014).

[12] Amir or Emir (in Arabic) stands for the commander, general or prince. Originally, the term indicated the commander-in-chief or leader, which is how it is now being used in Islamist groups.

An interesting point is that the characterizing words for the sides in conflict were used in everyday life, but the special words would be used when there were locals or strangers. It depended on the situation, as an informant said:

> When we see an unknown person, we translate the name Free Army into Armenian - *Azat banak*, or *banak* (army) - to avoid being understood by Arabs. We wanted to avoid any friction: we might have risked using the wrong name in front of a state official.

On the other hand,

> when we want to talk about them [the Islamist groups], we call them "the bearded ones", in Armenian *moruqavorner* (Informant 4).

We should take into consideration that the "Free Army" was not directly identified with terrorist groups or radical Islamists and was perceived as "armed opposition"; however, the religious factor played an important role in the perception of "oppositions". In this sense, the opposition was perceived as Muslim or Sunni opposition to Bashar Assad's power, who was associated with the Alawi minority. Accordingly, in the narrative of conflict the events of Homs and Hama are perceived as Sunni rebellions.

The situation in Aleppo also involved religion and it emerged in Muslim districts.

> One day we woke up and the radicals had already conquered some parts of Aleppo. They chose the parts of the city where the people's conditions were very bad and where religious people, Sunni radicals, lived (Informant 2).

The situation changed and became dangerous for all Christians, who became more vulnerable.

> If they kidnapped 10 Muslims, they could do it to 50 Armenians or Christians (Informant 2).

On the other hand, it became risky to continue working in Muslim suburbs:

> I changed my office; I moved to a good place among Christians and left that bad place (Informant 2).

## To Yerevan: Migration through War

The enduring war and the anxieties it produced led many Syrian Armenians to find safety beyond the borders of Syria.

The migration of Syrian Armenians to Armenia was based on both individual and family decisions. Migration was not the outcome of the community's collective decision. In general, the official position and policy of the community structures were based on a "community preservation" approach, not on the notion of leaving Syria.

Nevertheless, several thousands of Syrian Armenians migrated to Armenia through individual and family decisions. According to the data of the Ministry of Diaspora of Armenia, in the last three years (2012–2015) more than 21 000 Syrian Armenians have arrived in Armenia, with more than 16 000 living in Armenia now, 4 000 having returned to Syria during these years, and more than 1 000 having left Armenia for other countries.[13]

Though Syria and Armenia do not share a common border, the perception of Armenia as the "motherland" and the predominance of "Armenianness" in their identity steered the migrants' decisions to overcome both the distance, the dangers along the way, as well as the risks involved in reaching Armenia. It must be emphasized that being an Armenian is considered a dominant feature of the Syrian Armenian identity. "We are Armenians first of all, and then we are Syrians", and while Syria is considered a birthplace, Armenia is the motherland.[14] In this case, the Syrian Armenian identity is a form of "exilic nationalism", intended to emphasize the entire definition of Armenianness and support a "parallel" Armenian life in Syria (Migliorino 2008: 181). This dual understanding highlights the "social-political context" of the narrative (Eastmond 2007: 248, 251–252), corroborated by the existence of an Armenian institutionalized community in Syria that plays a major role in the formation of "Armenianness".

In this case, migration to Armenia acquires a higher meaning, one in which ethnic identity together with the idea of motherland play the most important role in selecting a survival strategy. Travel options to convey Syrian Armenians to

---

[13] "Housing and job major problems facing Syrian-Armenians", October 19, 2015 (http://www.tert.am/en/news/2015/10/19/syrian-armenians/18194). According to the data from May 2014, 11 000 Syrian Armenians were already established in Armenia (A short reference about the problems of Syrian Armenians, Ministry of Diaspora, Republic of Armenia, May 2014). According to UNCHR data for 2015, about 15 000 persons fleeing the conflict in Syria, primarily of ethnic Armenian background, have sought and found protection in Armenia. (Interview with UNHCR Representative. http://www.un.am/en/news/303#sthash.Sle68AnC.dpuf, July 28, 2015). According to the some non-official estimates, during the war around 15 000 Syrian Armenians migrated to Lebanon, around 2 000 Syrian Armenians to Jordan and around 8 000 to western nations (Mikael Zolyan, Refugees or repatriates? Syrian Armenians return to Armenia https://www.opendemocracy.net/od-russia/mikayel-zolyan/refugees-or-repatriates-syrian-armenians-return-to-armenia). It should be mentioned that these quantitative data are highly variable. They change dependant on the situation because the war and different migration flows are still ongoing.

[14] The present Armenian Community in Syria was formed after the Armenian Genocide (1915–1922). Syrian Armenians are originally from different parts of the former Ottoman Empire, including Western Armenia (currently Eastern Turkey). The Republic of Armenia is perceived as a symbolic motherland by the Armenian Diaspora (Abrahamyan 2000: 52–76).

Armenia varied according to circumstances: flights from Aleppo or Beirut to Yerevan, bus rides from Aleppo to Yerevan and transfers by individual cars. It is noteworthy that during the war the government of the Republic of Armenia allowed the Syrian citizens (of Armenian origin) to obtain Armenian visas thanks to corresponding resolutions and to apply for Armenian citizenship in order to obtain official passports from the country's legations in the Arabic Republic of Syria or Lebanon. Syrian Armenians were also exempt from the entrance visa fee and residence permit, thus simplifying the process to acquire Armenian citizenship.

Since 2012, the migration of Syrian Armenians to Armenia and their establishment in the country depended on varying circumstances. Migration to Armenia included various approaches: from temporary residence to permanent residency and repeated migrations from Armenia to Europe, Lebanon etc. These processes were affected by various factors. Initially, for example, some people migrated to Armenia to find temporary shelter from the conflict, mainly out of concern for their children's safety. These Syrian Armenians expected to return to Syria. In other cases, the Syrian Armenians relocated for 2–3 months (or a longer period) until the situation changed, but the prolonged conflict led to their staying in Armenia. It is important to note that family members or relatives continued to remain in Syria.

At the same time it is interesting that Syrian Armenians do not use the words "deportation" or "forced migration" to describe their departure, but rather "migration" or "displacement", noting that they were not forced to leave but left because of the war. Nevertheless, they mention that this "migration" was not voluntary, but "coercive".

The bus routes departing from Aleppo are interesting in the context of the everyday nature of war, where war and migration, danger and the process of escaping from danger are interlaced, various combinations of conflict converge, and new experiences and practices of coping with the dangers and risks in overcoming obstacles take shape and emerge.

The bus routes from Aleppo to Yerevan and Beirut are of particular importance. The buses run on roads controlled by various groups. The bus route to Yerevan[15] that existed before the conflict became quite useful for the Armenians of Aleppo, especially when the Aleppo airport stopped functioning and flights were cancelled. Despite these conditions, the bus route continued to function and many Syrian Armenians were transferred to Armenia. As an informant noted:

> [Armenian] brothers were managing an office [in Aleppo] [...] they would rest for two days, gather people and return to Yerevan. The ticket fee was 150 dollars including 30 kg of free luggage. The cost for each additional kilogram was 3 dollars (Informant 3).

---

15 As the informants note, it was a minibus.

The fact that the drivers were Armenians was important and guaranteed security for the Aleppo Armenians.

> The driver was Armenian. That was why we chose him; we wouldn't be safe with another person (Informant 6, male, 25, 2013 November, Yerevan).

So, how did migration work, what kind of risks and difficulties did the passengers face? An informant describes the route as follows:

> We drove out of Aleppo, after 500 m the Free Army guarded the road. They checked our papers, asked where we were going and why, were we going to return and told us to go back to our country, Syria. They inspected our ID cards from the window and asked the 18–20 years old people whether they served in the army or not (Informant 3).

The roads and various check-ups were dangerous especially for young people. The "oppositionists" determined whether the young people were soldiers of the Syrian state army. In that case, they would immediately become a target and the state army oversaw the people whom they regarded as draft dodgers:

> If you were able to serve in the army, they wouldn't let you leave (Informant 6).

A young informant of the Aleppo-Yerevan route said:

> We were afraid they would not let us go before we reached the border, as we are 20 and they require us to serve in the army. We had three friends sitting behind us as well as families. As we drove along, the "Free Army" stopped us. It turned out the driver was acquainted with those soldiers and was paid to get rid of them. He managed to establish contact with them as he drove back and forth on the route for a long time. We were afraid they would come and see the young people in the bus, but it did not happen. It took two hours to drive from Aleppo to the border. After we entered Turkey, the entrance visa was free and no problems occurred. That was why we were afraid [...] I served in the army, I showed my passport at the border [the state army was at the border], everything was legal and we drove into Turkey (Informant 6).

The route passed through territories controlled by the government and the Free Army, as well as by various Islamist groups:

> We drove almost 1 000 m after the Free Army stop, when Jabhat Al Nusra terrorists on armed jeeps stopped us. They said nothing, just wished us a good journey, God bless you. As the driver had always worked on that route, they were familiar with each other. There was no customs checkpoint on the Syrian border. The people from Jabhat Al Nusra with black hair and military clothes stopped us again, opened our luggage, checked

> and asked whether we had cigarettes as it was not allowed to transfer cigarettes from Syria. Following this, we changed our car on the Syrian-Turkish border and continued our trip (Informant 3).

All along the route, the driver negotiated with various "controllers" and "stations/checkpoints" when necessary. He took care of the passengers' security by bargaining and paying money:

> The "Free Army" stopped us. It was good that the driver had established contacts with them (Informant 4).

Nevertheless, there were risks and anxiety:

> We called our relatives and neighbours to tell them we had gone through safely, so if they wanted to drive out, there is nothing to be worried about (Informant 6).

For safety reasons,

> We hadn't brought any gold objects, as we were afraid they could be stolen [during check-ups] (Informant 6).

It must be mentioned in this context that although the "Armenian"[16] route was considered safe it was also a target of attacks and capture of civilians. The volatility and sensitiveness of the situation affected the safety of the bus routes. The problem of security became conditional and could be affected (or disrupted) depending on many differing circumstances. According to an informant, when Syrian state TV showed Armenians responding positively to the arrest of "oppositionists" by the governmental powers, the bus routes Aleppo-Beirut and Aleppo-Yerevan became more dangerous for Armenians.

> On our way from Aleppo to Turkey or Lebanon they [armed oppositionists] stopped us, asked if we were Armenians, wanted to take our money, threatened us [...] as I had other acquaintances, they solved our problem by paying money. They had to come to Armenia from Aleppo. On the border (Syria–Lebanon) they were stopped and asked if they were Armenian, Christian, because they were not allowed to live in their country since it was a Muslim country. Then they demanded money from them and if they refused, they said they would be slaughtered. If they had no money at that moment, they (passengers) asked to move to Lebanon to sell their houses in Syria and pay the money. Some people entered Lebanon and paid the money later. Sometimes they demanded a huge amount of money (Informant 6).[17]

---

[16] Organized by Armenians, the passengers were Syrian Armenians who left for Armenia, Yerevan.

[17] For example, in 2012 "Syrian rebels kidnapped an Aleppo-based Armenian, Hovsep Balmanoukian (born in 1990), on the border with Lebanon, with USD 20000 ransom

The important aspect is not that this attitude was conditioned by the TV broadcast of such a program, but that this explanation illustrates the sensitiveness of perception and the situation's volatility, which could be affected by changing factors. In general, other bus routes departing from Aleppo were not always safe and secure (for example, the regular bus routes from Aleppo to Beirut). Along these routes civilians risked kidnappings. The bus offices and drivers were often connected with various groups or members of these groups who were among them, gave information about bus passengers (who they were, their social status etc.) useful for kidnapping. "I was betrayed in Aleppo. Kidnappers, most probably, had informants in Aleppo, in that bus or in the office", noted an informant who was kidnapped and spent several days in confinement. He took the bus to leave Aleppo, reach Beirut and from there board a flight to Yerevan.

Kidnapping of civilians for different purposes was a result of the anarchic situation. As the informant recounts, those who were going to come to Yerevan, found the only way was a flight from Beirut to Yerevan, thus it was necessary to get from Aleppo to Beirut by bus first, but "They kidnapped on the way to Beirut ..." recalling that the bus was stopped at various locations from Aleppo to Beirut:

> There were places where the governmental army stopped them, and there were places where the oppositionists stopped them [...] There are other armies of oppositionists in other places, there were 1 000 such organizations in Syria (Informant 5).

The road check-ups by the various groups, nevertheless, became a part of war's everydayness, and even common, as

> They did not touch the elderly, checked the young people to determine if they served in the army or not, where they were going [...] and coming from, rich people were kidnapped, in contrast, they did not touch women (Informant 5).

Informant 5, who travelled this route Aleppo–Beirut several times, noted

> those extremists arrived, their faces covered, looked at us, greeted us [...], but the controller didn't ask for documents, only pointed at me. They already knew who I was because I was betrayed in Aleppo [...] He pointed at me and asked for the passport. [He ordered] me to get down [...] and then the bus left. I sat in a car followed by four soldiers; my head was covered by a hat so that I couldn't see where I was taken.

---

demanded". The kidnapped young Armenian was released when the ransom had been paid. Syria's Armenian community voiced readiness to pay USD 15 000 ("Kidnapped Syrian Armenian released" http://www.panarmenian.net/eng/news/119020/).

As Informant 5 notes, his pockets were emptied: his money, an old watch, even sandwiches and toothpaste were taken.

> They were thieves, but they said they were from the "Free Army".

It should be mentioned that in 2012 Human Rights Watch issued an open letter to the Syrian opposition (including the Free Army), accusing them of carrying out kidnappings, torture and executions, and calling on them to halt these unlawful practices.[18]

As the informant recounts, they then took him to a village in the desert, confined him in a "dirty" room and gave him a mattress and a pillow. In the adjacent room, as he mentioned, there was also a family of six.

Almost an hour passed and two male military "leaders" came, shook his hand [...] and said, "Sorry, it was a misunderstanding, we will set you free". They gave him back part of the money they had taken and promised to return the whole amount, but four days passed and they did not reappear. Once

> I saw them standing outside, they did not let me go outside, only to go to the toilet. There was always someone who followed me when I was there [...] I went out and asked, where are the things he said in the first day? After that, I realized that this was a different group (Informant 5).

He mentioned that "these people argued with logic" and reproached the people who kept him captive: "Whom have you brought here? He has no money, he has nothing." However, when he was originally abducted "no one harmed him, only threatened, they fed him, and he ate with them". At the same time: "I had discussions with them, we discussed the conditions and talked", including the subject of war and politics. He said,

> What are you doing, you are killing each other in vain (Informant 5).

And, amazingly, they replied,

> If it happens and we destroy this government, would it be of any good? They asked me (Informant 5).

According to the informant, he acted wrongly when he called his daughter, the kidnappers located the phone number and started to call demanding a ransom, threatening to have him judged by a religious court and to kill him. Because of these telephone conversations, the amount of the ransom decreased several times and was finally settled. The sum was sent through a Christian Arab driver whose passport and car were taken by force "to make him cooperate with them". "They

---

[18] "Open Letter to the Leaders of the Syrian Opposition Regarding Human Rights Abuses by Armed Opposition Members" (https://www.hrw.org/news/2012/03/20/open-letter-leaders-syrian-opposition). "Syria: Armed Opposition Groups Committing Abuses End Kidnappings, Forced Confessions, and Executions" (http://www.hrw.org/news/2012/03/20/syria-armed-opposition-groups-committing-abuses, 28. 10. 2015).

took us to Aleppo and set us free", the informant recounts, though he wanted to be taken to Beirut. Then he arrived twice to Beirut by bus.

That the perception of the conflict's sides, their self-representations, social images and boundaries, and their functional manifestations were constantly changing, depending on the situation and its circumstances, is vividly apparent in this story. The groups were "thieves" for our informant, though they checked them on the road as the "Free Army". These groups were also perceived in the same way by the people with whom they were communicating formally (for example, during bus check-ups). In case of kidnapping, liberation and ransom negotiations they were represented as "Islamists" threatening sentences issued by a religious court. These were people who were not extremely motivated politically and ideologically in their environment, village, everyday life; they had no perspective of their struggle and war, of what would happen in the future, if it would be good or bad. They even discussed questions contrary to their "political" orientation, and listened to reproach and criticism: "What are you doing, why do you kill each other."

At the same time, this opposition group was not homogenous neither in an organizational nor in a social sense since the various groups were not united: on the one hand "being the leading element with logical thinking" and "distinguishing marks", and on the other hand "thieves", most probably the inhabitants of that village. Relationships with each other were ambiguous and not always hierarchical. Their promise to liberate the hostage and return all the stolen money and items was not kept and for another group it became a way to "get" or "grab" money through quick and flexible "bargains".

This dual process shows the absence of a strict hierarchy inside the group, when one of the parties (the "leader" party) could not (or did not want to) veto the other party's ("villagers", "lower class") demands to leave the hostage imprisoned and to obtain a ransom. The integration of "lower" class into "oppositionist" powers could be silently encouraged. On the other hand, the application (realization) of the strict hierarchy to liberate the hostage could ruin their integration. Thus, in case of internal interrelations, the integration of the "oppositionist powers" became somehow important for the different layers (classes). It was more important than the realization of hierarchical power (rule). The other party was not against kidnappings, but regarded that as a "wrong" kidnapping, since the hostage was not rich.

A mechanism to organize kidnappings was established during the war with various functional manifestations and actors. The kidnapping net included actors, starting with spies, the people who carried it out and other people who were forced to participate (for example, the driver, whose passport and car were taken and who was forced to provide various services). The bus routes became a part of the kidnapping net. Despite the difficulties that occurred during to the war, the route from Aleppo to Yerevan was safe for Armenians. It was the "Armenian route" and the drivers were Armenians, though it was also attacked and Syrians abducted.[19]

In summary, it is important to note that local Armenians faced new challenges because of the Syrian war. The forced migration from Syria to Armenia was incorporated into the individual and family strategy of survival. The bus migration was not only a survival strategy that originated from war and conflict, but also an interesting social phenomenon, around which many everyday manifestations of war developed, and where new social interrelations, as well as connections and actors, were formed.

## Conclusion

The current anthropological research on violence, conflict and forced migration while the Syrian war is even now continuing, is interesting and problematic. It is very interesting because it provides the opportunity to understand some specifics of current processes through "hot" and "fresh" filed materials. It is problematic because people who deal with sensitive and traumatic stories are de facto refugees with uncertain further. At the same time, we should take into the consideration the social-political and war conditions in which they or their relatives lived or are still living. That is why the fieldwork and materials have such sensitive and problematic aspects.

Conflict perceptions among Syrian Armenians include some chronological and event points around which the war and conflict narratives are being constructed. It starts from events in Tunis, Egypt, Libya in 2011–2012. The other aspect of conflict perception is directly related to Syria and becomes the main axis to describe the Syrian conflict. These are events in southern Syria in the city of Daraa that escalated into armed conflict in 2011. Anyway, "Daraa" was the beginning of the conflict that afterwards spread to other regions and cities (Homs, Hama): Aleppo was also becoming a theatre of battles where the majority of Syrian Armenians lived.

The continuing and spreading conflict gradually gave rise to concrete dangers and threats that shaped conflict or wartime daily life with relevant manifestations and new individual and collective experiences.

Connections between people, violence and war differ in accordance with situations and events. The conflict may suddenly or barely surface in the district, at home, in the streets or in magazines. In this case, there is not a unified perception of the war or its related manifestations. Everyone has his own case, story, experience.

---

[19] For example, the driver and three passengers were kidnapped near the Turkish border in the summer of 2013.

In this situation, the war also conditions, dictates and forms different survival strategies at an individual or family level, one of which is migration to Armenia. The migration of Syrian Armenians to Armenia was based on personal or family decisions.

The process and ways to migrate to Armenia are in itself highly interesting manifestations of conflict's daily life.

The bus routes from Aleppo (Aleppo-Yerevan, Aleppo-Beirut) became part of war and migration daily life, where the war and migration, real dangers and ways to avoid them combine. This is where the different parts in conflict meet, where new experiences and practices to overcome risks and threats take shape.

## Bibliography

*A Short Reference about the Problems of Syrian Armenians* (2014): The Ministry of Diaspora, Republic of Armenia. Unpublished.

Abrahamyan, Levon (2000): Armyanskaya diaspora: raskhojdenie i vstrecha [Armenian Diaspora: Divergence and Meeting]. In: *Diaspori,* 1–2: 52–76.

Ayvazyan, Hovhannes (ed.) (2003): *Hay Spyurk: Hanragidaran* [The Armenian Diaspora: Encyclopaedia]. Yerevan: Hayk. Hanragidaran.

Cafarella, Jennifer (2014): Jabhat Al-Nusra in Syria: An Islamic Emirate for Al-Qaeda. In: *Middle East Security Report,* 25: 1–66.

Droz-Vincent, Philippe (2014): "State of Barbary" (Take Two): From the Arab Spring to the Return of Violence in Syria. In: *The Middle East Journal,* 68 (1): 33–58.

Eastmond, Marita (2007): Stories as Lived Experience: Narratives in Forced Migration Research. In: *Journal of Refugee Studies,* 20 (2): 248–264.

Holliday, Joseph (2011): The Struggle for Syria in 2011. In: *Middle East Security Report,* 2: 1–29

Holliday, Joseph (2012): Syria's Army Opposition. In: *Middle East Security Report,* 3: 1–57.

*Housing and Job Major Problems Facing Syrian-Armenians* (October 19, 2015): URL: http://www.tert.am/en/news/2015/10/19/syrian-armenians/1819461, accessed on December 16, 2015.

Ibrahim, Lina (March 20, 2011): *Syrians of Daraa, Baniyas Set Demands to End Protest, Watan Says*, Bloomberg News. URL: http://www.bloomberg.com/news/articles/2011-03-20/syrians-of-daraa-baniyas-set-demands-to-end-protest-watan-says, accessed on December 16, 2015.

Interview with UNHCR Representative (July 30, 2015): URL: http://www.un.am/en/news/303#sthash.Sle68AnC.dpuf, accessed on December 16, 2015.

Hovhannisyan, Richard (1974): The Ebb and Flow of the Armenian Minority in the Arab Middle East. In: *Middle East Journal,* 28 (1): 19–32.

*Kidnapped Syrian Armenian Released* (August 10, 2012): URL: http://www.panarmenian.net/eng/news/119020/, accessed on December 16, 2015.

Migliorino, Nicola (2008): *(Re)constructing Armenia in Lebanon and Syria: Ethno-Cultural Diversity and the State in the Aftermath of a Refugee Crisis*. New York: Berghahn Books.

Migliorino, Nicola (2006): “Kulna Suriyyin”? The Armenian Community and the State in Contemporary Syria. In: *Revue des mondes musulmans et de la Méditerranée*, 1–16. URL: http://remmm.revues.org/3020, accessed on December 10, 2014.

O’Bagy, Elizabeth (2013): The Free Syrian Army. In: *Middle East Security Report*, 9: 1–49.

*Open Letter to the Leaders of the Syrian Opposition Regarding Human Rights Abuses by Armed Opposition Members* (March 20, 2012): URL: https://www.hrw.org/news/2012/03/20/open-letter-leaders-syrian-opposition, accessed on December 16, 2015.

Sinjab, Lina (March 19, 2011): *Middle East Unrest: Silence Broken in Syria*. URL: http://www.bbc.com/news/world-middle-east-12794882, accessed on December 16, 2015.

Sanjian, Ara (2015): Armyanskie obshchini v usloviyakh grajdanskoy voyni: sravnenie Livana i Syrii [Armenian Communities in Conditions of Civil War: Lebanon and Syria Compared]. In: *Diaspori*, 1–2: 55–88.

*Syria: Armed Opposition Groups Committing Abuses End Kidnappings, Forced Confessions, and Executions* (March 20, 2012): URL: http://www.hrw.org/news/2012/03/20/syria-armed-opposition-groups-committing-abuses, accessed on October 28, 2015.

Zolyan, Mikael (October 15, 2015): *Refugees or Repatriates? Syrian Armenians Return to Armenia*. URL: https://www.opendemocracy.net/od-russia/mikayel-zolyan/refugees-or-repatriates-syrian-armenians-return-to-armenia, accessed on December 16, 2015.

# Ezidi Struggle for Survival

## From the Last Massacre in Sinjar to the New Temple in Tbilisi

*Marcello Mollica*

### Prologue

I first went to Tbilisi in August 2014 within the framework of an European Union research program.[1] My knowledge of Caucasia was limited. Research *loci* and ideas emerged through e-mails with a local colleague. First, there were mixed villages near Tbilisi, Georgian-Orthodox and Azerbaijan-Muslim (Tsodoreti, Tsikhisdziri, Vedzisi). Second, a bit farther off were other mixed villages (Dmanisi, Tetritskharo). Third, the Black Sea Coast in the Republic of Adjara was populated by both Georgian Muslims and Christians. Finally, there were sacred sites in Tbilisi city-centre (e. g., Father Vitali's grave within the Russian Orthodox Church complex).

However, that August of 2014 was to become known for events then happening in the Middle East, the product of the Syrian and Iraqi wars (Mollica 2015). Attention was drawn to minorities, above all to the Ezidis[2] then under attack by the terror group Daesh [Islamic State for Iraq and the Levant] (Açıkyıldız 2014). I was not new to studying Middle Eastern minorities and religiously-driven violence (Mollica 2011, 2012, 2014). Thus, when my colleague replied to another e-mail of mine saying that not only was there an old Ezidi community in Tbilisi, but that something was happening with Ezidi refugees coming from North Iraq, I realized that was the link I needed to conduct my research. Once I started, more intriguing and controversial components materialized, above all the building of an Ezidi religious structure. What follows connects the two events, framing the discussion within boundaries set by the encounter between a diasporic and a settled religious community.

[1] Marie Curie Project PIRSES-GA-2013-318961 (PSDEV).

[2] In this chapter I have chosen to use the word "Ezidi" and not the word "Yezidi". Ezidis argue that "Yezidi" is a name given by outsiders. Prof Çakır Ceyhan Suvari had a conversation with both Baba Sheikh and Baba Çavuş in Lalish on this issue two months after Isil massacre of Ezidis in Sinjar. Baba Sheikh explained that for them the word "Yezidi" has a negative meaning, above all because many Muslims argue that the word "Yezidi" comes from the Yezid/Yazid bin Muaviye, the murderer of Caliph Ali and his son Huseyin. Baba Sheikh added that "now even more than before that was not part of Ezidi history". On the other hand, for Baba Sheik the name "Ezidi" has a different meaning, that is, "Khuda/god worshipers".

## The Setting

It took a while to get in touch with the Ezidi in Tbilisi. There were telephone calls, visits and delays with respondents in the Ezidi Cultural Centre. The environment was never good to conduct interviews, as it was always crowded. In addition, some respondents had non-academic expectations and tried to exert control over data and its dissemination. People were generally friendly although highly suspicious.

I conducted the interviews mostly with Ana Ramazashvili, an MA student at Tbilisi State University. Ana translated the interviews with Dimitri Pihrbar (known as PirDima), who spoke Georgian and Kurdish, languages I do not speak, while I conducted English interviews with a UN-employed Ezidi refugee. Professor Keti Kutsishvili translated an interview with PirDima, when Keti, the Pir and I went for the first time to visit the construction site of the new Ezidi temple. Keti facilitated and translated the interview with another informant, Karim Ankosi. Additional information on the opening of the Ezidi temple was later collected by Boris Komakhidze, Ba student at Tbilisi State University.

The Ezidi Cultural Centre was on Tsinamdzghvrishvili Street. On the right side from the front door, below the stairs, many bags labelled *Kurdish Regional Government, Iraq, RGK* sat for weeks. In the main room there were usually an average of half a dozen aged men and half a dozen youngsters. The young men served tea or water to the elders. I remember just one occasion, somewhat formal, in which an old man entered the room and was addressed as *Sheik*. All stood and some kissed his hand. Most conversations were in Kurdish. The elders spoke Russian, but all spoke Georgian.

On another occasion, while I was interviewing a refugee, PirDima sat on the other side of the room counting money (mostly Euros). Then PirDima gave the money to the only woman in the room. I realized later that she was the secretary and in charge of the Women's Rights Community Initiative. On that occasion, we were shown a file on a PC screen called 'refugees': lists of refugees with names and addresses. A youngster printed that file for PirDima and put another copy into a folder. The young men never participated in the conversation with the elders. They all had Facebook accounts and one exchanged contacts with Ana. However, Ana never received any reply to her messages.

## The Ezidis

The Ezidis are a Kurmanji-speaking ethno-confessional group. Their ethnic homeland is a mountainous area in present North Iraq (Guest 1987 and 1993). Ezidis believe this region is the centre of the universe where God decided to live after the creation of the world. Old Kurdish religion components are dominant elements, but the influence of Islam on Yezidi religion is strong and undeniable (even if many Ezidis may not like to hear this.) The holy valley named Lalish

(Laleş), a place of temples and some buildings, in Nineveh Governorate, is their only place of pilgrimage, with its religious structure and the tomb of Sheikh Adi ibn Musafir (Muzaffar) (1073–1163).

Scholars often portray Ezidis as a mysterious people because of their religious practices or as followers of an esoteric faith blending Islamic, Christian and indigenous elements. The Ezidis are a closed society with prohibitions and strict endogamy. A number of categories characterize Ezidi hierarchy (Guest 1993: 35–37). Simplifying, the society consists of three hereditary castes: Sheikhs (highest religious authority), Pirs (saints, priests) and Murids (laymen, disciples). Each caste is divided into endogamous clans (Asatrian 1999/2000).

This intricate system of relations had an impact on both the transmission and the acquisition of knowledge. Attention to religious "purity" goes beyond the social dimension visible within the caste system to touch the belief in metempsychosis [migration of souls between humans following death]. It is an orally transmitted religion, based on orthopraxy [adherence to rules governing all life], where faith and social organization have been mutually reinforcing, providing means to survive in hostile environments, as they often had to hide their beliefs.

For Dalalyan (2011), there are about 200000–250000 people professing Ezidism, although some sources put this number closer to one million.[3] Recent figures coming from organizations working with refugees from Sinjar in the Kurdish Region put their number between 300000 and 450000. Complex and overlapping dimensions between Ezidism and Kurdishness have had and have an impact on censuses. However, Ezidis represent a tiny percentage of the Kurdish population, presumably between 26–33 million (Mollica 2011), although some would put it to 40 million, 37 in the Middle East and 3 in diaspora (Piot and Goldstein 2012).

A 2008 UNHCR Report estimated the Ezidis in Iraq between 120000 and 500000, with significant communities near Lalish and Sinjar. Around 15000 Ezidis lived in Syria. In Turkey, there were a few Ezidi villages southeast of Diyarbakır. A growing number of Ezidi migrants lived in Western Europe, mostly in Germany (40000), mainly originating from Turkey, with additions from Iraq during the 1990s. In former Soviet territory, Kurds and Ezidis were concentrated in Russia, Azerbaijan, Armenia and Georgia (Chikhladze and Chikhladze 2003).

[3] Kurmanji-speaking Muslim Kurds live mostly in Turkey (10–15 million), Northern Iraq (4–6 million), Syria (1–2 million), Azerbaijan, Russia and some European countries (mainly in Germany). Groups professing Ezidism live in the same countries, except Azerbaijan (Dalalyan 2011).

## Ezidis in Georgia

Nodar Mossaki (2014) has recently argued that the old belief of an Ezidi migration in the XII century in Georgia is simply a myth. He shows that Ezidis migrated to Georgia (and mainly to Tbilisi) only in Russian and especially in Soviet and even more so in post-Soviet times. However, from the XV century the Ezidis were caught in the hostilities between Persia and the Ottoman Empire. Georgia remained a non-Muslim state that attracted neighbours living under Turks (Chikhladze and Chikhladze 2003). Large-scale Ezidi migration took place in a series of waves dating from the XVII century.

When the Russian army withdrew from Anatolia after the 1828–29 War, many Ezidis moved to Erivan province [today central Armenia, Turkish province of Iğdır, and eastern Azerbaijan]. In the 1830s, following new turmoil in Anatolia, more Ezidis crossed the border. Another migration occurred between 1879 and 1882. In 1881, Ezidis in Tbilisi were 4 697 and the imperial census in 1897 enumerated 14 726 Ezidis under the Tsar (Guest 1993: 196). By the beginning of 1912, Ezidis increased to about 24 500. Another wave occurred in 1915–1917 (Chikhladze and Chikhladze 2003). In 1918, yet another wave of Ezidis came from Kars (Yepiskoposian et al. 2010).

Georgia was a destination to escape from persecution in both the Ottoman and Persian empires. Nevertheless, the Southern Caucasus served as home to Kurds (and Assyrians) since the early XX century. However, in 1937–1946, nearly all Muslim Kurds (and Meskhetian Turks) were deported from Adjara (Chikhladze and Chikhladze 2003).[4] According to Nasidze et al. (2005), who studied Kurdish groups in Georgia, during their migration to the Caucasus they experienced a bottleneck effect [a sharp population reduction due to natural or human activities] and since then have not mixed with the Georgians. However, in the Soviet Union the Ezidis "disappeared" from official sources, since the Soviets used language rather than religion as the marker of national identity.

The 1960s–1980s were the best time for Ezidi Kurds: they had a theatre and a folkloristic dance group; Kurdish culture was a regular feature, while the radio ran weekly broadcasts in Kurdish (directed by Karim Ankosi under the Georgian State Radio) and there were Kurdish newspapers (above all "Glavezh" [The Morning Star] founded in 1999 by Karim Ankosi).

This is what the 2008 UNHCR Report calls the "Kurdish cultural renaissance in Georgia". In the 1989 census, 33 331 Kurds were recorded in Georgia, the vast majority Ezidis (UNHCR Report 2008). However, in the early 1990s the theatre and dance group closed and the radio stopped broadcasting. Migration began.

---

4 The 2008 UNHCR Report gives these numbers: in the 1939 census, 12 915 Kurds were recorded in Georgia (around 6 000 outside Tbilisi, mostly Ezidis); in 1944, some 9 000 Kurds were deported from Georgia. This dramatically altered the Kurdish profile, depleting it of its Muslim component.

## Migration

Migration is a constant theme in Ezidi history. In Georgia, most Ezidi left during Eduard Shevardnadze's time (1992–2003). In 2003, according to Chikhladze and Chikhladze (2003), the Ezidi Kurds were even afraid that their community might disappear, to the extent that migration became an opportunity for cultural survival. According to official figures, between 1989 and 2002 they lost 37 per cent of their population – the most prominent Ezidi community decline in the South Caucasus. The 2008 UNHCR Report ascribed the decline both to state policies (nationalism, discrimination) and to Ezidi cultural features (endogamy, caste system). Moreover, the departure of businessmen and community leaders reduced their ability to interact with Georgian civil society, just when state support was withdrawn. On the one hand, emigration changed the proportions of religious castes. Sheikhs and Pirs fell in respect to Murids, while the latter's capacity to pay for Sheikhs' and Pirs' religious services declined. On the other hand, economic collapse affected their language, while depriving the community of public spaces to gather and thus keep endogamous marriage practices alive. However, migration must be seen in light of wider Ezidi migration flows. There was migration from Turkey in the 1980s and from Iraq in the 1990s after the first Gulf War. Ezidi migration from the South Caucasus was mostly toward Germany, with few cases of return migration (UNHCR Report 2008). An implication of this trend is that the diaspora[5] lacks horizontal relations and is capable only of vertical relations, as we shall see in reference to state financial support.

## Education

The same 2008 UNHCR Report argued, however, that in the late 1990s there was a reinvigoration of the Ezidi community (that is, a number of cultural activities). It is already worth noting that what the report calls "reinvigoration" was helped by government assistance and funding received from the Regional Government of Kurdistan, a point we will return to when discussing the new Ezidi

[5] Main definitions of "diaspora" are, of course, based on Jewish, Armenian and African communities; however, in the "past two decades this concept has been extended to various groups of migrant or ethnic origin" (Kokot et al. 2013: 10). In this chapter my definition of "diaspora" refers to the latter theoretical frame, thus including "all expatriate groups who consider themselves as members of a worldwide network of common origin and identity, regardless of individual legal status or citizenship"(Kokot et al. 2013: 9). On a methodological level, in order to avoid the trap of the so-called "methodological nationalism" which takes for granted that diasporic units "are a compact entity from homogeneous countries of origin", I endorse Giordano's (2013: 218) approach in his analysis of Penang's Chinese diaspora, which instead reveals both cultural and social diversification.

temple. In 2003, according to the 2008 UNHCR Report, four schools in Tbilisi taught Kurdish, although none had books for students or teachers. Karim Ankosi contests this information.[6] Education is here an important variable. The capability to adapt to a changing environment seems conditioned by prohibitions associated with Ezidism, still visible in Georgia, although to a diminishing extent.

Ankosi argues that Chikhladze and Chikhladze (2003) used fake data on schools and that later those data were used by the UNHCR in their extensively quoted 2008 Report. According to his chronology of events, Kurdish classes in Georgia used Armenian Methodist textbooks for many years, but he never liked their methodology. The first textbook, based on Armenian, was used between 1921 and 1923. The second, again based on Armenian, was used in the early '30s. The third was used in the mid-sixties, when in Tbilisi Public School Number 7, Kurdish classes were opened, again with an Armenian teacher teaching in Kurmanji. The fourth was used at the end of the '70s, again in Tbilisi Public School Number 7, when Ankosi started working on the direction of the programme. Classes were offered weekly by an ethnic Kurdish teacher, while the methodology was changed. The school closed due to financial problems at the beginning of the new century. A last experience was in 2008, when Ankosi was given some space by the NGO "Caucasian House" to teach Kurmanji to an average of 25 students. The rationale behind his classes was linguistic, not cultural, although when asked for religious information he said he "had a chance to explain". Ankosi is critical of international organizations, blaming them for not providing support and for relying on fake data. Part and parcel of Ezidi recent cultural life, he is also critical of past and present Ezidi political and religious leaders.

In 1978, Ankosi formed an organization called "Runai", which lasted until 1998. In 1992, he founded the NGO "Society of the Kurdish Citizens of Georgia", later renamed "Union of the Ezidis of Georgia". By early 2002, Georgia had several Kurdish/Ezidi structures. In 2003, the Union of the Ezidis, supported by the New Rights Party, started publishing a Russian-language newspaper.

If we look closely at Armenia, the negative attitude towards education is associated with both religious directives and the Ezidi family economic system (engaged in seasonal cattle rearing). Education was seen as an "unnecessary luxury". Ezidi identity is thus constructed upon a conservative attitude toward education and traditional upbringing of children. According to Delalyan (2011), the ideologists (here meaning priestly castes) of the Ezidi identity failed to elaborate mechanisms for modernizing their socio-religious heritage.

---

[6] Born in Tbilisi in 1937, a self-defined "Kurd of the first Georgian generation", he came from a family of refugees from Van, Turkey. He was an activist in the Kurdish liberation movement and a member of the Georgian Communist party, as well as a scholar and the founder of many Ezidi/Kurdish organizations.

## Population Picture

In a 2003 survey, the majority of Ezidis were reported as urban dwellers, but just a few years before, there were some Kurdish villages in Kakheti. In Tbilisi, they formed a compact community mainly living in the poorer districts. The majority was engaged in hard manual labour (Chikhladze and Chikhladze 2003) and many were taxi-drivers.

A 1999 census reported 13 100 Kurds in Azerbaijan. A 2001 census reported 40 620 Ezidis in Armenia. According to a 2002 census, there were 18 329 Ezidis in Georgia. (Adding 2 514 Muslim Kurds, the overall Kurdish community was 20 843.) Some 93.4 per cent of Ezidis in Georgia lived in Tbilisi; a few hundred were recorded in the eastern industrial cities of Telavi and Rustavi. However, Ezidi community leaders argue that official data are inflated, and some estimate there are just 6 000 Ezidis in Georgia. According to the censuses, some 60 000 Ezidis lived in the South Caucasus. Georgia and Armenia had small populations of Muslim Kurds, so that within the Kurds, Ezidis form majorities, which is unusual in their experience. In contrast, in Azerbaijan they form a tiny minority within a larger Muslim Kurd minority (UNHCR Report 2008). Finally, thousands of Ezidi migrants from Armenia live in Georgia, mostly in Tbilisi (Dalalyan 2011).

Today, the most important Ezidi organization in Georgia is the "Ezidi Spiritual Council of the Ezidis in Georgia", officially registered in 2011 but informally already operational, of which PirDima is the head.[7] The council acts as an umbrella organisation for all Ezidi groups (e. g., "Ezidi Cultural Centre", "Women's Right Community Initiative" and "Ezidi Centre for Ezidis").

## The Ezidis within the Georgian Religious Panorama

Georgia contains a large majority of Orthodox Christians (83.9 %).[8] The Constitution acknowledges the special role of the Georgian Orthodox Church in Geor-

---

7 Thirty-six years old and a self-defined "Ezidi of the fifth generation", his family came during the Ottoman time from Van, Turkey. Since December 2013, he is the spiritual leader of the Ezidi Council in Georgia. He argues that his mission is to keep Ezidism alive in Georgia, despite all financial problems.

8 Other religious groups: Muslim 9.9 %, Armenian Apostolic 3.9 %, none 0.8 %, Catholics 0.8 %, Jewish 0.1 %, others 0.8 %. Georgians belong mostly to the Georgian Orthodox Church. Then there are Catholics, Muslims and other groups. Azerbaijani are both Shia and Sunni. Armenians are Eastern Orthodox, Gregorian, and Uniate. The few Abkhazians are Sunni and Orthodox. Russians are Orthodox and followers of Russian Spiritual Christianity (Dukhobor, Molokans) and Starovers. Ossetians are Orthodox and Protestants. Greeks are Orthodox. Jews are Jewish. Kurds are almost all Ezidi. Besides them, there are followers of "non-conventional religious organiza-

gia's history, reiterated in the 2002 "Concordat" between the Church and the Republic of Georgia. Religious teaching in the national education system has been dominated by a focus on Orthodox Christianity (UNHCR Report 2008). The influence of the Church has grown in recent years (Dafflon 2014: 162). In Soviet times, there was no tension since ethno-religious issues were avoided. This time of partial assimilation ended in the early 1990s. Since then, conflicts have increased (Chikhladze and Chikhladze 2003).

Ezidis started defending their rights under Shevardnadze (1992–2003). However, assimilation had already affected the religious sphere. Ezidis were used to celebrating Georgian national holidays and Orthodox and Catholic Christmas like the rest of the country (Chikhladze and Chikhladze 2003). Syncretism[9] was visible in the public holiday of Saint George, when Ezidis used to go to cemeteries, as did locals. This led to tension on the sensitive issue of burial rituals. For the deceased Ezidis who had converted to Christianity, priests would first celebrate the function and then usually Pirs would expel the priests from the house, since conversion is not allowed in Ezidism.

According to Ankosi, young Ezidis got involved in religion some ten years ago following a general religious revival. The Ezidis have not been subjected to forced conversions; rather, the impact has been subliminal since they have been exposed to Georgian Orthodox discourse. Along with an Ezidi religious revival, there were also conversions to Orthodoxy. Unlike Ezidism, Georgian Orthodoxy allows conversion. The UNHCR 2008 Report goes further, suggesting that, once converted, Ezidis had a chance to expand their possibilities for marriage as they would avoid any religious-driven stigma.

PirDima argues that there are increasing attempts today to convert Ezidis to Protestantism and psychological indoctrination from Jehovah's Witnesses (apparently the latter approach Ezidis saying that they will offer financial support). PirDima recalls the case of Georgian missionaries converting three Ezidi villages in Armenia.

Some informants told me of cases of people who have been baptized and *are* still Ezidi. For PirDima, neighbours and friends play a role here; he also mentioned that a quite common saying is "let me baptize you". PirDima argues that sometimes people are said to have been converted in official documents, even though they were not consciously converted. There are cases of Ezidis becoming

---

tions": splitters from the Georgian Orthodox Church (Mkalavishvili); newly established churches (Fire of Prometheus); "Foreigners" groups (New Apostolic Church, Pentecostals, Jehovah's Witnesses, Adventists, Evangelists, Healing Army, Boston Group, World Christians); groups with eastern roots (ISCON); Islamic groups (Salafi); and "Special Groups" (Anthroposophy, Scientology) (personal communication by Keti Kutsishvili).

9 For a detailed account on Ezidi cultural mixing dynamics, see Langer (2010) and Spät (2013).

aggressive toward those who have misleadingly converted them and cases of others becoming aggressive toward other Ezidis once converted.

After all, since 2011, when Ezidism was officially acknowledged as a religion, Ezidi religious leadership has allowed some converts to return to Ezidism. Major problems (sometimes manifest within the same hierarchy) are here linked to indoctrination, religious structure and access to information. This emerged, for instance, when many Ezidis were refused asylum in some European countries precisely because as Murids (laymen) they were unable to explain the basis of their religion (UNHCR Report 2008).

## The Issue of Language and Ethnicity

Ezidis in the South Caucasus may speak the language of countries where they live as their first language while having variable degrees of fluency in Kurmanji. According to a 1989 Soviet census, 75 per cent of Georgia's Kurds recorded Kurdish as their native language, while 11.5 per cent and 12.3 per cent recorded Georgian and Russian respectively as their native languages. The 2008 UNHCR Report suggests that, in Georgia, the Ezidis identify broadly with the Kurdish community while "rejecting notions of Ezidi particularity". However, the terminology seems confused. If the term "Ezidi" refers to adherents of Ezidism, Ezidi self-identification with the Kurdish community fluctuates in accordance with political developments. The religious distinction gave rise to claims that the Ezidis are not Kurds (i. e., in Armenia, where the issue produced a longstanding "acrimonious" debate)[10].

In Armenia, however, constructing Kurdish/Ezidi national identities among the Kurmanji-speaking population means considering the largest minority group: according to the 2001 census, 42 139 people or 1.3 per cent of the total population (Dalalyan 2011). This census (as previous censuses) considered Kurmanji as the Ezidis' mother tongue, but now they have learnt Armenian and the census does not differentiate between those self-defined "Kurds-Ezidi" and those self-defined "Ezidi-Kurds". Thus, among the Kurmanji-speaking population of Armenia, many terms are used ("Ezidi", "Kurd", "Kurd-Ezidi", "Ezidi-Kurd") (Dalalyan 2011). Mamoe Halit, quoted in Dalalyan (2011), argued that Soviet Ezidi-Kurds considered themselves "Ezidis and not Kurds" (meaning Muslim Kurds). An elderly Ezidi would still get offended if called "Kurd". However, in recent years, some Ezidis preferred to be called "Kurds", so that in the 1999 book "Nationalities of Armenia", published by the Academy of Sciences of Armenia, quoted in Dalalyan (2011), Kurds and Ezidis are listed as separate communities.

---

[10] See on this "Ezidis in Armenia" blog, edited by the photographer Onnik James Krikorian.

The Issue of Human Rights

Besides a peculiar internal structure and the debate over identity, according to the UNHCR 2008 Report, the human rights context in the South Caucasus should also explain Ezidi decline. Despite freedom of association, they experienced obstacles to enjoying socio-economic rights. Lacking an external kin-state and an organized diaspora (horizontal relations), Ezidis remained unprotected, while other minorities could rely on alternative sources of support (external kin-states). This became manifest once the Soviet state support policy for minorities ended and a policy of groups competing for resources started. The issue of self-identification then played a major role: Kurdish or Ezidi identity? It is here worth mentioning that it was in the post-Soviet time that an Ezidi Member of Parliament was elected, Mame Raiki (1995–99), who could allocate a budget for Ezidi cultural development. However, since then, as the Ezidi groups associated with diverse political parties, no ethno-religious Ezidi candidate has entered the Georgian Parliament (UNHCR Report 2008).

According to the UNHCR 2008 Report, in the South Caucasus there is little interest in adopting international minority rights standards or specific laws on national minorities, as envisaged by their membership in the Council of Europe. National minorities are still protected under general non-discrimination provisions. In reality, the accession to the Council of Europe had a detrimental effect on Georgia's compliance with international standards, while a 2005 parliamentary resolution defining "national minority" excluded those living in cities where most Ezidis live, who thus, by implication, cannot be considered *national minority*.

Soviet legacy had numerous consequences on policies toward national minorities. First of all, the status granted to ethnic groups is related to their presence in Georgia (e. g., Ossetians are not considered an indigenous people but an *invited* people [Dafflon 2014: 156–158]; while Armenians' presence is also contested). In addition, Georgian language and Orthodox faith lie at the heart of the national project and, by implication, exclude persons belonging to national minorities. As Dafflon (2014) argues, in terms of policies towards national minorities the years since independence can be divided into three periods: 1. under Zviad Gamsakhurdia (1990–92): peak of nationalism culminated in interethnic conflicts; 2. under Eduard Shevardnadze (1992–2003): politics of ignorance in the context of a failing state; 3. under Mikheil Saakashvili (2004–2013): strengthening state's authority and more inclusive national discourse (Dafflon 2014: 156–158). It is too early to consider incumbent president Giorgi Margvelashvili's policy toward national minorities.

The Ezidis are accepted in the South Caucasus as a "historical minority", that is, a minority tolerated as long as it makes no demands (UNHCR Report 2008). Perceptions of Ezidis in Georgia, however, have been dominated by their socio-economic position. The least prestigious professions are associated with them (street sweepers, rubbish collectors, street vendors). According to the UN-

HCR 2008 Report, some sources suggest concern over the similarity between the Georgian words Kurd *(kurdi)* and thief *(kurti)*, to the extent that some incidents of police brutality towards Ezidis have been motivated by perceived impunity. Finally, according to Chikhladze and Chikhladze (2003), Georgian society did not respond to Ezidi/Kurdish desire to become its component part, and, when Kurds voiced their disapproval at a conference in October 2002, several newspapers accused them of anti-Georgian sentiments.

## The Issue of the Temple in Ezidism

Ezidis usually do not have temples. Even Lalish is rather a complex of tombs and other elements than a shrine, while the Parestgeh in Lalish is a huge sanctuary consisting of several units. In the villages, there were shrines (which may or may not contain tombs/mazar) often outside the houses of Sheykhs and Pirs. Caucasian Ezidis lack such installations. In any case, Lalish is considered unique, enhanced by the believers' duty of pilgrimage. There are however cultural centres in the diaspora where people meet for festive events, both secular and religious. Thus, reintroducing something like a shrine might be seen as a move of those who consider Ezidism as a form of Zoroastrianism, which needs something like a temple. Some traditionalists do not support claims of Kurdishness. On the contrary, they claim that Ezidi language has nothing to do with Kurdish and that Ezidism is a separate religion. This is a general split in Ezidi communities, especially in Caucasia.[11] In fact, in Tbilisi, those defending "Kurdishness" were at best sceptical about the construction of an Ezidi temple.

Many Ezidis would argue that the only temple should be Lalish. On their part, religious authorities were satisfied by different forms of prayers in other *loci*, held at Pirs' or Sheiks' houses. The uniqueness of Lalish is often explained by reference to the sun's importance for Ezidis. They say "our temple *is* the sun", thus it does not need walls. However, new generations are building new temples, like the Alevis.[12]

A similar discussion took place a few years ago in Armenia. A monument was erected in Armavir Province to represent both Ezidi faith and Lalish Sanctuary, the so-called temple of Shamiran (Armenian) or Shemiran (Kurdish). On that construction, in 2013 Christine Allison produced one of the very few accounts available in academic literature. Articulating on the relationship between monuments and publics, she encounters semantic problems similar to those I met in Georgia in regards to the word "temple" as used by my informants to refer to the Georgian construction. In Armenia it is "referred to not as a *pamiatnik* (the Russian word for monument, which is normally used for such large pub-

---

[11] Personal communication by Dr Robert Langer.

[12] Personal Communication by Dr Çakır Ceyhan Suvari. See also Mollica 2012b.

lic constructions) but as either a *ziyaret* (shrine) or a *nîşan* (symbol)" (Allison 2013: 161). Neither Christine Allison nor Robert Langer, on whose unpublished data she relies, are able to substantiate the issue (Allison 2013: 179). However, what was constructed in Armavir Province was not a building, but a freestanding monument to which there was a yearly pilgrimage at the time of the Lalish feast. Traditionalists boycotted the event.[13] The businessman and philanthropist Mirza Cholo built this monument near the graves of his relatives. The Armenian Ezidi religious leader, Hassan Hasanyane, blessed it.[14] Similar constructions stand in the Russian Black Sea coastal town of Krasnodar and, a much more famous one known as Bingehê Lalish is in the city of Dohuk.

"Temple" (here denoting what in English would be a "shrine") was the word respondents used during interviews up to March 2015. The new structure was meant to contain all current Ezidi organizations in Tbilisi, while an educational centre will be built nearby. The official name I was given was "The House of the Ezidis". Yet, "house" was also the name some elder Ezidis opposing the construction used in reference to old places used in Ezidi rituals in Tbilisi, that is, (private) "houses" of Pirs and Sheiks. "Mala Ezidiyan" or "House of the Ezidis", however, is also used in Germany in reference to the Organization of Ezidis. "Mal"/"house" is also used to refer to the house/lineage of Sheikhs and Pirs possessing special abilities in Iraqi Kurdistan.[15]

Ezidis refer to the main Sanctuary in Lalish (that of Sheikh Adi) as "parestgeh" ("the protected place" in Kurdish).[16] Many argue that Parestgeh is singular,[17]

---

[13] Personal communication by Dr Robert Langer. See on this also "Ezidis in Armenia" blog, edited by the photographer Onnik James Krikorian.

[14] The Religious Council of the Ezidis has however approved the construction of a new Ezidi temple [Quba mere diwane] which will be built in the town of Aknalich (http://www.horizonweekly.ca/news/details/71632).

[15] An example is that of late Sheikh Bardan and his wife, famous for being able to cure *jinn-* [supernatural beings] induced maladies. People still talk about them as "Mala Bardan". Some still say, "I was always afraid, so I went to Mala Bardan to get some sacred earth". Another example is that of "Mala Mira", the princely family; people refer to anybody from princely lineage as "Mala Mira" (personal communication by Dr Eszter Spät).

[16] Lalish structure is also called "parestgehan" ["parestgehekan" in Aramaic]. The root is parast- ("worshipper"), parastesh, "worship". It also means somebody who serves (guard, slave). The Arabic word for "temple" is "ma'bad", which also has the meaning of "to serve". "Parast(iš)gâh" is common Iranian for "worship-place". The Zoroastrians use it for their shrines and temples. However, it could be used in Persian for any place of worship. "Parastin" means "to defend" in Kurdish, and there is also some intelligence called Parastin, Parastin u Zanyarî (assisting intelligence agency) (personal communications by Dr Robert Langer and by Dr Eszter Spät).

[17] However, others argue that *parestgeh* can also be plural, depending on its use. Some scholars would not consider Parestgeha Lalish a temple, but rather a complex grown around the mausoleum of Sheikh Adi over time. In Ezidism there is no "temple" tra-

unique, as is Lalish, being the throne of God. Earthly Lalish is a reflection of heavenly Lalish, while the earth only settled and became green when Lalish came down to earth. Then there are the sacred places, "qob" (conical spire) or "mazar" (grave), but they are not necessarily graves. Sacred places are many and built in different ways. However, a "qob" or a "mazar" cannot be built anywhere, as the presence of the Khas (holy beings) is what makes places sacred.[18]

A case in point is what Baba Sheikh told one journalist: "We cannot make new ones [meaning "qob" or "mazar"]. These are all originals. Muslims will build a mosque on top of a dumping ground after clearing the garbage. We could never do this." He also added, "We have no 'mazars' in Europe. Only in the Middle East and in Russia". If the journalist is to be trusted, there are "mazars" in Russia.[19] Yet, there are ways to avoid the ban on constructing new sacred places (e. g., having visionary dreams). Then, permission is needed from religious authorities, and, since they usually prefer to keep people satisfied, it is not too hard to get. However, to make a location really sacred, people get material from Lalish, like water from the Ava Zimzim/Zemzem (a holy well in Lalish) earth, tops (round stones) and curtains. In one place, believers apparently got a piece of the *khirqe* (Hirka/kirqa) (cloak) of Feqir Haji - then guardian of Lalish - and buried it under a fake tomb in the new shrine. In other words, Ezidis act pragmatically and do whatever needs to be done for the survival of the community.[20] As long as Ezidis in Georgia do not claim the new temple is equal to Lalish, there will be no serious controversies with higher Ezidi religious authorities.

## The "House of the Ezidis" in Tbilisi

According to a 2003 survey, Ezidi Kurds in Georgia believed that the lack of a temple was their main problem. There were plans to build a temple in 2002, but Ezidis could not pay for the land on which the temple was expected to stand (Chikhladze and Chikhladze 2003). The project however resumed a few years later. Nevertheless, controversies on the issue persisted in the community, as an article written by Karim Ankosi in 2010 proves. Ezidis kept renting a hall for big ceremonies.

The main problem the *ad hoc* Tbilisi Municipal Council had to resolve regarding the land to be given to the Ezidis concerned *land* itself, whether it had

---

dition to carry out religious practices. Some scholars would ask: "if the Sanctuary of Sheikh Adi in Lalish is a temple and used for this purpose, why not have another one in Georgia?" (personal communication by Dr Birgül Açıkyıldız; see also Açıkyıldız [2014]).

[18] Personal communication by Dr Eszter Spät.

[19] See on this "Middle East Journal" webpage and, above all, blogs edited by the journalist Michael J. Totten.

[20] Personal communication by Dr Eszter Spät.

to be donated, sold, or rented. Land extension or the dimensions of the building were never an issue.[21] The *ad hoc* council supported Ezidis' request, allowing however the construction in the suburbs of Tbilisi, on Javakheti Street in Varketili. Permission was granted in 2007.

The Ezidis chose a Georgian architect, Paata Kurdiani, for the construction. They brought him to Lalish, as the new temple had to resemble Lalish architecture. They got the land from the Saakashvili Government for a "symbolic" price.

Besides the land given at a symbolic price, donations came from private donors: first an unknown Ezidi businessman from Tbilisi, then Masoud Barzani (incumbent president of the Autonomous Region of Kurdistan) and Jalal Talabani (incumbent president of the Republic of Iraq), and finally Mir Tahsin Beg Saied (world leader of the Ezidi community and of its Religious Council), known as the "Prince of the Ezidis".

## The Refugees from Sinjar

In August 2014, 63 Ezidi Iraqi citizens (28 females and 35 males) applied for refugee status to the Georgian Ministry of Refugees and Resettlement for religious and social reasons. Those who applied for the status were to be granted the status of applicant refugees within ten days. The status of refugees was later granted to 29 applicants. Six were granted the humanitarian assistance status, while procedures stopped for the remaining 27 because of problems with their application forms or because of their absence. One application was still pending at the time of my last inquiry (late summer 2015).

Refugees mainly settled in two districts of Tbilisi: Zahesi and Ponichala. The Ministry and UNHCR jointly supported them financially by paying their rents, giving them 45 Lari [20 USD] each per month and guaranteeing insurance and healthcare until their economic conditions improved.

With Decision N. 15 (29. 1. 2015), the Georgian government granted assistance to teach Georgian to the children of those with the status of refugee, applicant refugee and humanitarian assistance, as well as support for secondary and further education. With Tbilisi Municipal Decision N. 2–5 (3. 2. 2015), the children were also granted access to kindergarten programmes. Aside from the case of Ossetia and Abkhazia, refugees in Georgia are mostly citizens of the Republic of Iraq, Syria and Ukraine. Procedures are usually simplified for those coming from conflict zones.

The refugees belonged to the same group and had relatives in Georgia; they went from Dohuk to Arbil and then directly to Tbilisi. Georgian immigration

---

[21] Personal communication by a member of the *had hoc* "Tbilisi Municipal Council for the Issue of the Yezidi Temple".

law changed on September 1, 2014. Unlike Armenia, refugees did not need a visa to enter the country.

Refugees came from what my informant[22] called a collective town[23] of around 18000 people (not far from Sinjar). It was June 10, 2015 when Daesh entered Mosul. They first killed Arabs who did not accept their ideology. Then they asked Christians to pay 300 USD per month if they wanted to stay, or to convert, leave or face death. The Peshmerga (Army of the Kurdistan Regional Government) told Ezidis to stay, as they would protect them. In July, my informant went dozens of times to Sinjar until, on the 2nd of August, Daesh arrived. Those who could escape ran for seven days to Mount Sinjar, but they had assistance for just half of the distance. Then the PKK (Kurdistan Workers' Party) came and opened the border with Syria, transporting half of them in their cars.

Daesh killed 3500 Ezidis in seven days – 2000 near Sinjar Mountain and the surrounding region (when they tried to escape to nearby Arab villages) and 1500 south of Mount Sinjar (as they tried to enter other Arab villages). While writing (late summer 2015), there are almost half a million IDP (Internally Displaced People) in the camps in North Iraq assisted by the UNHCR out of more than two million IDP.[24] Camps are created according to different ethno-religious groups. Ezidis cluster in the Khanki Refugee Camp, north of Mosul (Rushing 2014).

I asked Ankosi why the entire planet was talking about the Ezidi. He replied that this diaspora is different from previous ones:

> Compare us with Armenians in Turkey, which was so openly discussed by the lobbies. If you do not use proper means nobody will pay attention. Like the Jewish in Germany. If the Israeli state was not so active it would be lost because somebody makes the memory (Karim Ankosi).

Here the issue of education emerges again:

> Our religion was against education, but if you are not educated you have no chance to get information. Now things have changed, everybody watches Kurdish satellites. For the record, this is the 74th documented oppression we have memory of (Karim Ankosi).

---

22 Originally from a town 20 km from Dohuk, he worked for the UN Child Protection Unit, helping unaccompanied children. He came to Georgia for two reasons: 1. work, as in 2002 he took part in a training programme for youth named "Wealth Youth Together to Peace" with Ezidi associations; 2. although they had relatives in Europe, they needed a *special* visa to go there. It was nevertheless possible to buy the so-called *Schengen Visa* for 40000 USD. Since Georgia immigration law has changed, he cannot go back to Arbil directly from Georgia, but needs to go there via Istanbul.

23 See on this Recchia 2012.

24 See UNHCR webpage at http://www.unhcr.org/cgi-bin/texis/vtx/page?page=49e486426&submit=GO.

Local Ezidi were happy to help refugees. Yet, even ordinary Georgians started talking about them. Two Georgian ministers showed interest. The Administration of Muslims of all Georgia, the Baptist Church and the Ombudsman of Georgia, on behalf of all traditional and some non-traditional churches, all paid their respects. The Patriarchal Administration of Georgia released a statement against what was happening.

## The Peacock Angel in Tbilisi

Ezidis have often been the subject of derogatory characteristics ("devil worshippers"), mostly in reference to their relation to the peacock. In Islam, the peacock is controversial; on the one hand, it is the world's most beautiful creature and symbol of wisdom, but on the other hand it is known for its demonic characteristics (friendship with the biblical snake, punished by God by making its legs ugly) (Asatrian and Arakelova 2003).

Malak Tavus (literally "the peacock angel") is a key figure in Ezidism and has been the subject of various interpretations because as "the head of all angels" it is often depicted, mostly in Sunni Islam, as a peacock. This representation shaped stereotypes of the Ezidis as followers of Satan, since the peacock was considered one of his symbols (Asatrian 1999/2000, Asatrian and Arakelova 2003). In reality, the peacock was *the* symbol of the new intercessor for the Ezidis (Guest 1993: 28).

However, the rivalry between Ezidis and Muslims (mainly Sunni, including Sunni Kurds) goes deeper than that. Muslim Kurds adopted written traditions quite early; Ezidis used a secret alphabet for religious purposes and over time forgot it. Thus, most Ezidi heritage (traditions and their two holy books) was passed down generations verbally (Dalalyan 2011). One of Sheikh Adi precepts was indeed "a warning against written books" (Guest 1993: 33). In addition, during the Ottoman time, Ezidis benefited neither from membership in the Muslim *millet* (community) nor from the rights accorded to non-Muslims *(dhimmi)*. Those conditions prompted their migration to the South Caucasus.

An understanding of Ezidis' relations with surrounding faiths is needed to grasp Ezidis' relations with surrounding majorities (including recent attitudes in ethno-religious exclusive refugee camps in Iraq). In a Muslim-majority context, Ezidis perceived themselves as occupying a position similar to that of persecuted Christians. However, even if they do not see themselves as Muslims, Islam plays an important role. On the one hand, there is both intimacy and hostility between Ezidism and Islam, while on the other hand, there are affinities between Ezidis and Christians who have shared (Menant 1892: 39–40, Guest 1993: 64, 135, 174) and are sharing the same political space (UNHCR Report 2008) as well as tensions linked to Christian proselytizing activities (Muhamad 2015).

Within Kurdish peoples, at least before Abdullah Ocalan (incumbent, imprisoned leader of the PKK), there was distance between Ezidis and Muslims. The former were not treated well and they feared Muslims. Some Georgian informants argue that Ocalan made Ezidis part of the Kurdish people. He proposed establishing a Kurdish Parliament among autonomous bodies, which many saw as a reference to various ethnic groups. When he was arrested in 1999, as Karim Ankosi recalls, most Ezidis felt Kurdish and there were protests even in Tbilisi.

In recent times, Ezidis of the South Caucasus have been affected by developments in their traditional homeland. Ezidis are regarded as infidels by Sunni extremists and have thus been targeted. Ezidis living outside the Kurdish Regional Government were considered vulnerable to sectarian attacks by Arab armed groups well before Daesh came to the fore. In August 2007, almost 800 Ezidis were killed by four coordinated suicide bombers affiliated with al-Qaida in an attack near the settlement of Kahtaniya (Wander 2010), the second deadliest act of terrorism in history after 9/11 in New York. Because of security conditions, if any Ezidi migration from the South Caucasus to Iraq seemed already unlikely in 2008 (UNHCR Report 2008), now it seems beyond imagination. In Georgia, however, stereotypes related to the peacock are known only to Muslims. Locals, according to PirDima, knew Ezidis as sun worshippers.

## Epilogue

This Tbilisi ethnography examined an old Ezidi community and a small unit of recent Ezidi refugees. Security-related issues were the concern of the newly arrived group from North Iraq, victims of both terrorism and state weakness. A revitalization attempt, instead, was the concern of the long-settled community. To different extents, both groups wavered between feeling part of the state and feeling forgotten by it. Both interacted upon foreign soil while lacking horizontal relations with a non-existent institutionalized homeland.

We do not need to recall the terrorists of Daesh here to talk about hostility towards Ezidis, as their association with "devil-worship" was already encountered by European ethnographers centuries ago (Menant 1892: 13–14). Yet, for all my Ezidi informants, migration is by definition linked to persecution. Ezidis are exposed to other groups to the extent that paradoxically their religious revival is explained in terms of a generalized religious revival in Georgia. This led to tension between members of the old group and, by implication, with some of the newly arrived migrants based exactly on the priorities to be given to communal markers (Kurdish or Ezidi).

When I first met PirDima in August 2014, he told me that the new temple was going to open in two months; the same answer was given the following November and again in March 2015. The temple was eventually opened on June 16, 2015 and a new name was actually given: "Sultan Ezid". Three Georgian MP representing the Superintendence of Cultural Heritage and the Georgian Minister of Integration, Paata Zakareishvili, attended the opening together with Georgian representatives of the Georgian Armenian Church, Roman Catholic Church, Baptist Church and the Jewish and Muslim communities. Groups of Ezidis from Iraq, Armenia, Russia and ten members of the German Oldenburg Ezidi community attended too.

The congregation first gathered in the Conference Hall where Agit Mirzoevi introduced PirDima who welcomed the assembly, later speeches were given in Kurmanji or translated from Georgian to Kurmanji. The floor was then given to the son of Mir Tahsin Beg who spoke on behalf of his father who could not attend the opening and then to the representative of the Presidency of Georgia, who read a letter from President Giorgi Margvelashvili, and finally to the Minister Paata Zakareishvili. Then the guests were led to the temple, where people took their shoes off, while women were handed white veils by Sheik Nuri. The congregation then gathered in front of the image of Malak Tavus where some threads were placed into a fireplace made of olive wood. Doors were then closed for a few minutes and a short ritual was held inside; in the meantime, an Ezidi flag was unfurled on top of the temple.

PirDima had entered the temple with a large tricolour (red, yellow, green) satin scarf. When he came out he was praying. He then gave the scarf to one of his young attendants who laid it on the top of a shrine. Some informants explained the tricolour scarf as a sort of representation of the Turkish Kurdish flag (that is, the Kurdish flag as used by Kurds in Turkey, since in Iraq it is red, white and green with the sun disc in the centre). Karim Ankosi was there, too, and when asked about the event he replied, "it is a great day". The Ezidi refugees from Iraq were there as well, although not all of them, as controversies have recently arose between some of them and the Georgian Ezidi leadership.

When I started my research, different interpretations upon the *locus* were clashing, mirroring deeper understanding, expectations and even reliabilities. Those tensions seemed to be mitigated by a unifying decision; the opening of the new temple was not going to be a lavish celebration because of the 2014 dramatic events at Mount Sinjar. Yet, even this was to be challenged.

On July 16 the opening was solemnly celebrated, including an evening dinner for foreign guests and Georgia government representatives offered by the Tbilisi Ezidi businessman Suliko Simaev who had also paid for the opening of the cultural centre. It was actually the only public gathering of that week in Tbilisi as all other events were cancelled following a dramatic flood in the Vere River Valley two nights before, resulting in more than 20 casualties and massive damage. What was eventually cancelled was a local Ezidi group's performance of Kurdish folk songs and dances at the opening.

## Acknowledgements

This research was supported by a Marie Curie International Research Staff Exchange Scheme Fellowship within the 7th European Community Framework Programme (grant no: PIRSES-GA-2012-318961). The author is also grateful to

Birgül Açıkyıldız, Boris Komakhidze, Keti Kutsishvili, Robert Langer, Ana Ramazashvili, Eszter Spät and Çakır Ceyhan Suvari for their critical comments.

## Bibliography

Açikyildiz, Birgül (2014): *The Ezidis: The History of a Community, Culture and Religion*. London: I. B. Tauris.

Allison, Christine (2013): Addressivity and the Monument: Memorials, Publics and the Yezidis of Armenia. In: *History and Memory*, 25 (1): 145–181.

Ankosi, Karim (2012): Once again about the construction of the Ezidi religious temple in Tbilisi. In: Karim Ankosi (no date): *Problems of Studying Ezidism*. Tbilisi: no publisher, 92–94.

Asatrian, G. S. (1999/2000): The Holy Brotherhood: The Ezidi Religious Institution of The Brother and the Sister of the Next World. In: *Iran and the Caucasus,* 3–4: 79–96.

Asatrian, Garnik S. and Arakelova, Victoria (2003): Malak Tāwūs: The Peacock Angel of the Ezidis. In: *Iran and the Caucasus,* 7 (1–2): 1–36.

Chikhladze, G. and Chikhladze, I. (2003): Georgia's Kurdish Community Say They Are in Danger of Losing Their Culture, Language and Faith. In: *IWPR Caucasus Reporting Service,* No. 166.

Dafflon, Danis (2014): National Minorities in Georgia in the Context of Nation-Building and State-Building (2004–2012). In: C. Giordano et al. (eds.): *Does East Go West? Anthropological Pathways through Postsocialism*. Wien: Lit, 153–166.

Dalalyan, Tork (2011): Construction of Kurdish and Ezidi Identities among the Kurmanj-Speaking Population of the Republic of Armenia. In: Sophia Khutsishvili and John Horan (eds.): *Changing Identities: Armenia, Azerbaijan, Georgia*. Tbilisi: Heinrich Boell Foundation, 177–201.

Giordano, Christian (2013): Corporate Groups, Factions and Networks: Social Organization of the Chinese Diaspora in the Straits of Malacca – the case of Penang. In: Waltraud Kokot, Christian Giordano, Mijal Gandelsman-Trier (eds.): *Diaspora as a Resource. Comparative Studies in Strategies, Networks and Urban Spaces*. Fribourg Studies in Social Anthropology 36. Münster: Lit Verlag, 199–221.

Guest, John S. (1987): *The Ezidis – A Study in Survival*. London: Routledge & Kegan Paul.

Guest, John S. (1993): *Survival among the Kurds: A History of the Ezidis*. London: Kegan Paul.

Kokot, Waltraud, Giordano, Christian and Gandelsman-Trier, Mijal (eds.) (2013): Introduction. Diaspora as Resources: Cultures, Networks and Urban Space. In: Waltraud Kokot, Christian Giordano, Mijal Gandelsman-Trier (eds.): *Diaspora as a Resource. Comparative Studies in Strategies, Networks and Urban Spaces*. Fribourg Studies in Social Anthropology 36. Münster: Lit Verlag, 9–24.

Krikorian, Onnik J. *Ezidis in Armenia* [blog and webpage]. URL: http://onnik-krikorian.com/2013/08/more-on-Ezidis-in-armenia/, accessed on 13. 4. 2015.

Langer, Robert (2010): Ezidism between Scholarly Literature and Actual Practice: From "Heterodox" Islam and "Syncretism" to the Formation of a Transnational Ezidi "Orthodoxy". In: *British Journal of Middle Eastern Studies,* 37 (3): 393–403.

Menant, M. Joachim (1892): Les Yézidis. Épisodes de l'Histoire des Adorateurs du Diable. Paris: Leroux

Mollica, Marcello (2011): Understanding Determinants: Syrian Orthodox Christians and Security Related Issues in Diyarbakır. In: *Urban Anthropology,* 40 (1–2): 109–150

Mollica, Marcello (2012a): Political Manipulations: Death and Urban Graveyards Northern Ireland. In: Giuliana Prato and Italo Pardo (eds.): *Anthropology in the City: Methods, Methodology and Theory*. Aldershot: Ashgate, 155–172.

Mollica, Marcello (2012b): The Alevi Cultural Centre in Horn-St Gallen, Switzerland: An Exploratory Study. In: Aykan Erdemir et al. (eds.): *II. Uluslararasi Tarihten Bugüne. Alevilik Sempozyumu (23–24 Ekim 2010)*. Ankara: Cem Vakfi, 133–150.

Mollica, Marcello (2014): When the Ethnographer Encounters War. In: Andrea Boscoboinik and Hana Horakova (eds.): *Anthropology of Fear. Cultures beyond Emotions*. Münster: LIT, 205–218.

Mollica, Marcello (2015): Geopolitica del conflitto in Siria. Ad un anno e mezzo dal rapimento di padre Paolo Dall'Oglio. In: Chiara Lapi (ed.): *Padre Paolo Dall'Oglio. Uomo di dialogo ostaggio in Siria*. Pisa: Pisa University Press, 41-62.

Mossaki, Nodar (2014): Yezidis in Censuses in the USSR and Post-Soviet Countries. In: Khanna Omarkhali (ed.): *Religious Minorities in Kurdistan: Beyond the Mainstream*. Studies in Oriental Religions, 68. Wiesbaden: Harrassowitz Verlag, 97–135.

Muhamad, R. (2015): URL: http://www.basnews.com/en/news/2015/06/08/yazidis-unhappy-with-christian-missionaries/, accessed on 9. 7. 2015.

Nasidze, Ivan et al. (2005): MtDNA and Y-Chromosome Variation in Kurdish Groups. In: *Annals of Human Genetics,* 69 (4): 401–412.

*New Yezidi temple in Armenia*. URL: http://www.horizonweekly.ca/news/details/71632, accessed on 18. 8. 2015. Piot, Olivier and Goldstein, Julien (2012): Kurdistan. La colère d'un people sans droits. Paris: Petits Matins.

Recchia, Francesca (2012): From Forced Displacement to Urban Cores: The Case of Collective Towns in Iraqi Kurdistan. URL: http://architexturez.net/doc/az-cf-123984, accessed on 13. 4. 2015.

Rushing, Josh (2014): URL: http://america.aljazeera.com/watch/shows/fault-lines/FaultLinesBlog/2014/10/16/yazidi-slideshow.html, accessed on 22. 4. 2015

Spät, Eszter (2005): *Ezidis*. London: Saqi Books.

Spät, Eszter (2013): On Soil and Jinn: Ritual Practices and Syncretism among the Ezidis of Iraq. In: Andreas Pries et al. (eds.): *Rituale als Ausdruck von Kulturkontakt: "Synkretismus" zwischen Negation und Neudefinition*. Wiesbaden: Harrassowitz, 111–130.

Totten, Michael J.: *Middle East Journal* [blog and webpage]. URL: http://www.michaeltotten.com/archives/001064.html, accessed on 13. 4. 2015.

UNHCR [webpage]. URL: http://www.unhcr.org/cgi-bin/texis/vtx/page?page=49e486426&submit=GO, accessed on 22. 4. 2015.

UNHCR Report (2008): *The Human Rights Situation of the Ezidi Minority in the Transcaucasus (Armenia, Georgia, Azerbaijan)*. URL: http://www.academia.edu/7912818/The_Human_Rights_Situation_of_the_Ezidi_Minority_in_the_Transcaucasus_Armenia_Georgia_Azerbaijan_

Yepiskoposian, Levon et al. (2010): Genetic Affinity between the Armenian Ezidis and the Iraqi Kurds. In: *Iran and the Caucasus* 14 (1): 37–42.

Wander, Andrew (2010): URL: http://www.aljazeera.com/secretiraqfiles/2010/10/2010102216102542 8625.html, accessed on 22. 4. 2015.

# Religious Aspects of Structuring the Ethnocultural Identity of the Assyrian Community in Georgia

*Ketevan Khutsishvili*

After achieving independence in 1992, Georgia underwent the painful process of the "death" of the "old" societies and their "rebirth". By its very nature, the complex process of adaptation to a new environment is extremely difficult and involves the reconstruction of identities. In the process of reconstructing their identity or working towards new ones, the ethnocultural groups living in Georgia have actively exploited religion as one of the most important markers of their ethnocultural heritage.

After undergoing the experience of challenging atheism, the post-Soviet society has turned to its religious roots. Due to the reassessment of the Soviet priorities, personal and public priorities have changed significantly and religiosity has become the determining factor of public life. The interest towards religion has sharply increased, thus also the influence of religion. As a major element of ethnic self-consciousness, religion clearly determines the character of the processes of inner-ethnic consolidation and of differentiation between the ethnic groups. Religious creed is crucial in terms of the inner orientation of individual and ethnic group self-identification, and as carrier of cultural values. Religious representations have emerged as a system of values playing a major role in ethnocultural identity within the group, in the integration process of ethnocultures in a poly-ethnic society and in developing a stable environment for the entire society. During its process of transformation, Georgian society has addressed religious belonging as a main marker of identity construction; however, since Georgian society has never been homogenous, the situation is rather complex.

At the crossing of the West-East and North-South axes, Georgia has always been a poly-ethnic and multicultural state with a population comprised of various ethnic and confessional groups. After independence was announced in 1991, the country's ethnical structure underwent serious changes and the economic and political processes triggered a high percentage of migrations. Yet, about one hundred ethnic groups, whose members belong to various religious confessions, are still present in Georgia. According to the last census, 88.6 per cent of the entire population is Christian, 9.9 per cent Moslem, 0.1 per cent Jewish, 0.8 per cent other confessions, and 0.6 per cent has no religious affiliation (Beridze 2004). It is necessary to note that almost none of the nationalities living in Georgia is mono-confessional, among these the Assyrian community, which is a small minority group with specific characteristics.

* * *

The majority of Assyrians living in Georgia came from the region of Urmia, currently in Iran, close to the border with Turkey. Assyrians are an ethnic group indigenous to present-day Iraq, Iran, Turkey and Syria believed to descend from the ancient Acadians. In the course of time, Aramaic tribes were assimilated into the Assyrian empire and their language became dominant, while the different cultures merged to form the ancient Assyrian culture, Urmia was the Assyrian homeland for many centuries, but at the end of World War I, in the summer of 1918, Assyrians fled the area, as Turkish troops along with Persian and Kurdish irregulars were on the move against them. The Assyrians migrated in various directions, including the Caucasus (Songulashvili 2005). Scattering throughout Georgia, they established close-knit settlements.

Nowadays, the Assyrians live in Tbilisi's Kukia neighbourhood, in the village of Kanda, Mtskheta Municipality, and in the village of Vasilievka, Gardabani Municipality. A small number of Assyrians also lives in Kutaisi, Zestaponi, Samtredia, Senaki, Batumi and Akhaltsikhe (Beridze 2004). According to the 1998 State Census, the number of Assyrians in Georgia was 6206 (0.1 per cent of Georgia's entire population) decreasing to 3299 (but still 0.1 per cent of the population) in 2002 (Beridze 2004).

The Assyrian community became more known recently thanks to the Orthodox Father Seraphim (Bit-Kharibi). Anyone interested in Orthodox chants or religious music in general is bound to have heard about the Georgian priest who chants in the "language of Christ". Father Seraphim of the Mtskheta diocese of the Georgian Orthodox Church guides the church in the village of Kanda, not far from Tbilisi. He is an ethnic Assyrian and the only one granted permission by the Catholicos-Patriarch of All Georgia to officiate in Aramaic. Orthodox Christians of the Assyrian community in the village of Kanda consider him a spiritual and cultural leader.

* * *

Kanda is located in the Mtskheta-Mtianeti region, formerly owned by the Georgian landed aristocrats Mukhran-Batoni. In the late 18th century, under Russian empress Catherine the Great, German colonizers settled in the area. The first wave of Assyrians, construction guest workers from the Urmia region for the new houses being built in Tbilisi, arrived in the village in 1867 (Songulashvili 2005). In 1900, Ioane Mukhran-Batoni sold the village and its land to a rich Assyrian, Usta-Alaverdi. In 1918, Georgia proclaimed its independence and the new government launched a reorganization of the administrative composition and land distribution throughout the country. During this period of the first Republic, the village experienced some economic problems; the villagers, mainly ethnic Assyrians, lacked tillable land, since it was distributed among the neighbouring villages.

The village of Dzveli Kanda [Old Kanda] had a mixed ethnic composition but became an Assyrian village during World War I, when Assyrian refugees from Persia's Urmia-Salmas district fled to the Caucasus and settled in Kanda.

The Germans, a minority though, stayed in the village up to 1941 (Basilia 2008) when Nazi Germany attacked the Soviet Union; they were deported to Central Asia, never to return. Only one German woman who had married a Georgian was allowed to stay. Her son, an artist, still lives on Kanda's main street, which is still known to the villagers by its old name, German Street, where only two crumbling houses survive from German times. The village currently consists of about four hundred houses.

Nowadays, nearly all of Kanda's inhabitants are Assyrian; it is one of the few compact settlements of Orthodox Assyrians, whose main economic activities are agriculture and crafts. The villagers narrate that Kanda means town in Persian and, since they have Urmia-Persian roots, the first settlers gave this name to their new place. Dzveli Kanda is the oldest and largest Assyrian settlement in Georgia.

As mentioned above, the majority of Assyrians arrived in the Southern Caucasus in the early 20th century when they fled from present-day Turkey and Iran (Songulashvili 2005), which coincides with the first appearance of Assyrians in Dzveli Kanda. Yet, narratives about the appearance of Assyrians in Georgia can be traced back to the sixth century, when the Thirteen Assyrian Fathers (monastic missionaries from Assyria) reached Georgia (Javakhishvili 1979, Japaridze 2009). According to some scholars, the thirteen Orthodox "Assyrian" fathers (David Garejeli, Ioane Zedazneli, Abibos Nekreseli etc.), were actually ethnic Georgians (Kekelidze 1960) educated in Assyrian religious centres. Aiming to spread and strengthen Orthodoxy, they founded monasteries and religious retreats throughout Georgia and are among the most venerated saints of the Georgian Orthodox Church.

Assyrians came in contact with Georgians once again in the 1760s. Under Ottoman rule, the Assyrians sought protection from religious and ethnic persecution (Songulashvili 2005, Basilia 2008). The Patriarch of the Assyrian Church of the East Mar Avraam petitioned Georgian King Erekle II Bagrationi (1720–1798) of Kartl-Kakhetian (Eastern Georgia) for protection for the Assyrians and for the Yazidi of present-day Turkey. In April 1770, Georgian troops under Russian command headed towards the city of Akhaltsikhe (Southern Georgia). At the same time, the Assyrian Bishop Isaiah left Tbilisi carrying letters to Assyrian and Yazidi leaders in which the Georgian king exhorted them to fight together against the Ottomans.

The plans for military cooperation failed, but, during the war, an Assyrian community of several dozen families arrived in Georgia from Persia and the Ottoman Empire. King Erekle II provided asylum for the Assyrian refugees and settled them in Kakheti (East Georgia). The Assyrians gradually spread to the Vake and Kukia districts in Tbilisi, to the villages of Kanda and Gardabani in East Georgia and to Batumi, Kutaisi and Senaki in West Georgia. In the late 18th century, Assyrian-Chaldeans and Nestorians from Persia petitioned the Georgian Orthodox Church to grant them permission to join Orthodoxy. Soon after, an Orthodox church was built in Kanda.

The next wave of Assyrian immigrants occurred in 1828 when Russia signed the Treaty of Turkmenchay with Persia by which a new boundary was set between Russia and Persia and Russia gained control of several areas in the South Caucasus. In the 1830s, Assyrians and Kurds from Iran arrived in Georgia as workers.

In 1860, a group of Assyrians migrated to West Georgia. Around the same time, Assyrians settled in the village of Vasilevka in East Georgia (nowadays Gardabani district). More arrived in the second half of the 19th century and settled in Tbilisi. By the end of the 19th century, over five thousand Assyrians lived in Georgia. The largest number of Assyrians arrived between 1915 and 1917, as they fled from Ottoman mass slaughters (Basilia 2008, Katsitadze 2014).

* * *

Since Assyrians came to Georgia at different periods, they also had different ethnocultural backgrounds. In terms of language, religion or cultural belonging and features, the new settlements' different locations further diversified the groups into distinct sub-ethnic groups, such as the Urmunjai, Shapnai, Salmsnai, Turanai and Botanai amongst others (Ghutidze 2014). The differences in everyday life are noticeable in their economic activities and social organization (each group is organized according to kinship and has its own group leader, *Malik* [leader]). The groups are not socially subordinate to each other. Further differences are determined by the type of settlement (urban or rural, compact or dispersed) and language preferences. Georgian is the inter-group communication language for the majority of East Georgian Assyrians and for all West Georgian Assyrians, whereas certain groups, mainly in Tbilisi and Gardabani, use Russian. Assyrians in West Georgia have adopted the local Georgian patronymic patterns, especially newcomers who were not used to these systems (e. g. Azerbaijanis, Ossetians).

The Georgian patronymic system first appeared in the early Middle Ages. The earliest historical document in which a person is identified by first (given) name, first name of the father and surname dates back to the 9th century. The surnames of Assyrians who settled in West Georgia are formed like those of the local Georgians, with the suffix – *dze*. In East Georgia, the Assyrian surnames are formed like the Russian ones, ending in *-ov* or *-ev*. Some Assyrians have surnames formed according to their kin names, e. g. *Bit-Batkashi* [descendant of Batkashi], which subsequently became *Batkashi*.

The important markers of Assyrian identity appear to be language and religion. Most Assyrians speak a modern form of Syriac, an Eastern Aramaic language (neo-Aramaic) and its dialects: Urmian, Salmasurian, Vanian and Jilubotanian (Ghutidze 2014). Assyrians living in Georgia speak Syriac at home, whereas Georgian and Russian are their communication languages. Their language is also linked to their religion. Assyrians in Georgia belong to two religious groups: Orthodoxy and Chaldean Catholicism. The language of most of the Orthodox Assyrians is Georgian, whereas for the majority of Chaldean-

Catholics it is Russian. Orthodox services are held in Georgian, except in the village of Kanda where, as mentioned above, the ethnic Assyrian Father Seraphim celebrates service in Aramaic. Chaldean-Catholic services are held in Aramaic.

Overall, Assyrian culture is determined by religion. Assyrians are proud of their heritage, their Christianity, and of speaking the language of Christ, as they affirm. When Assyrians meet representatives of another ethnic group they are bound to mention that they are "the first Christians".

"You learned Christianity from Assyrians, you should show more respect for our sacred sites", a young Assyrian man (28 years old from the village of Kanda) told the driver who would not drive us to the Orthodox Church of the Assyrian village because the road was damaged. I heard the oldest villager (81 years old from the village of Kanda) tell the Assyrian children that they are the descendants of Christ, speaking in his language and they should preserve their language and identity.

* * *

Assyrians living in Georgia call themselves *Suraia*. They also use the ethnonyms Aturai and *Kaldai,* whereas their endonyms are both Assyrian and Aisori. Their language is termed Lishana Suraia, Lishana Ashorai and Lishana Atorai, where Lishana means language, i. e. language of Suraia, Ashorai or Atorai. They always emphasize the historical importance of their language, as already mentioned, deeming it the one spoken by Christ.

> We should keep the language of Christ (30 years old man from Kanda).
>
> So sad that the youth is not speaking Christ's language anymore (57 year old man from Kanda).
>
> We have special courses to teach our children our native language – the language of Christ (62 year old man from Kanda).

Dialectal variations are also evident. For example, the inhabitants of Kanda can hardly understand those living in Gardabani or West Georgia since they belong to different regional groups and the dialectal differences where already present when they first reached the territory of Georgia. In time, the new language environment (neighbours, communication channels, mixed families, religious belonging etc.) reinforced these differences making them even more distinct. Thus, the idea of being the carriers of the "language of Christ" became a unifying idea and marker for all Assyrians, but, in practice, the language similarity has weakened.

Some years ago, the Assyrian language was taught in Kanda 2–3 times a week in the public school at private expense. Today the elective course is no longer available. There are twenty people in the village that read and write Aramaic. In terms of language assimilation, the process continues. Assyrians appreciate their heritage, yet it is very common to give the new generation the Georgian surnames of their mothers or grandparents. Our informants explain this as a means to make life easier for the children within Georgian society. Children are often given Christian or Assyrian first names such as Ashur, Sargon, Ninos, etc., but Georgian, Greek and Russian names are also common, especially nowadays. Assimilation processes can also be traced in these tendencies.

* * *

Nowadays, the lifestyle of Assyrians is not that different from the Georgians' one, except for some characteristic eating habits and religious rituals. Baptism and marriage rituals are similar to those of other Christian denominations, the only difference being the national dances performed during the celebrations. Baptism (and First Communion among Catholics) is a lavish celebration.

The burial ritual is also similar to the Georgian one, expect for the massive funerary monuments. When an Assyrian dies, people gather to celebrate his ascension to heaven three days after burial (like Jesus). After seven days, they gather again to commemorate the person's passing. Close family members wear only black clothes for forty days or one year as a sign of respect; Georgians practice a similar custom. Neighbouring Georgians and Assyrians mutually assist each other during the mourning ceremonies and are involved in shared activities. In places where Assyrians, Georgians, Armenians, Azerbaijanis and other groups live close to each other, they will have cultural elements in common: in some cases just aspects of everyday life, in others even syncretic religious practices.

* * *

Since 1992, the National Congress of the Assyrians of Georgia (ANCG), supported by donations from a number of wealthy Assyrians, has been offering financial aid as well as social and educational assistance to local Assyrians. The Congress is connected to the Cultural Centre located in Tbilisi's Saburtalo district, a densely populated and thriving area. The building's architectural style harks back to ancient Assyrian temples. It includes a religious space (which belongs to the Chaldean-Catholics) and an educational one offering language and history courses (teachers are volunteers, sometimes expressly invited). Students cover the expenses of art classes: dance, music, theatre.

In the late 1920s, there were four active Catholic churches in Tbilisi (Songulashvili 2005) attended by Catholic Assyrians. At that time, Catholic Assyrians from the village of Vasilievka collected money to build a church, but the project fell through. Chaldean-Catholics began a campaign to rebuild their religious life after the collapse of the Soviet Union.

The general growth trend of religious people in Georgia also relates to Chaldean-Catholics. This has led to the call to build a Chaldean church in Georgia. In Soviet times, they would pray at home or in nearby Catholic churches.

In May 1995, the parish priest Rev. Father Benny Beth Yadegar established an Assyrian-Chaldean mission in the Republic of Georgia under the direction of the Vatican. He began the construction of the Mar Shimon Bar Sabbae Assyrian Chaldean Religious Cultural Centre in 2004. With the support of his bishop, Mgr. Giuseppe Pasotto (a leader of the Catholic community in Georgia), he sought help from the Catholic charity Aid to the Church in Need (ACN). ACN supported the community. Completed in October 2009, the Centre became a religious space for Chaldean-Catholics. Father Benny invited Cardinal Mar Emmanuel III Delly, the Chaldean Patriarch of Babylon, for the consecration of Mar Shimon Bar Sabbae in 2009. The celebration was attended by his Excellency Mar Shlimo Vardoni from Iraq and his Excellency Mar Thoma Meriam from Urmia, Iran, and by several priests from France, Germany and USA. The Consecration was scheduled for October 17, 2009 at 4:00 p.m. Chaldean-Catholic Assyrians had come together for the celebration.

A large group of demonstrators from the Georgian Orthodox Church, however, started to gather in front of the building and quickly reached over several hundred, waving banners and blocking the entrance to the compound, protesting against the establishment of a new non-Orthodox religious centre. The immediate intervention of the local police avoided any clashes. Once the situation was under control, the ceremony was performed. After the ceremony, the community held a banquet in the building's banquet hall. On October 18, 2009, the first Sunday Mass was celebrated. Following the ceremony, First Communion was celebrated for over 20 boys and girls followed by the baptism of an infant girl. In the afternoon, the choir gave a concert for all the guests and spiritual leaders, and the locals (mainly Tbilisians). On Monday October 19, 2009, a funeral mass was held. Thus, the Church became active. Despite the initial protests of Orthodox Tbilisians, the Assyrians slowly accepted the place as a Cultural Centre for the entire Assyrian community, i. e. both Catholics and Orthodox. Now Orthodox Assyrians, too, attend the centre; they are involved in different kinds of activities, which they regard as a tool for ethnic mobilization. This is what they narrate:

> This centre is good as we are meeting with each other, we are sharing information, we are involved in social activities. For example, we took part in a sports competition and have travelled abroad (28 years old Orthodox man).
>
> There we are together (34 years old Orthodox man).
>
> We are seeing each other and feeling that we are Assyrians (68 years old Catholic man).

The Orthodox and Catholic religious spaces are separated; the religious life of both groups is developing independently. At the same time, the Cultural Centre claims to be the unifying element for all Assyrians, providing a space for non-religious activities.

The students perform scenes from Assyrian history in the cultural centre's theatre. According to their explanation, they are trying to transmit this knowledge to the younger generations. In the 1990s, because of the difficult economic and political situation, some Assyrians migrated to Russia and Europe. This is the reason for their dwindling number in Georgia.

In general, the centre helps Assyrians maintain their cultural belonging and historical memory; this is also the centre's official intent. At the same time, Assyrians who attend the centre also claim that it provides the only possibility to support their identity. As mentioned before, Orthodox Assyrians who attend the centre also narrate how great it is to feel united. This unity, however, is rather shaky.

Tension between the Orthodox and Catholic Assyrians has been noticeable ever since their appearance in Georgia and was often expressed in open conflicts in everyday relations (Songulashvili 2005). They tended to avoid each other and mixed marriages with members of other ethnic groups, apart from Catholic Assyrians, were regarded favourably. The effects of Soviet ideological pressure on the attitude towards religion, however, altered the situation. The spread of atheism during the Soviet period left its mark. One of its consequences was the disconnection from religious knowledge and values, if not their utter annihilation. A lack of traditional religious knowledge or its fragmented character has produced a society alienated from traditional religious representation. Religion appeared to be remote from real life and, in a number of cases, gradually led a certain part of society to deny religion.

We need to bear in mind that the Soviet state's ideological machine shaped the negative attitude towards religion and that entire generations were reared in an ideology contrasting both atheism and the negative representations of religion and the church. It may seem paradoxical that religious ideas appeared to be appreciable, yet the negative attitude towards religion was counterbalanced by the people's stronger perception of their religious identity. In the post-Soviet era, there were the added difficulties of the transition period, which created the right environment to spread religious emotions and ideas. As previously mentioned, in the nations established after the collapse of the Soviet Union, besides the political and economic crisis, there was also a deep spiritual crisis due to the collapse of the system of values. Problems of identity, distinctions between cultures, minority-majority, globalization-localizations and so forth began to emerge. In these circumstances, the Assyrian community began the process of seeking its identity and the group appeared to be divided in two: those trying to be more associated to Georgians (Orthodox Assyrians) and those who started to focus on and maintain the differences.

At the same time, in both groups the revitalization process of their ethnocultural features was noticeable. In the last decades, they have started to celebrate *Habnisann* – the New Year celebration in spring. *Kha b' Nisan* or *Ha b' Nisin* [Head of the Year in Syriac], also known as *Akitu,* is the spring festival celebrated on April 1st. In April of 2015, they celebrated the year 6765, according to the Assyrian ancient calendar officially reinstated by the Assyrians World Congress in 1968. However, in addition to the traditional Assyrian New Year on

April 1st, all Assyrians also celebrate the Gregorian calendar New Year on January 1st along with the rest of the world. Celebrations include parades and parties.

The main holiday is Christmas, *Idasura*. They also celebrate *Sharad'martmariam* and *Marezoba* [Holiday of Marezi/Marzaia]. *Marezoba* is celebrated twice, on June 14th and January 14th. In the village of Kanda, the Orthodox Assyrians come together, slaughter the animals and share meals. The usual practice for the day is to invite guests and to share the special dish *Murtukha* - cooked in the church's yard with the involvement of the entire parish. This holiday is peculiar to Orthodox Assyrians, but they also use the space of the Cultural Centre in Tbilisi for this celebration where young Orthodox Assyrians organize the banquet. Another important celebration is the day of St. Mary, which Assyrians regard not only as a religious holiday, but also as a national Assyrian feast like *Marezoba*.

* * *

Thus, the processes under way among the Assyrians can be defined as an assimilation on the one hand, and an integration on the other of this community as an ethnic group. However, language and religious differences hinder the process. The community is divided into two religious groups and though members of both groups are trying to communicate, the religious institutions are not.

The connection of the Orthodox Assyrians with the Georgian Orthodox Church, thus with Georgians in general, was strongly supported by the arrival of the ethnic Assyrian Orthodox priest within the Georgian Orthodox Church; in fact, Father Seraphim represents a bridge over this gap. In 2005 the villagers of Kanda petitioned the Georgian Catholicos-Patriarch to have a priest with the same ethnic background at their village, thus Archimandrite Seraphim became their spiritual leader. The village's spiritual and cultural life was galvanized by his arrival. He has renovated the existing church and built a new one. Father Seraphim does not reside in Kanda, but celebrates the liturgy there every Sunday. He is highly respected in the Georgian Orthodox parish as well. His endeavour is to consolidate the Assyrian and the Georgian communities through Orthodoxy. This is not surprising since Orthodoxy, as the religion of the dominant nation, has a large influence on public stability and on the integration and cooperation processes. Orthodoxy has preserved its standing and importance in everyday life.

Georgia has been a Christian country since the 4th century; its population is historically Orthodox. To this day, the majority of Christians living in Georgia - 83.9 per cent - belongs to Orthodoxy. They represent 83.8 per cent of the entire population and 94.7 per cent of them are ethnic Georgians. Orthodoxy has historically played a major role in shaping the Georgian culture and nation. Article 9 of the Constitution of Georgia reads: "the State shall declare absolute freedom of belief and religion. At the same time, the State shall recognize the outstanding role of the Apostolic Autocephalous Orthodox Church of Georgia in the history of Georgia, and its independence from the State" (http://csb.gov.ge).

The exclusive role of Orthodoxy established by the constitution became the legal basis for the constitutional agreement between the Georgian state and the Orthodox Church of Georgia decreed on October 14, 2002. These events also strengthened the position of Orthodoxy. Together with the main trend of being religious, Orthodoxy is in a leading position and the readiness of the Georgian Orthodox Church to make adjustments for present-day issues attracts the smaller groups under its umbrella. In 2002 the Catholicos-Patriarch of Georgia Ilia II declared: "Times are changing and together with them we are changing too; therefore, the church should take into account the new spiritual and material problems that we encounter in life."

On the other hand, the Catholic community of Georgia is also very active, including the Chaldean-Assyrian group. So far, however, no cultural leader (with a political project) has emerged among the Assyrians.

Thus, the case of Assyrians is special in the sense that a small community is facing the problem of becoming divided. The binary opposition we/they present at a religious level, together with the social-political problems, may worsen the tension. The Assyrians are constructing new markers of their ethnocultural identity; one group has chosen integration in the Georgian culture and they at least have a spiritual leader (Father Seraphim), whereas another group tries to maintain the differences, though seeking assistance from the Catholics. This latter group does not have an outstanding leader yet.

Today the stable development of the Assyrian community is contingent on the degree of peaceful coexistence between representatives of various confessions within the ethnic group. Religious creed as an inner orientation of the individual and ethnic groups' self-identification, as well as carrier of cultural values, is highly important. Yet, though religion promotes an inner-ethnic integrating process, it is also a differentiation element between the groups and even within the same ethnic group. At present, religion acts as a factor of ethnocultural integration and identification and if the religious opposition should escalate, the inter-confessional tension could hinder the construction of a consolidated ethnic group.

## Bibliography

Basilia, Merab (ed.) (2008): ეთნოსები საქართველოში [Ethnoses in Georgia]. Centre of Tolerance by Ombudsman of Georgia. Tbilisi: Library of Ombudsmen of Georgia, 171–182.

Beridze, Teimuraz (ed.) (2004): საქართველოს მოსახლეობის 2002 წლის პირველი საქართველოს ეროვნული აღწერის ძირითადი შედეგები [Basic results of the first general census of Georgian population 2002]. Tbilisi [no publishing house].

Constitution of Georgia. URL: http://csb.gov.ge/uploads/2081806.pdf.

Ghutidze, Inga (2014): The Assyrians in Georgia – Language Situation (According to materials obtained in Kanda). In: *Journal of Kartvelological Studies,* 159–168.

Japaridze, Anania (2009): მიტროპოლოტი ანანია ჯაფარიძე, საქართველოს სამოციქულო ეკლესიის ისტორია, თბილისი, გამომცემლობა ალილო [History of the Georgian Apostolic Church]. Tbilisi: Alilo.

Javakhishvili, Ivane (1979): თხზულებანი თორმეტ ტომად [Works in 12 volumes], vol. I. Tbilisi: Metsniereba.

Katsitadze, Papuna (2014): საქართველოს ასურელების სამოქალაქო ინტეგრაციის პრობლემები [Problems of Civil Integration of Georgian Assyrians]. In: კავკასიის ეთნოლოგიური კრებული [Ethnological Journal of the Caucasus], XV, Tbilisi Universali, 24–32.

Kekelidze, Korneli (1960): ქართული ლიტერატურის ისტორია [History of Georgian Literature], vol. 1. Tbilisi: Rustaveli Institute of Georgian Literature.

Songulashvili, Avtandil (2005): ეროვნული უმცირესობანი და კონფესიები საქართელოში [Ethnic Minorities and Confessions in Georgia]. Tbilisi: Orbeliani Pedagogical University.

# Molokans in Georgia: A Changing Culture and the Search for New Identities

*Tamar Antadze*

## Introduction

This chapter is based on ethnographic data and interviews collected from 2011 to 2013 in Tbilisi and Southeast Georgia among the Molokan communities. Molokans are an ethno-confessional minority group whose subsistence was based on inter/intra-group economic relations.

Molokans are among the "Spiritual Christian" sects whose members were exiled from central parts of the Russian Empire to its periphery in the Caucasus. Displaced to Georgia in the 19th century, they settled in the eastern part of Georgia and in the Rikhe district of the capital Tbilisi where they had compact settlements. Molokan communities were chiefly agricultural ones with a communal economic system: sharing land for food and forage production. However, when the Soviet Union was established, their communal settlements were transformed into kolkhoz, i. e. collective farms, and they lost ownership of their land, private property and goods.

Researches on this topic mainly have an historical approach. I have analysed the Molokans current everyday life, examining how their economic basis was destroyed and how the group is exposed to various impacts: on the one hand, they influence the region's societal organization and live in a multiethnic place, but on the other hand, changes in political organization are modifying their group's composition. Yet, Molokans have somehow adapted to the changes and, by adding public secular events and holidays to their religious calendar, have actualized their practices. Consequently, if their identity's defining factor used to be religion, nowadays it is increasingly connected to nationality.

Research questions included why and how they changed their identity, what are the main factors that preserve the group's existence and unity and what are the main factors that endanger their unity.

## Historical Background

Among the ethno-confessional minorities residing in Georgia, Molokans are Russian "Spiritual Christians" displaced to the Caucasus in the 19th century. Founded in the 17th century by Semion Uklein, the sect was denominated Molokan by the Consistory of Tambov district in 1785, officially because Molokans used to drink milk during fast time. According to other sources, the sect's name may derive from the faith in God as spiritual milk молоко [Moloko, milk] for the believers, their primary resettlement's place name молочные воды [Molochnie Vodi, Milky Water), or a small number of Molokans [мало/malo, little]. Members of the community dismiss these versions, stating that "like a child needs milk to grow physically, they need spiritual milk to grow spiritually" (Remizova-Kiriakova 2014: 191).

Russian Spiritual Christians include Doukhobors[1], Molokans[2] and Starovers[3]. They broke away from the Russian Orthodox Church and established the "Protestant" sect. From the 14th to the 16th century, several sectarian movements emerged in the Russian Orthodox Church. They were not popular in the Russian Empire so the movements, unlike Protestantism in Western Europe, did not have a reformative character (Khutsishvili 2000: 133).

For the greater part, members of the Molokan sect were peasants. Molokans rejected the Orthodox liturgy, icons and crosses, and at their meetings would solely chant spiritual themes from the Bible. Their communities were led mostly by the elders. Internal dissents divided the sect into several branches: Constant Molokans, Priguny or Jumpers, Communist Molokans, Maksimisty and so on. Constant Molokans adhere to the teachings of their founder Semion Uklein. Jumpers leap or dance while chanting the psalms. Maksimisty stemmed from Priguny in the 20th century (Lane 1978: 101).

Russian rulers were concerned that Russian Spiritual Christians would spread their "heretic ideas" that could spark protests. Moreover, the government wanted to establish new settlements with reliable forces in the peripheries of the Empire and the Caucasus was a newly conquered region. This is why Paul I of Russia (1796–1801) persecuted members of the Doukhobor and Molokan communities, some of which were exiled to Siberia. In 1839, the Tsar issued an ultimatum: either the sectarians converted to orthodoxy or they would be resettled in the newly conquered Caucasus region (Lohm 2006: 5). Though some Molokan communities believed they could find salvation in the Caucasus region, thus went voluntarily, most of them were forcibly exiled to Georgia, Armenia and Azerbaijan in the Caucasus. Nowadays the majority of Molokans live in Russia.

---

1 Духобор, "spirit-warrior". Emerging in the 17th century, this subgroup, which had its own spiritual leaders [вожди/vozhdi], believed in Jesus Christ and rejected the authority of church and state.

2 Emerging in the 17th century, this sect's social composition differs from the Doukhobor's one. It elected its leaders among the elders [пресвитер/presbyter].

3 Старовéры/Staroveri, "old believers". Emerging in the 17th century, this subgroup adheres to the Russian Orthodox Church liturgy antecedent the reform enacted by Patriarch Nikon of Moscow in 1652.

## Molokans in Georgia

A small ethno-confessional minority group in Georgia, Molokans lived almost in isolation in accordance with their confessional practice. They settled in the village of Eliatsminda in the Kakheti region and in the Rikhe district in Tbilisi (Lineff 1912: 552). Eventually, they separated into three independent communities in the Saburtalo, Sanzona and Navtlughi districts.

Members of these communities were mostly peasants and land workers, thus strongly agriculture-oriented and, like the Doukhobor, had a communal system. Under the Soviet Union, they worked in kolkhozes (collective farms), which were among the most profitable in the entire Soviet Union.

> They lived in separate homesteads, but within compact villages where pasture was held in common, and land was regularly redistributed depending on the needs of families: if someone died or if another got a new child they shared the lands accordingly. This was called a *mir* [communal] system (Lohm 2006: 7).

In Georgia, Molokans were not a homogenous group. After the resettlement, new sectarian denominations emerged: "Priguny" [jumpers], a sect founded in 1841 in Tbilisi, "new Molokans", "Evangelist Christians", "Sukhoi" [dry], "Baptists", "Liberal Molokans", "Progressists" and so on. In Tbilisi and in the village of Eliatsminda (Kakheti region) Molokans are Constants.

An interesting event occurred on August 20, 1867. Voronin, the Presbyter of the Tbilisi Molokans met with Martin Kolveit, a German Baptist who persuaded him that baptism with water was essential. Voronin was impressed by Kolveit and was baptized along with other members of the Molokan community. After that episode, the number of Molokans decreased (Papuashvili 2008: 244).

In the 19th century, the Molokans of Tbilisi were active in public life; they established two private schools for Orthodox Christians and Molokans and founded the Kukia district civil society in Tbilisi whose members included not only Molokans, but also Baptist believers. The Tbilisi Molokan society also established several schools, boarding houses, science societies and so on (Papuashvili 2008: 243).

## The belief of the Molokans and organization of the community

Molokans were hard workers and strong believers. The Bible, which Molokans read every day, plays a crucial role in the lives of every believer. The Holy Book is kept on a table at the centre of their home (Remizova-Kiriakova 2014: 201). Molokans interpret the Bible in a symbolic way. For example, they do not practice baptism by water because they do not view the word "water" literally, but rather allegorically as "living water" according to the Gospel of John (7, 38). Their ideology included important social and political elements, by which they were conscientious objectors and pacifists (Breyfogle 2007: 225). Their customs and interpretation of the Bible are recorded in a book called "Obriadnik" (Papuashvili 2008: 239). Molokan rituals differ from Orthodox Christian rituals. For example, as mentioned above Molokans practice Spiritual Baptism, i. e. baptism without water. Religion is transmitted at birth: whoever is born within the community is Molokan.

Molokans reject religious and secular authorities and do not recognize Orthodox Church crosses and icons, believing that an artificial connection with God is unnecessary. Molokans have Prayer Houses where they convene for Sunday service denominated Sobronya. The Presbyter leads services and prayers (Remizova-Kiriakova 2014: 202).

The spiritual leader-Presbyter should be the man with the most extensive life experiences. As informants told me, he must not necessarily have a higher education, but he must have the personal traits of a leader, be honest and true to his way of life. Molokans hold elections to choose their leader and everyone has the right to vote. In most cases, Presbyters are the oldest members of the community (Remizova-Kiriakova 2014: 203). At elections, members of the community write the name of their candidate on a piece of paper and the leader is elected by popular vote. The Presbyter is elected for life, but there are some exceptions, as one informant told me:

> When the leader is not fulfilling a commitment, the community rejects him and elects another person (Informant 1, Tbilisi, May 2012).

In the case of the Tbilisi Sanzona district community, the Presbyter was fulfilling every above-mentioned requirement. In the village of Gorelovka, the Presbyter is middle-aged rather than elderly and was elected for his personal qualities. The Presbyters of two other communities in Tbilisi (Navtlughi and Saburtalo districts) are women because there were no men left in their communities.

Molokan appearance and eating habits are aspects of their belief. Molokans have a characteristic attire: women wear long dresses, long-sleeved shirts and printed veils: middle-aged men wear caps, long trousers and shirts (Remizova-Kiriakova 2014: 205). As for eating habits, Molokans are not allowed to eat pork or drink wine. They cannot smoke cigarettes. They explain that according to the Bible, one is not allowed to do any of the above-mentioned things. At times, however, preaching and practice diverge. Molokans living in the urban environment of Tbilisi adhere to these prohibitions and act accordingly. However, in the rural environment of the village of Eliatsminda, local Molokans smoke, drink wine and eat pork; they even sell pork to other villagers.

Molokans live in small communities. Elders control every change and discuss every case in the community. Hierarchy by age is evident during their services, where Molokans in the front seats are elders while younger people sit at the back. They call each other brother and sister because they believe that God's spirit is equally present in every individual (Remizova-Kiriakova 2014: 204).

Molokans are active in social life: Presbyter Fyodor Niudakhin was awarded the citizen's Medal of Honour by the Tbilisi municipality. Members of the Molokan community attended the worldwide meeting of Molokans on July 21–24, 2005 in Stavropol Krai, district of Kachubei. The meeting marked the 200$^{th}$ anniversary of the Molokan separation from the Russian Orthodox Church. Delegates arrived from different areas of Russia as well as from Armenia, Georgia, Azerbaijan, Ukraine and USA. From Georgia, seven Molokans with head presbyter Fiodor attended the celebration (Antadze 2013: 35).

Molokans are strong believers and in Georgia there is a general narrative about their honesty. In the village of Eliatsminda in the Kakheti region, Georgians were helping Molokans prepare the celebration dinner. Other Georgians, too, had been invited to the dinner. One Georgian woman recounted:

> They are very nice and honest people. We commemorate celebrations together. We have lived peacefully for so many years. I remember their marriages, how beautiful they were and how they sang and danced in the streets (Informant 2, Eliatsminda village, May 2013).

A woman who bought her house from her Molokan neighbours, stated:

> I bought this house from Molokans. They are really clean, hardworking and kind people. They are great cooks. Sometimes I ask them for recipes and study them to learn how to cook well (Informant 3, Eliatsminda village, May 2013).

This explains why there is no historical record or narrative about conflicts between Molokans and other ethnic groups; besides, Molokans were pacifists and one of their main ideals was peace. Though Molokans were an endogamous group, mixed marriages with Georgians and even with Azeri people have occurred in rural areas (Eliatsminda village in the Kakheti Region, eastern Georgia). An interesting fact is that Azeri people are not only ethnically different from Molokans, but their confessions of Christianity and Islam are also different from each other, yet some ideals of Molokanism are akin to those of Islam and Judaism. For example, in accordance with Mosaic rules they do not eat pork, as the main customs of the Molokans derive from Judaic and Islamic traditions (Papuashvili 2008: 240).

All the above-mentioned Molokan characteristics helped me during fieldwork. As mentioned, the main data-collection methods were in-depth interviews and participant observation. I attended and took part in celebrations and Sunday services with the Tbilisi community during 2012–2013. Members of the community were open and forthcoming. Several weeks into our acquaintance, I was helping them prepare dinner when one elder told me that I looked like a real Molokan. After that they regarded me as an insider and there were no barriers between us. Besides these subjective factors for their openness, there are also some objective ones: the group has few members and they are trying to talk about their culture and faith with others to hold on to their history. The main challenge I encountered while collecting data was winning people's trust in the village of Eliatsminda. Another group interested in Molokan culture had worked in this community and offered them money in exchange for information. After that experience, several Molokans expected the same from me and refused to talk for free. At the start, this really hindered my fieldwork, but eventually I was able to win their trust.

## Religious and secular ethics of Molokanism

Christel Lane (1975) writes that Soviet literature always points up that Molokan communities were more united by their secular ethic than by their religious views. The reason for their secular ethic – equality, brotherhood, diligence – lies in their understanding of God's nature (Lane 1975: 224). This democratic ideal stems from their belief that God's spirit blesses men equally (Lane 1975: 223).

Before the Soviet Union era, Molokans already lived in segregated but not isolated communities. They implemented their ideals and beliefs in the organization of communes. In most communities, the ideal of equality was not fully achieved since social differences between members were noticeable, but Molokans successfully realized their ideal of brotherhood in communal life (Lane 1975: 224). To this day Molokans in Tbilisi call themselves brothers and sisters. They collect money for shared needs, such as communal bills, celebration dinners and so on. The rule for collecting money is interesting; members leave as much as they can under a scarf placed on a table so no one can see the amount each one donates. The secular ethic is extremely important for our purposes because Molokans have turned a specific secular celebration into a religious one. Before delving into this aspect, I will first describe the process of decline in Molokan communities chronologically.

## The process of extinction

In the 1970s, scholars were already discussing and researching the problem of the dwindling Molokan communities, which had once been among the strongest and influential in pre-revolutionary Russia, but were now moving towards extinction (Lane 1975: 221). Lane (1975) discussed the reasons underlying the sect's decline.

After the establishment of the Soviet Union, citizens faced a new reality. The sects in particular had to cope with radically different social relations. During the Tsarist period ($17^{th}$–$19^{th}$ century), Molokans were opposed to three different social institutions: the Tsarist state, landowners and the Orthodox Church. After the beginning of the Soviet Era (1922), the church was destroyed and the state's ideology became anti-religious (Lane 1975: 225). During the revolution, Bolsheviks respected 'rationalist religious sects' such as the Spiritual Christians. They supported Molokans who started to create new communes. The reason was similarities between the ideology of the Soviet government and the Molokan belief: equality and brotherhood were key concepts for both. This stance was maintained after the revolution too. Soon after, however, Molokan communes started to close down (Lane 1975: 226). The first reason was that Molokans refused to serve in the armed forces for religious reasons and the second was the enactment of a new policy that would affect villages. Though from the very beginning Molokans had worked in their own communes, after the reform process known as collectivization their ownership was taken over by the Soviet government. Literature mentions that following collectivization Molokan communities started to dissolve or changed their dogmas and created new schismatic groups, for example the Maksimisty in Armenia (Lane 1975: 227). Many Molokans joined the Baptist sect. Even today, young Molokans in Tbilisi are increasingly joining the Baptists. When asked why, their reply is that the teachings and dogmas are actually the same; moreover, it guarantees material security. In a number of cases, the parents are Molokans but their children decide to become Baptists. An elder explained:

> We don't have money and even our prayer house is crumbling. Baptists have good furniture, good musical instruments and so on. Therefore, the young decided to become Baptists. Moreover, the belief is really alike (Informant 4, Tbilisi, May 2012).

Lane (1975) mentions that the key reason of the Molokan decline in the 1970s was that their secular communist ethic and their religious views were so similar that they abandoned their religious ideology. However, this was in the 1970s; the migrations caused by the subsequent dissolution of the Soviet Union accelerated the decline process.

Since the collapse of the Soviet Socialist system in 1991, the political situation has radically changed in Georgia. The post-Soviet political changes - growing nationalist feelings, the migration process among the ethnic minority groups and the collapse of the economic base - impacted the life and practice of Molokans: the once strong community became a small and weak one.

> The analyses of the events of the last decade enable us to state that the painful processes of the "death" of the "old" societies and their "rebirth", during which they undergo a complex adaptation to the new environment, is ongoing. This process, by its very nature, is extremely inconsistent (Khutsishvili 2004: 1).

The process of change was detrimental because the character of the historical changes taking place in post-Soviet societies like Georgia is determined by the replacement of the communist principles of a socialist society and of the Soviet people by absolute other values: civil society, the individual citizen and state institutions (Khutsishvili 2004: 1).

Molokans had to change their way of life once again. In these circumstances, the role of religion increased and somehow replaced ethnicity (Khutsishvili 2004: 1). My aim is to examine the current processes in the communities.

## Celebrating the 9th of May

The 9th of May is Russia's World War II Victory Day: the war ended on May 8, 1945 and the 9th of May was established as Victory Day. In Georgia, this secular celebration is an official public holiday. Molokans commemorate Victory Day every year not as a secular celebration, but as a religious holiday: the day of victory and All Souls' Day.

When asked which religious celebrations they celebrate, one informant listed the following: Christmas (7th of January), Epiphany (19th of January), Easter, Ascension (40th day after Easter), Holy Trinity (50th day after Easter), Transfiguration (19th of August), Day of Gratitude (last week of September) and the 9th of May. Their service for the 9th of May is similar to their other celebrations.

On May 9, 2012, I attended their service at the home of one of their community's members. It was a special service for her father who had died in World War II. After service, they had a traditional dinner, which consisted of tea, lapsha (traditional homemade noodle soup) and boiled meat. The Presbyter Fiodor told me:

> On the 9th of May our ancestors died. No one knows the exact number of casualties. I remember wartimes, I was a child and I remember poverty. Everyone knows what happened during the Leningrad Blockade [September 8, 1941 - January 27, 1944]. We haven't forgotten their valour and we have to celebrate the day of victory. It's tragedy and glory at the same time because it's the day of victory (Presbyter Fiodor, Tbilisi, May 2012).

The special service was attended by members from all three communities in Tbilisi - Saburtalo, Sanzona and Navtlughi: in total, thirteen elders and two middle-aged persons. Women wore multicolour scarves. The Presbyter had a long beard and wore a long white shirt and long trousers. The Presbyter told me that in the past everyone wore traditional dresses but not nowadays. An interesting aspect is that the three leaders of the three communities held service together. They were seated next to the table reading the prayers. The other members, seated around the room, were chanting psalms. The chanting and praying was so stirring that some of them were moved to tears. Every member of the community was involved in reading, chanting or explaining the scriptures freely. During the service, which is not strictly established, they freely decide what to read and chant.

> He [the presbyter] read aloud the first words of the psalm, and one of the brethren intoned a prayer. The others thereupon took up the melody and raised it by an interval of a 4th or of a 5th, and then they divided into two

> parts. The women joined in later, and in their turn sang in two parts, and sometimes in unison. The result was an interesting and peculiar counterpoint. The relation with the Russian folk-song was felt very strongly, but the parts here moved more closely; and the cautious manner in which the high parts moved within the compass of two or three degrees lent to these psalms a peculiar, stern character. Everybody sang with enthusiasm and with a serious, concentrated expression; the women sang with their mouths half screened by their hands, and therefore their voices sounded shrill; but on the whole the choir sounded beautifully, was full of colour, and bore that expressive conviction which is inherent to folk improvisation (Lineff 1912: 552).

Even nowadays, their singing is much the same. Molokans clearly pass on their traditions from father to son. They call each other brother and sisters according to their social organization. As mentioned above, their ideology is based on egalitarian principles, as every member of the community is equal: an ideal rooted in their belief that God's spirit blesses every man equally (Lane 1975: 223).

The service is divided into two parts: during the first part they sing and pray sitting on the long bench next to the main table on top of which lie the Psalms and the Holy Bible. During the short break between the first and the second part, they move the table and chairs against the walls. In the second part of the prayer, Presbyters stand and pray while the other members stand in one corner chanting. At the end, they pray on their knees.

The location for their services is quite simple: a table covered by a white veil on top of which are the Holy Bible and Psalms. For celebrations, they also have bread and salt on the table:

> For celebrations, we necessarily have bread and salt. Like Orthodox Christians have holy water, we have bread and salt for blessing (Informant 1).

Apparently, this tradition derives from their being an agricultural community. Bread and salt are symbolic of fertilization so they pray for a good harvest. They are an agricultural community, which is also apparent in their style of fasting. Their Day of Gratitude at harvest time celebrates their gratitude to God for abundance. This is a movable feast celebrated in October after the grape harvest.

> We call it the day of gratitude. We have a harvest in springtime. For good harvests, in autumn we give thanks to God (Informant 5, Tbilisi, May 2012).

Their fasting and holidays clearly indicate that years ago they were an agricultural community, but now this surfaces only in rituals, since in Tbilisi they have no connection to agriculture.

The 9th of May service lasted two hours. After prayer, they had dinner. The dinner after celebrations is very important and strictly defined according to the Russian tradition: tea in a samovar (traditional Russian tea urn), lapsha, boiled meat, pancakes and sweets. The women prepared the dinner while the men took care of the meat and bread. During the dinner, they chanted and prayed. Molokans hold this traditional dinner on the 9th of May, on the Day of Gratitude, on the Day of Transfiguration, and at marriages and funerals.

## Identity

During this dinner, they spoke about themselves, who they are, about their identity. Different levels of identity emerged in the interviews:

> Molokans are Russian, but now we live in Georgia; therefore, our home is Georgia (Informant 6, Tbilisi, May 2012).
>
> Molokans are neither Georgian nor Russian but the descendants of Jews. When some Jews became Christian, they maintained most of the traditions and rules from the Old Testament. We follow the Mosaic rules. For example: Molokans are not allowed to eat pork, touch anything unclean or enter the place where a dead person lies. In the past, those who buried the dead were considered unclean and were not allowed to sit with others at the funeral repast. We had some Molokans who were real Jews. We Molokans also observe the Ten Commandments and have prayers for the dead that come from the Jews, also reading and singing Psalms is an essential part of our Sunday Service (Presbyter Fiodor).
>
> When someone asked my aunt where she came from, she answered, "I am Molokan". She thought that Molokans were a nation. She also believed that Molokans and Russians were different people; of course, that's not true. When I go to Russia, I say that I am Georgian and when I am in Georgia, I say that I am Russian. Georgia is our homeland because we were born and raised here. Sometimes people laughed at us: "even you don't know where you come from", but that's not true. We are not like foreigners in Georgia because we were born here, but we are Russians" (Informant 7, Tbilisi, May 2012).

As the head Presbyter of Tbilisi told me:

> From the first to the fourth century, we were called "Pavlikans", apostles of the apostle Paul. In the 3rd century, Pavlikans lived together in communities and married amongst themselves. After the first church council, the churches divided. One part believed in icons and another was against it. Those who were against icons were called iconoclasts and were persecuted. We are the descendants of those iconoclasts. We are close to Orthodox Christians except that we don't have baptism but a spiritual baptism. We also have the same Psalms and prayers as the Orthodox Christians (Presbyter Fiodor).

When Molokans talk about themselves and the features that distinguish them from the others, they always mention their eating habits, that they do not eat pork, do not smoke cigarettes and do not drink alcohol. In the minds of outsiders, these markers always create the image of honest people. The general stereotypical image of the Russian in their conquered territories is that of an unreliable drunkard, but since Molokans do not match this image, they are seen as trustworthy. About their reputation among Georgian citizens, we have to mention Internet discussions on forums:

> They are hardworking, diligent, honest. They don't smoke and don't drink alcohol. They made the best dairy products in the Caucasus. They sold their products in the Tbilisi bazaar called "Malaknebi" [the Molokans in Georgian]. Sometimes they speak four languages: Georgian, Russian, Armenian and Azerbaijani. That's why they feel free in interethnic relations (Remizova-Kiriakova 2014: 221).

The image of honest people also arose from trade relationships. A Georgian informant said they always bought honey and milk from Molokans because their products are natural and uncontaminated: another reason why they were perceived as honest people.

In addition, the 9th of May is a secular celebration but Molokans included it in their religious calendar. It happens quite often when

> Religion replaces ethnicity and carries out an appropriate political role. It's natural since religion, as a major element of ethnic self-consciousness, determines the character of processes of inner-ethnic consolidation and, at the same time, differentiation between the ethnos (Khutsishvili 2004: 1).

However, in the case of Molokans ethnicity comes before religion. They state that it's not a bad thing when a younger generation migrates as long as Russia remains their homeland, their nation. In this way, Molokans underline their Russian identity and a means for reunion-survival.

## A Taylorian approach to present-day Molokanism

Religion has always played an important role in the history of mankind. Throughout the epochs, human beliefs and forms of social organization have undergone changes. In earlier times, there was a distinct boundary between sacred and profane. According to Charles Taylor (2006), the sacred consisted in special places, special actors, special time periods and special actions: for example, service (action) held by the priest (actor) during fast time (time period) in the church (place) (Taylor 2006: 281).

Nowadays this model of interaction between mankind and God has been replaced by a new one combining the cosmos and the state. Taylor calls this era the time of mobilizations. New communities emerge and unite around new kinds of identities defined by political identity, thus the group is not necessarily united around one ethnos or religion. The connector can be religious confession, general state principles and historical connections. By mobilization, Taylor implies the actions enforced by influential actors that give rise to new types of social and religious unities. These agents, actors who have the power and the influence, can be the authorities of the government or religious groups and so on (Taylor 2006: 282).

The case of Molokans changing identities can be explained by the "neo-Durkheimian effect". Taylor divides religious mobilizations into three types: evangelical revivals akin to the Protestant current, the neo-Durkheimian phenomenon, i. e. the interweaving of religious confession and political identity, and civilizational links (Taylor 2006: 294).

For our purposes, the most interesting is the neo-Durkheimian effect. According to Taylor, this occurs when the world is not strictly divided into sacred and secular. The neo-Durkheimian effect, as mentioned above, emerges when group and confessional belonging overlap and the moral issues of the group's history tend to be coded in religious categories (Taylor 2006: 281).

As discussed above, at the beginning of the previous century Molokans were able to blend secular and religious ethics. However, this was not a forced artificial process because it happened naturally. This was possible because of the strong connection between the ideology of the Soviet government and the beliefs of the Molokans; brotherhood and equality were key concepts for both. The era of mobilizations for Molokans began after the dissolution of the Soviet Union in the late 1990s when they were forced to adapt to a new structure and organization of social life. The Socialist State machine turned into a capitalist one and in the process, Molokans lost their formalized kolkhoz collective farming. As a means to survive in this heterogeneous state of affairs and new social system, they blended their sense of belonging to the group with that to their confession, not artificially but naturally. Their identity changed as they tried to adapt to the new conditions. One of the outcomes is that they commemorate a secular celebration as a religious one.

Victory Day on May 9, 1945 was highly significant for Russia itself. Soviet Union leaders exploited its symbolic value to empower Soviet identity, but it ultimately became the symbol of Russia's power, the successor to the Soviet Union. This is why Molokans connect it to "being Russian" and as a way to empower their connection with their homeland Russia and Russian identity.

## Conclusion

Based on field notes, interviews, participant observations and literature, I examined how Molokans adapted to changes in economic organization, how they preserved their culture and why they have slightly changed their identity. They experienced extreme conditions first when they were exiled to Georgia and then when the Soviet Union collapsed along with its kolkhoz.

The political changes had a huge influence on the small group's existence. The main factor was the aftermath of the Soviet Union's collapse in which the Molokans lost their formalized unit, the kholkhoz, which supported their way of life based on collective farming. For the Molokans and other Russian Spiritual Christians (Doukhobors), the kolkhoz, the Soviet form of economic organization, was an officially recognized unity on which they grounded their traditional farming collective, which was also the basis of their confessional unity. The destruction of this formal structure was the main endangering factor to the unity of the groups.

Because of the current migration processes, Molokans have fewer members especially among the younger generation, thus the group's members are decreasing. These factors give us reason to think that this minority group is going to disappear. Yet, they have found ways to survive. Molokans have included public secular events and holidays in their religious calendar, thus are trying to actualize their practices. One of these public secular holidays is the 9$^{th}$ of May. This celebration does not empower their religious belonging, but rather their national identity-belonging to Russia, as proven by the event in itself and by the perceptions of the group's members.

This is the type of religious mobilization Charles Taylor defines as the neo-Durkheimian effect: the condition in which the sense of belonging to a group and to a religious confession are fused and the ethical issues of the groups' history tend to be coded in religious categories. Celebrating the 9$^{th}$ of May is the factor that still unites the group.

## Bibliography

Antadze, Tamar (2013): მოლოკნები საქართველოში [Molokans in Georgia]. Unpublished Master thesis, Department of Ethnology, Tbilisi State University.

Breyfogle, Nicholas B. (2007): Prayer and the Politics of Place: Molokan Church Building, Tsarist Law, and the Quest for a Public Sphere in Late Imperial Russia. In: Mark D. Steinberg and Heather J. Coleman (ed.): *Religion and Spirituality in Modern Russia*. Bloomington: Indiana University Press, 222–252.

Lane, Christel (1975): Socio-Political Accommodation and Religious Decline: The Case of Molokan Sect in Soviet Society. In: *Comparative Studies in Society and History,* 17 (2): 221–237.

Lane, Christel (1978): *Christian Religions in the Soviet Union: A sociological Study*. Albany: State University of New York Press.

Lunkin, Roman and Prokofyev, Anton (2000): Molokans and Doukhobors: Living Sources of Russian Protestantism. In: *Religion, State and Society*, 28 (1): 85–92.

Haytian, Aram (2007): The Molokans in Armenia. In: *Iran and the Caucasus*, 11 (1): 33–44.

Khutsishvili, Lia (2000): მოლოკნები [The Molokans]. In: კლიო [*Klio*], 2: 133–148.

Khutsishvili, Ketevan (2004): რელიგიური სიტუაციის ცვლილება და უსაფრთხოების პრობლემა თანამედროვე საქართველოში [Changing Religious Situation and Problems of Public Security in Georgia]. Tbilisi: Artanuji.

Lineff, Eugenie (1912): A Musical Tour in Caucasus. In: *Sammelbände der Internationalen Musikgesellschaft,* 4: 552–564.

Lohm, Hedvig (2006): *Dukhobors in Georgia: a Study of the Issue of Land Ownership and Inter-Ethnic Relations in Ninotsminda Rayon (Samtskhe-Javakheti)*, ECMI working paper #35. URL: http://www.ecmicaucasus.org/upload/publications/working_paper_35_en.pdf.

Papuashvili, Nugzar (2008): მალაკნები [The Molokans]. Religions in Georgia. Tbilisi: Georgian Public Defenders Library, 239–245. URL: http://dspace.nplg.gov.ge/bitstream/1234/8483/1/Religiebi_Saqartveloshi.pdf.

Remizova-Kiriakova, Nadejda (2014): История возникновения и происхождения секты духовных-христиан Молокан [The History of the Origins of Molokans]. In: ისტორიულ ეთნოლოგიური ძიებანი [Studies in History and Ethnology], 16: 190–223.

Taylor, Charles (2006): Religious Mobilizations. In: *Public Culture*, 18 (2): 281–300.

# Ways to Maintain Ethnic Identity

## Folk Festivals of Georgians in the Artvin Province (Republic of Turkey)

*Rozeta Gujejiani*

One of the defining factors of Georgian ethnic identity in the Republic of Turkey is folk festivals, many of which, however, have been lost. This chapter is based on historic-ethnographic sources and field-ethnographic data collected between 2006 and 2014 on two surviving celebrations, შუამთობა [Shuamtoba] and მარიობა [Mariobа].

*Shuamtoba* and *Marioba* are celebrated in the historical Tao-Klarjeti area. *Shuamtoba* relates to livestock breeding. Georgian city dwellers still come to the area from different parts of Turkey, often taking their vacations simultaneously. *Marioba* celebrated the Assumption of the Virgin Mary (August 28th). In some villages, it is a large-scale celebration lasting three days, with a traditional song festival and performances in traditional costumes culminating in a theatre play.

The festivals' transformation began in the 1960s, when local administrations decided to establish specific venues for *Shuamtoba* and *Marioba*. The celebrations are currently organized and planned by local administrations and include welcome speeches delivered in Turkish or translated into Turkish. Nevertheless, some Georgians are struggling to keep the tradition of celebrating *Shuamtoba* as a distinctly Georgian festival as a way to preserve a segment of their ethnic identity.

* * *

In the 16th century, the Ottoman Empire conquered part of the Georgian territory, thus nowadays millions of ethnic Georgians live in the Republic of Turkey (Guchua 1973). In 1878, a large portion of Georgian territory situated in the Ottoman Empire was ceded to the Russian Empire; in 1921, part of the Georgian historical territory was reoccupied by the neighbouring Republic of Turkey. Georgians in the Republic of Turkey are Sunni Muslims, but have maintained their Georgian identity, language and many elements of the Georgian culture: family life, material culture, folklore, festivals, rituals and so forth.

Unfortunately, in the Soviet period, Georgian academics did not have the possibility to study the life and culture of the Georgians in Turkey, thus there is no information available for the period between the 1920s and the 1980s to compare ethnographic materials of different periods. Consequently, my research is based entirely on my own field-ethnographic information and on a reconstruction of the past according to the informers' stories (oral history).

The study is based on historical and ethnographic sources and on field ethnographic materials that I collected from ethnic Georgians of Turkey during the years 2006–2014. The research was accompanied by some difficulties, e. g. the lack of ethnographic reference materials. During the research in Tao-Klarjeti (Artvin province), I was the first citizen of Georgia the population had ever met; therefore, they were very interested in Georgian life and I often became the subject of the interviews myself. During the last century, Georgia and the Artvin province lacked mutual information about each other's culture and life. The local population's distrust must also be mentioned and overcoming this factor took time. However, in my case there were no restrictions from local administration.

The Georgian folk festivals are one of the determining factors of the ethnic identity of Georgians in the Republic of Turkey. Many of these traditional festivals have been lost and nowadays only the *Shuamtoba* and *Marioba* festivals are celebrated, along with bull fights, i. e. bull against bull, which have already acquired a character of a festival, though in some areas rituals are still carried out in a traditional way.

Areas in which the festivals take place include the historical area of Georgian settlements whose population's identity is still Georgian: Imerkhevi, Upper Machakheli, Klaskuri, Borchkha, Murghuli Gorge, Devskeli and Baginistskali Gorges, Shuakhevi, Araveti, Akhaldaba, Adaguli, Ebrika, Kartla, Tkhiladze, Omana, Orji, Kheba, Maradidi, Katapkhia Gorge, Beghlevani Gorge, Chkhali Gorge and Parkhlistskali Gorge. The population of Georgian descent that now identifies as Turk celebrates modified versions of these holidays ("festivals") (Gujejiani 2010, Gujejiani 2011a, Gujejiani 2011b). According to the nomenclature of territorial units, this is the Artvin Province.

Folk festivals of the Georgians of Turkey are particularly important from the general perspective of Georgian religious culture, since rituals and festivals of traditional everyday life of the Georgians of Turkey are identical not only to ethnographic material in Adjara and Meskheti, neighbouring the historical Tao-Klarjeti area, but also to festivals held in Svaneti, Pshavi and Khevsureti, which are territorially distant.

* * *

Historical Tao-Klarjeti was conquered by the Ottoman Empire in 1551. After the Russian-Turkish War (1877–78), most of this area was ceded to the Russian Empire. In 1921, this historical land was separated from Georgia again and became part of Turkey. Local Georgians endured a difficult experience. Due to the influence of the state's assimilation methods, some of them gradually lost their Georgian identity, though the majority still identifies as "Georgians" (*The Constitution of the Republic of Turkey* 2000: 104, Sordia 2002: 36, Makaradze 2009: 161–166).

An interesting mechanism that represents and has preserved the ethnic identity of Georgians of Turkey is the tradition of the Georgian folk festivals through which they handed down an entirely different worldview and rituals compared to that of other citizens of Turkey with different ethnicities.

Changes in the way of celebrating festivals and rituals were first introduced in the second half of the 20th century. From this period on, local administrations took over the management and planning of festivals.

*Shuamtoba* and *Marioba* festivals were characteristic to every region of the historical Tao-Klarjeti area and are part of the folk festivals' annual calendar in southwest and southeast historical Georgia.

At present, festivals are celebrated in a comparatively authentic way on the villages' pastureland, where people still practice cattle breeding. Regrettably, traditional forms of animal husbandry and intensive agriculture were abandoned due to internal migration processes that began mainly in the 1980s.

*Shuamtoba* is related to the traditions of cattle breeding and is celebrated on summer pastures ("mountain"/*"Yayla"* - a Turkish term assimilated into Georgian). The Georgian term is აგარა [Agara], which is still used in some regions, e. g. Yusufeli District, Artvin Province. The Georgian areas and villages of the Artvin Province have their own summer pastures, where there are shelters for people and cattle. მემთევრი [Memtevri, one or several members of a family, i. e. farmers, milkers and dairymen] go to the "mountains"/*"Yala"* in spring and stay there until the early autumn. The Shuamtoba folk holiday is celebrated during the Memtevri period, i. e. from when cattle are led to the summer pastures to when they are led back to the plains. *Memtevries*, families and guests take part in the holiday, which lasts from one to three days with guests staying overnight. People living in towns try to visit their home areas at least during the *Shuamtoba* festival and often attend the *Shuamtoba* festival during their vacations. During this festival, people dine together, organize round dances, wrestling, bull and male goat fights, ჭეჲობა [Chedoba], horse racing, shooting tournaments and so on. Relatives living in various areas of Turkey come together at this time.

The alternative name of the *Shuamtoba* festival, *Marioba,* is still in use in several communities: for example, in several villages in the Imerkhevi Valley (Bazgireti, Ustamis) and the Nigali Valley, in some villages of the Baginistskali and Devskeli gorges and in the entire Upper Machakheli Valley. Obviously, among these populations, aside from several exceptions, the religious concept of the Assumption holiday to which this festival was related is lost, although they are aware the festival is Georgian and try to preserve it.

Among the Bazgireti community, the *Marioba* festival is celebrated in every village on a particularly large scale and has retained its authenticity. The locals do their best to preserve traditions as much as possible. The festival lasts three days (any Friday through Sunday in August) and is attended by many guests. A vast field north of the village becomes the centre of the festival celebration where Georgian songs and music are performed on a raised platform. Groups of young people in traditional Georgian costumes, to the accompaniment of folk music played by bagpipes and garmon, parade throughout the community at midday, inviting people to the square. Families carry their food, plates and teakettles to their tables and invite passers-by to join them. Local songs and a round dance are played on bagpipes and garmon. The festival's high point is a theatrical performance, ფადიკო [Phadico], which raises a great interest and sometimes is performed several times. The *Phadico*'s scenario subsumes elements of the ბერობანა [Berobana] too. The next day, the local folk sports event, ბილა [Bila], takes place on the slopes of the same square. On Sunday evening, guests return to their homes. The festival is significant under many aspects, most importantly for its marked Georgian character. Welcome speeches and conversations among participants are mainly in Georgian and the musical background is Georgian likewise. Typical Georgian features of the *Shuamtoba* and *Marioba* festival are prominent in regions where communities organize the festival independently, without the local administration's involvement. Scenes and elements of the festival rituals, as well as the ethno-musical folklore, are similar to traditions found in various regions of Georgia. The most significant aspect is that a certain part of the population regards festivals as a way to maintain and develop their ethnic identity whereas the rest of the population is not interested in maintaining their ethnic identity because the process of ethnic assimilation has gone too far.

* * *

Since the 1960s, the festivals' process of transformation has been ongoing. The Turkish administration has established the venues for the official festival in every settlement (Imerkhevi - Satave, Upper Machakheli, Klaskuri, Borchkha, Murghuli Gorge, Devskeli and Baginistskali Gorges, Shuakhevi, Araveti, Akhaldaba, Adaguli, Ebrika, Kartla, Tkhiladze, Omana, Orji, Kheba, Maradidi, Katapkhia Gorge, Beghlevani Gorge, Chkhali Gorge, Parkhlistskali Gorge), in an attempt to supplant local *Shuamtoba* and *Marioba* festivals. Local administrations control the management and planning of the official festival and choose the festivals' names, such as Honey Festival, Potato Festival, Kada Festival etc. Since the 1990s, when Georgia freed itself and the borders with Turkey were opened, Georgian scientists and visitors have been attending these festivals periodically and in some cases the local administration allows them to give speeches and greet the participants: an involvement previously restricted. The government of the Republic of Turkey has become more permissive over the last decade and the strict assimilation policy has ceased. Unfortunately, a great part of the ethnic Georgians has already been assimilated.

For the Imerkhevi official festival, called Satave, the government has established a plain venue located in the middle of the forest in the farthest reaches of the historical Diobani community (present-day Meydanchik). The Satave festival currently serves as a *Shuamtoba* festival for all Imerkhevi. For the Satave festival the administration organizes fairs and sets up a clearing where the concert is held: the list of invited singers and repertoire is prearranged. Welcome speeches and presentations are strictly in Turkish, though for us visiting guests from Georgia they made an exception and allowed us to speak in Georgian (with translation).

Large-scale festivals of this type have also been introduced in Upper Machakheli (Honey Festival), Parkhlistskali and Murghuli gorges etc. Of the official festivals, the Upper Machakheli "Honey Festival" has not been fully transformed yet. The local folklore group's repertoire is obviously Georgian and in recent years, a delegation from Lower Machakheli (Republic of Georgia) attends the festival, which is considered a highly important event by both locals and Machakhelians from Georgia. In 1921, the historical-ethnographic area of Machakheli was split in two: Upper Machakheli is in Turkish territory.

In parallel with the *Marioba* and *Shuamtoba* festivals, "festival" traits have been attributed to another element of Georgian traditional culture – the tradition of bull fights, which had a ritual nature before being turned into a festival. Ethnographic materials clearly indicate that the rules of bull fights and of men against bulls are present in several historical-ethnographic areas of Georgia (Svaneti, Racha, Adjara, Meskheti and Tao-Klarjeti). Bull fights are part of the traditional Georgian culture and were performed within the framework of several rituals.

In previous times, bull fights were organized in various Georgian festivals, but this tradition is currently followed only in Svaneti (during Easter Week), in the Adjara Mountains and in the historical Tao-Klarjeti area, though nowadays the tradition of bull fights in these areas too has features of a competition. Aside from several mountainous villages, bull fights mainly occur within the framework of "festivals" and are no longer part of a ritual. From the second half of the 20th century, the state of Turkey officially classified bull fights as a festival and the local administration became involved in its management. Public officers are now responsible for the preparatory work and management of the festival, which is currently celebrated as described above.

The majority of Georgian folk festivals famously involve elements of military drills. Up to the early 1980s, festivals included competitions in rock-lifting, long jump, running and archery. Some of the drill-like competitions are still organized: for example, the Svaneti ელიაობა [Eliaoba, *Hulish/Ulish*] festival includes horse races; during festivals devoted to St. George (ლიგერგი [*Ligerg*] in autumn (November 23rd) and spring (May 6th) wrestling competitions are arranged, at კვირიკობა [Kvirikoba] there is a rock-lifting competition etc. In addition, a number of Georgian folk holidays include the traditional performance of ritual round dances, which, besides a ritual connotation, also had a military training function (Bardavelidze 1968, Alaverdashvili 2012). In some of the ravines in Tao-Klarjeti, sports games are still arranged during festivals and every gathering is accompanied by the traditional performance of ხორუმი [Khorumi, round dances].

The tradition includes not only bulls, since also ram and male-goat fights are present in traditional Georgian everyday life; for example, in Svaneti ram fights were set up during the community and village festival ლიხვდიში [Likhvdishi]. Ram fights are a common event also during *Shuamtoba* festivals in Tao-Klarjeti.

Until recently, bull fights were part of a religious ritual organized in Svaneti during the Easter Week [უფლიშიერი, Uplishier, the Day of the Lord] holiday cycle. According to material gathered by Vera Bardavelidze, the holiday cycle of *Uplishier* lasted a long time – from two to six weeks. The holiday cycle included the prayers ritual [ლიმზირ, Limzir] as well as days for bull fights (Bardavelidze 1952, Bardavelidze 1957: 158). Calves with no flaws would be selected and reared for three years specifically for the Easter Week. The calf would be dedicated to St. Barbara (December 17$^{th}$). The selected calf would be carefully looked after; in winter it was kept in a hayloft and fed peas and barley, it would be bathed and never hit with a stick (Bardavelidze 1957: 157–158). At the age of three, it would be prepared as a sacrifice for the Easter Week. It would then be taken to the competition, held in the village square, two or three days before the Easter Week. Every village (within the territorial community) would select one winning bull and arrange its fight with the winning bull of another village. Different communities would also compete with one another. The bull that made its opponent retreat from the field was considered the winner. Besides Turkey, there are large historical Georgian diasporas in Azerbaijan and Iran, but this type of tradition has not survived in any of these cultures.

In Adjara, bull fights were organized in early spring. The bull that had been readied for the fight was considered a sort of honourable animal, but after the spread of Islam in this area, the tradition of celebrating the Easter Week and the idea of offering a sacrifice gradually disappeared. In general, the Ottoman Empire restricted many Georgian traditional festivals in Adjara; therefore, these traditions were mainly lost or transformed. The Christian idea disappeared from the above-mentioned tradition and only the ritual of bull fights was maintained. According to materials collected through field-ethnographic research by Vakhtang Shamiladze in the 1970s, in Adjara the calf that would become the sacrificial bull was selected and reared with particular care: 3–8 years was regarded as its ideal age. Afterwards, they would be castrated, fattened and finally slaughtered. Fighter bulls had to have a wide neck, big head and well-shaped and inward curved horns, wide nostrils, thick short coat, long tail, and protruding eyes, forehead and horns area. In Adjara, selecting and rearing the best bull was considered a great accomplishment. The calf's horns needed to be scraped and sharpened; therefore, a tin plate would be nailed to a post at the proper height so that the calf itself could sharpen them. Trainers would use their hands, knees and head to coach the calves in fighting, after which the calves would be pitted against other calves and encouraged by cheers. Bulls would take part in fights from the age of three. By the age of five, bulls became mature and at the age of 8-10, they would be good fighters (Shamiladze 1973: 45–46). Bull fights used to begin in the first week of April and lasted the whole week. Under the influence of Muslim culture, bull fights would begin on Friday, which according to Vakhtang Shamiladze occurred at a later period (Shamiladze 1973; 46), since

Friday is the most important day of the week for Muslims – comparable to Sunday for Christians.

* * *

Based on ethnographic materials of the years 2006–2014, all ethnic Georgians in the Tao-Klarjeti area are familiar with the tradition of bull fights; non-Georgians as well participate in this activity, officially referred to as "Artvini Tradition".

The tradition of bull fights has also been observed in the Nigali Valley (Kheba, Maradidi, Katapkhia, Beghlevani, Devskeli, Baginistskali Gorge, Imerkhevi [Ustamis community, Diobani community, Manatba community, Khevtsurili community, Bazgireti community]) and in historical Tao-Klarjeti (Parkhlistskali Gorge).

In some gorges of historical Tao-Klarjeti, in the past the tradition of bull fights merged with the cattle-breeding traditions and was chiefly associated with the *Shuamtoba* festival. From the 1960s, except in a number of high mountain villages, bull fights are arranged separately and accepted as a "festival". Obviously, the tradition has been transformed. Nowadays, the traditions of *Shuamtoba* Festival and bull fights reveal some innovative elements that will gradually turn into traditions as well.

Traditionally, bull fights were arranged in summer mountain pastures [*Yaylas*], where *Memtevries* [farmers] along with their guests celebrated the *Shuamtoba* festival. For example, in historical Nigal/Ligan/Livana, the town of Artvin and its neighbouring territory populated by Georgians, pastures are mainly near the Tetritskali area and in Karchkhali on the right side of the Coruh River whereas in the Mount Triala area they are on the left side of the Coruh River. Under every "mountain", on the plains there are ყიშლა [Kishles, a Turkish term assimilated into Georgian] in which farmers live from spring-early summer to early-late autumn when they drive the cattle back to their villages. Summer shelters are located in Agara as well as in mountains. During the *Shuamtoba* festival, people dine together and take part in round dances, wrestling and bull fights. Traditionally, certain mountains are visited by locals and their relatives, friends and neighbours from town. Numbers of people come from various neighbouring ravines of Tao-Klarjeti. In the highest lush summer pastures, *Memtevries* [a family member who tends the cattle and makes dairy products] would arrange venues for bulls, the so-called ხარების იატაღი ["bulls" iataghi'] where the bull fights were traditionally held.

> We used to have horse jumping, wrestling, shooting tournaments and bull fights. When the snows melt, we would bring the bulls to the mountains up until the grape harvest (informant 1, male, age 56, August, 2007).

For the bull fights, families would select a yearling calf. When the bull was three years old, it could take part in bull fights. Bulls for fighting were selected specifically; they were particularly cared after and bred – the ethnographic term used to describe this process is ხარებ ვაპატივებდით ["respecting the bulls"].

> We showed the bull respect. We boiled black beans for the bulls, we mixed honey in water and gave it to the bulls to drink" (informant 2, male, age 72, August, 2012).
>
> The bull had to have big horns. The bull's horns could not be sharpened, the bull could not be hit with a stick (informant 3, male, age 67, August, 2011).

Nowadays, the major bull fights are held in the Nigali Valley during the კავკასორი [Kafkasör] festival. Kafkasör is a plateau located several kilometres from the town of Artvin, a location with relaxing and entertaining infrastructures for visitors.

> In olden times, bull fights were held in Kafkasör too, and the same is done today; everyone bring bulls here. Now they hold a festival there (informant 4, male, age 27, August, 2012).

The festival has been held there approximately for the last 30 years. Murghuli Gorge is in the historical Nigali area. Nowadays the major bull fight event in Murghuli Gorge is held at the Tkhirapuna Arena.

> We used to arrange bull fights. Here, down in the village there is a place where bull fights are organized. Our mountain is near the black ridge over there [indicating], at Komrali, there is a ხარების იატაღი ["bulls" iataghi']. Cows are kept in another place. Bull fights once took place in *Yala*. We used to have a master for bulls (informant 4).

The owner of the winning bull receives a certain amount of money as a gift. Bull fights are also characteristic of the historical Tao-Klarjeti areas populated to this day by ethnic Georgians. In this respect, with its three large communities (Kvabai/Kobai, Khevai and Balkhi) entirely populated by Georgians, along with other villages of the same gorge populated by relatives of these three communities, the Parkhlistskali Gorge is distinctive. In this area, the tradition of bull fights appears to have spread in olden times. Narrators remember traditional forms of bull fights:

> Bulls grazed in Tevnari and it was there that the bull fights were arranged. When snows melt, we used to take the bulls to the mountains where they stayed up to the grape harvest (informant 5, male, age 77, August, 2011).
>
> Bull fights were also arranged in Sarigola [Sarigolis, Sarekeli/Sarikeli in Georgian]; on this side of the ravine, bull fights were set up in two-three places, in the Zapori Mountains, too, and in Devtisai. Now everyone does them in Tutlughi. We breed bulls and make money. Khevaels' bull fights took place in Dudguri, above Devsakarai. Now they have a festival there (informant 6, male, age 82, August, 2010).

> We Kvabavrians used to go to Tsalivkan. That was where the bull fights were held (informant 5).

Khevaelians used to arrange bull fights in Chanchakhi too.

> There used to be huts but they are ruined now. Bull fights were set up from May. We respected the bulls by feeding them barley and arranged the fight there. A bull calf is not a bull. We used to have ram fights too. We stayed there in Agara for three-four days and performed round dances. Men also used to wrestle and rams too. We also used to arm-wrestle (informant 7, male, age 74, August, 2014).

Khevaelians took particular care of bulls for bull fights in the Satsoria Mountains.

> Satsoria was in Devskarai. We call it Satsoria. It is behind Devskarai, near Olvilodziri. We used to drive bulls there. There is a "bulls" iataghi' there where they are kept at night. Another shepherd watches over the bulls as they graze in the grassland. We used to pound barley, pour hot water over it and when it became soft, we would feed it to the bulls. This made the bulls grow (informant 8, male, age 43, August, 2012).

> People from Balkhi, Khevai and Kobai used to gather in Satsoria. After the bull fights they would bake Kadas, we lit up twigs that shone brightly, had fights and arm-wrestling ... you had to have a strong wrist (informant 9, male, age 32, July, 2008).

In the villages of Parkhlistskali in which *Shuamtoba* festivals are organized nowadays, they still have round dances, wrestling and bull fights. Traditionally, other Georgians (Chans and Murghulelians amongst others) arrive from the neighbouring ravines. In this respect, the Tsalikvani festival draws a particularly high number of people.

> We used to have horse-racing in Tsalikvani. At first the festival in Tsalikvani was held only by the people from Kobai [...] We used to have wrestling, shooting tournaments and bull fights in Tsalikvani. There was cockfighting. There were many cocks and we used to make them fight. Then we started to play football (informant 10, male, age 72, August, 2009).

Nowadays, the largest bull fights in the Parkhlistskali Gorge are organized in the village of Akhalta. Near its main street, there is a special arena where the best bulls arrive from the entire Yusufeli district. This is an official festival called Bulls Festival. The owner of the winning bull receives a certain amount of money as a gift.

* * *

The current ritual of bull fights has been adapted to the modern so-called festival system and structure, which includes faded elements of the Georgian ethnic traditions. Bull fights are clearly an ancient tradition dating back to the earliest historical stages.

In the Christian era, this tradition was held on the Sunday after Easter [კვირაცხოვლობა, Kviratskhovloba], but after the spread of Islam, the day of the celebration changed and the bull fights became related to *Shuamtoba* festival.

All the modern festivals resemble each other and lack individual characteristics. These festivals have acquired an official character because they are performed under the permission and control of the administration.

According to ethnographic materials regarding the last years, there are several reasons for the transformation of the local Georgian folk celebrations: 1. the interference of the administration (the state) and the formalization of the celebration with authorities involved in the organization process; 2. internal migration processes with the widespread movement of the local population from the villages to cities and industrial centres; 3. the destruction of the local cultural-economic life.

Some of the locals, for whom ethnic culture and its originality are important, try to maintain the tradition of celebrating village Shuamtoba festivals. They consider festivals as the way to maintain and develop ethnic identity.

## Bibliography

Alaverdasvili, Ketevan (2013): საწესო ფერხულების შესწავლისათვის [A Study of Ritual Round Dances]. In: Vera Bardavelidze (ed.): *Collection of the Papers of the International Scientific Conference in Tbilisi*, 110: 29–38.

Bardavelidze, Vera (1968): სიცოცხლისა და სიუხვის ხე ქართველთა სარწმუნოებაში [The Tree of Life and Abundance in Georgians' Religion]. In: საქართველოს ეთნოგრაფიის საკითხები [Issues of Ethnography of Georgia], 44–64.

Bardavelidze, Vera (1952): Бардавелидзе Вера, Главное божество древнегрузинского пантеона Гмерти, Вопросы этнографии Кавказа [The Main Deity of the Georgian Pantheon Gmerti]. In: Issues of Ethnography of Caucasus, 301–318.

Bardavelidze, Vera (1957): Древнейшие религиозные верования и обрядовое графическое искуство грузинских племен [Ancient Religious Beliefs and Ritual Graphic Art of Georgian Tribes]. Тб. Академия Наук Грузинской ССР. Институт истории [Academy of Science, SSR, Institute of History, Tbilisi], 157–158.

Guchua, Viktor (1973): ბრძოლა ქვეყნის მთლიანობის აღდგენისათვის და აგრესორთა წინააღმდეგ XVI ს. პირველ ნახევარში [The Fight for the Recovery of the Integrity of the Country and against the Aggressors in the Early 16th Century]. In: საქართველოს ისტორიის ნარკვევები [Essays of Georgian History], 4: 87–150.

Gujejiani, Rozeta (2010): ტრადიციული ქართული კულტურის მოტივები ტაო-კლარჯეთში [Motives of Traditional Georgian Culture in Tao-Klarjeti]. კრ. სამხრეთ-დასავლეთ საქართველოს ეთნოლოგიის პრობლემები [in coll. Problems of Ethnology of the South-Western Georgia], III. Batumi: Batumi Shota Rustaveli State University, 86–110.

Gujejiani, Rozeta (2001a): ეთნიკურ ქართველთა თანამედროვე ყოფა და კულტურა (თურქეთის რესპუბლიკა) [Contemporary Life and Culture of Ethnic Georgians (Republic of Turkey)]. ინტერდისციპლინარული არქეოლოგია [in coll. *Interdisciplinary Archaeology*] I, 130–146.

Gujejiani, Rozeta (2011b): პარხლისწყლის ხეობის ეთნიკურ ქართველთა ტრადიციული ყოფა და კულტურა (თურქეთის რესპუბლიკა, იუსუფლის რაიონი) [Traditional Life and Culture of Ethnic Georgians of Parkhlistskali Gorge (Republic of Turkey, Yusufeli District)]. In: საქართველოს ეროვნული მუზეუმის მოამბე [Bulletin of the National Museum of Georgia] 2 (47-b): 409–432.

Makaradze, Emzari (2009): მუსტაფა ქემალ ათათურქის დამოკიდებულება ისლამისა და ლაიციზმის საკითხისადმი [The Attitude of Mustafa Kemal Ataturk on the Issues of Islam and Laicism], coll. The scientific research centre of South-west Georgia of the Faculty of Humanities. Batumi: Batumi Shota Rustaveli State University, vol. VI, 161–166.

Shamildze, Vaxtang (1973): კორიდასადრეულიფორმებისისტორიისათვის საქართველოში ეთნოგრაფიული მონაცემების შუქზე [A History of the Earliest Forms of Bull fighting in Georgia in Light of Ethnographic Data]. კრ. სამხრეთ-დასავლეთ საქართველოს მოსახლეობის კულტურისა და ყოფის საკითხები [coll. Issues of Culture and Life of the South-Western Georgia Population], 1: 43–50.

Sordia, Giorgi (2002) დემოკრატიულ ნორმათა პრობლემები თურქულ კანონმდებლობაში [Problems of Democratic Standards in Turkish Legislation], Davit Katsitadze (ed.). Tbilisi: Tbilisi State University, 1–36.

თურქეთის რესპუბლიკის კონსტიტუცია [2000] [The Constitution of the Republic of Turkey], transl. by Giorgi Sordia. Tbilisi: Artanuji.

# Negotiating and Maintaining Identity in the Urban Jungle

## Alevi Organizations and Alevi Identity in Izmir

*Kayhan Delibas*

### Introduction

Due largely to the process of globalization, culture and identity have emerged as the key elements of social relations. Identity is people's source of meaning and experience (Castells 2004: 6). "We know of no persons without names and no languages or cultures in which some manner of distinction between self and other, we and they, does not exist" (Calhoun 1994: 9–10 in Castells 2004: 6). Since the beginning of the 1990s there has been a widespread debate focusing on identity and identities in Turkey. In this chapter, I will investigate the newly emerging Alevi organizations, the mechanism that creates them and their role within the new urbanite Alevi communities, as well as how they are perceived and whether they have any role within their perceptions and functions.

*Alevi* is a blanket term for a large number of heterodox communities with appreciably different beliefs and ritual practices (Bruinessen 1996). Historically, Turkey's Alevis used to be concentrated in central Anatolia; however, since the 1950s many have left their isolated villages for big cities (Bruinessen 1996: 7). The mass migration of this rural population gained new momentum with the neoliberal restructuring policies of the 1980s. For various reasons, in the course of this process Turkey's Alevis almost deserted their traditional homeland and by the mid-1990s, had gained visibility in metropolitan cities such as Istanbul, Izmir and Mersin. This process, expectedly, brought about a crisis of identity that needed to be renegotiated within and with the *others* and required new strategies and mechanisms to sustain Alevi identity in the new urban setting. Thus, a variety of new Alevi organisations emerged. The main aim of this chapter is to discover the objectives, importance and activities of the Alevi organizations that emerged around the 1990s in Izmir. In addition, this empirical sociological study intends to uncover the importance of Alevi organizations for the survival of the Alevi identity as well as their roles and functions in protecting and reproducing the Alevi identity. This paper will draw on long-term participatory observations, in-depth interviews and a quantitative survey of (N 200) carried out in the field from 2008.[1]

---

[1] Part of the 2008 data used in this work is taken from an unpublished MA Thesis I supervised and with the permission of the author, Bahadır Serap (2008).

Who are the Alevis?

The problem of a clear definition in this regard continues to this date. The shortest definition usually applied is *Alevilik* (Alevism), referring to a group who followed Ali, the son-in-law of the Prophet Muhammad. This evolved into a belief system or a way of thinking (Bozkurt 1990: 1–2). In the Alevi belief system the Twelve Imams play a central role. Although Alevis are generally located within the tradition of the Shia denomination of Islam, their religious practices, rituals and cultural codes are quite different.[2] Furthermore, Alevis give great importance to the equality of men and women in their group ceremonies known as *cem*, which are led by the religious leader, known as *dede*. *Dedes* usually play the *saz*.[3] Men and women attend these ceremonies together and have equal roles. Aside from the *Buyruk*, the Alevi-Bektashi belief system is not based on a sacred text. Alevism is a varied movement, without a central authority, whose main teachings are based on oral tradition, passed on through generations, which until the 1990s had generally been secluded from the outside world.

Alevis comprise diverse groups with various ethnic, cultural, linguistic and historical roots. As Martin van Bruniessen put it, *Alevi* is a blanket term for a large number of heterodox communities whose beliefs and rituals practices differ significantly. For example, in the eastern province of Kars there are communities that speak Azerbaijani Turkish whereas the Alevi communities of southern Turkey speak Arabic (particularly in Hatay and Adana). These Arabic-speaking Alevis are ethnically part of Syria's Alawi (Nusayri) community and have no historical ties with other Alevi groups. The larger Alevi groups predominantly speak Turkish and Kurdish, both appearing to be descendants of rebellious tribal groups that were religiously affiliated with Safavism[4] (Bruinessen 1996: 6). Beside the different regional, ethnic and cultural diversities, other differences also exist that need to be mentioned shortly. When discussing Alevis one must also include another quite closely associated group of people who are called Bektashi *"Bektaşi"*.

---

2 For example, Shiism has become the religion of the Prince/state authority in Iran, while Alevism remained as the belief system of the periphery and/or the religion of the "others" within the Ottoman Empire.

3 The *Saz* is a long-necked stringed instrument of the lute family and one of the most important instruments in Turkey. It is believed that it originated in Central Asian Turkish culture.

4 Due to Mongol invasions in the 13th century, Turkish and Mongolian tribes migrated to Iran and adopted Persian customs as well as the language. Although Safavism emerged in the 13th century, the Sufi order having begun under Sheikh Safi od-Din Ardabili (of Ardabil: 1252–1334), Safavism became state religion under the Turkish king Shah Ismail. The announcement by Shah Ismail at Tabriz in 1501 that the Ithna 'Ashari, or "Twelver" form of Shiism was to be the official religion of the newly established Safavi state was his most significant decision (see Savory 1980, Shapour 2015).

For some authors it is important to stress that Alevism is a tradition within Islam. Others more easily conceive Alevilik as a conglomeration of groups that do not necessarily define themselves as religious, but rather as a basis for the formulation of alternative life-styles. Some stress the theological roots in Shiism; in contrast, other groups incorporate liberal traditions for their interpretation of religion (Olson, Ozdalga and Raudvere 1998: IV). In addition, it is widely claimed that the Alevi-Bektashi religious belief has its roots in Central Asia. Turks who migrated from Horasan to Anatolia were originally from Central Asia, where Shamanism was widely practiced.

## Where does the Alevi belief system originate?

Many scholars have noted the relationship between the Turkish tribes' pre-Islamic belief systems such as Shamanism[5] and Alevism. It is widely acknowledged that "from the beginning of the 10th century, Turkish tribes had begun to accept Islam; nevertheless, they did not entirely abandon their Shaman traditions. In fact, they mixed the Shaman traditions with their newly adopted religion. There is one reality that unifies researchers who have studied the transition of Turks to Islam, which took hundreds of years, and their failure to completely abandon their Shaman traditions" (Livaneli 2001: 3–4). It is known that "Anatolian Alevism appeared in the 11th century during the reign of the Anatolian Seljuks. The greatest factors in the rise and spread of this religious orientation were the wandering dervishes who came from Horasan to Anatolia" (Livaneli 2001: 4).

"By mixing Shamanistic elements with Islam, Ahmed-i Yesevi developed a religious orientation that was different from Orthodox Islam. He sent the students that he trained to a variety of countries, with the intention of spreading this novel religious understanding. Yesevi's ideas, which appeared as a heterodox form of belief, spread to Anatolia and the Balkans through the efforts of these wandering dervishes. One of Yesevi's students, Hacı Betktash (Hacı Bektaş), came to Central Anatolia where he founded the religious order known as Bektashisim" (Livaneli 2001: 4). Over the centuries, the Alevi-Bektashi communities were persecuted by the Ottoman Empire's Orthodox Sunni authorities. They were the "others" for the followers of Orthodox Sunni Islam. Due to their unorthodox belief system and closeness to Shah Ismail, who was of Turkish origin, the Alevi-Bektashi communities rose to power in Iran. When the oppression increased, especially at the beginning of the 16th century, the inclination of the Alevis in Anatolia to support Shah Ismail began to trouble the Padishah Yavuz

[5] It is widely argued that up to the beginning of the 10th century Turkish nomadic tribes of Central Asia had practiced a shamanistic religious belief system. They subsequently adopted/converted to Islam (early 10th century) but never entirely abandoned their shamanistic traditions since some elements – beliefs, practices and rituals – endured (see also Boyle 1972).

Sultan Selim. Before the start of the Iran-Ottoman War (1514), a great massacre of Alevis was carried out in Anatolia. The survivors fled to the mountains and had to continue their worship and lives in hiding (Livaneli 2001: 5). Under the assumption that the Alevis might support Shah Ismail, thousands of Alevis were massacred and displaced in Eastern Anatolia. This historic tragedy has never been fully erased from the collective memory of the Alevi-Bektashi communities. As such, the collapse of the Ottoman Empire and the establishment of the Turkish Republic in the early 1920s appeared as a hopeful new era for Alevi communities across Turkey. This optimism, however, was short-lived. In the early years of the republican area, the closure of Islamic Sufi brotherhoods' houses *(tekke)* and lodges *(zaviye)* in 1925 showed that the new regime would hardly recognize the Alevi cultural and religious rights. The regime's long-term denial policies affected the Alevi's perception as a minority throughout the republican history. Moreover, in the late 1970s, there were also a number of violent phases during which Alevi communities were attacked and hundreds lost their lives (like in Çorum, K. Maraş, Sivas) that left a mark on the Alevi collective memory. This phase reoccurred, with some differences, in the early 1990s culminating in the widely censured Sivas Madımak Hotel Arson during an Alevi celebration in which thirty-seven intellectuals - writers, poets, artists, musicians - were killed. Further incidents include the Gazi Mahallesi (1993), Istanbul, in which several people were killed and some recent attacks to the *Cem houses*, or terror attacks, suicide bombings in Ankara (2015) during demonstrations, all of which have been rekindling fear and anguish among Alevi communities.

Collective memory, Halbwachs showed, is not a given but rather a socially constructed notion. As Halbwachs specifies in *On Collective Memory:* "While the collective memory endures and draws strength from its base in a coherent body of people, it is individuals as group members who remember ... It follows that there are as many collective memories as there are groups and institutions in a society" (Coser 1992: 22). Collective memories can play a significant role in terms of today's political, religious, cultural or ethnic conflicts, as in the case of the Alevi collective memory throughout the Ottoman Empire and the republican period. It seems Alevi collective as well as historic memory plays an important role in terms of how current political, religious, ethnic, or even international conflicts, such as the Syrian crisis, are perceived and understood in everyday social life. It can shape or direct attitudes and collective action, social mobilization, political realignment and voting behaviour in contemporary Turkey. Probably one of the most important developments in this context is the rise of the pro-Islamic political movement in Turkey in the mid-1990s. In this process, the rise of political Islam in Turkey, the long-term AKP government policies (since 2002) and some of the authoritarian/undemocratic attitudes and practices have been a significant determinant of the Alevi identity movement (Delibas 2015).

### *The Modern, Secular Republic and the Alevi Belief System*

When Mustafa Kemal Atatürk established the Turkish Republic in 1923, it was a poor peasant society. Traditional agriculture and craft-based production systems were destroyed during the lengthy wars and its small industry was severely damaged (Stirling 1994: 6). The Kemalist revolution of 1923 shaped the direction and characteristics of the modern Turkish political system (Feroz 1977: 2). By the mid-1930s, the new regime consolidated itself. Modernization, secularization and rationalization were established in the urban areas, where 20 per cent of the overall population lived. The Republican ideology was stronger especially amongst the younger generations. Kemalist elites were convinced that unless the people's mentality (their beliefs, values and norm systems) were radically altered, Westernisation and modernisation would not be possible. Therefore, they began the task of secularising both the public and private spheres. The Alevi communities viewed the principle of secularism in itself as a great achievement and a significant step forward. It was more than a change of regime for them; the prospect of an independent, secular nation state was seen as the end of hundreds of years of oppression, discrimination and prejudice during the Ottoman period.

For the Alevi-Bekthasi communities, Mustafa Kemal and his new order (a modern, secular republic) were seen as freedom of religious beliefs, teachings and traditional sacred rituals and freedom for the Alevi-Bektahshi traditions and cultural heritage. However, despite the initial expectations, the religious and cultural freedom Alevis had hoped for never materialised. Up to the early 1990s, most Alevi-Bektashi rituals, ceremonies, celebrations, gatherings and prayers like *cem* had to be performed in concealment for fear of persecution or cultural condemnation.

In addition, secularism did not bring about the end of the widespread Sunni prejudice against Alevis. First of all, the experience of secularization in Turkey has distinct characteristics. For example, since the 1920s and 30s the Turkish official discourse of secularisation has been dominated by the separation of state and religion. However, this separation narrative has been challenged by a number of scholars according to whom separation has rather been controlled by the state (Davison 1998: 155, Delibas 2006: 384). Mardin (1989) argued that the Kemalist regime failed to provide a social ethos that would appeal to the hearts as well as to the minds of the Muslim Turks (Mardin 1989: 32 cited in Davison 1998: 155). It can be argued that since the experience of secularisation in Turkey was problematic, there are bound to be some repercussions. If the secularisation process is not achieved, it can lead to problems such as discrimination, prejudices or anti-minority sentiments in a given society.

The Alevis' gradual integration into wider society through migration to towns, presence in educational institutions and careers in public services brought them into closer contact, and sometimes into direct competition with strict Sunnis. However, this new proximity between Alevis and Sunnis did not entirely eradicate the existing anti-Alevi sentiments, rhetoric and prejudices (Bruniessen 1996: 8). These anti-Alevi sentiments and attitudes, latent or otherwise, can have various outcomes and can be traced in public as well as private sectors. For instance, the ratio of Alevis in high-ranking public positions, as managers, military officers, district governors, high-level judges, public company CEOs and so on, has been negligible or non-existent in some cases. Recently it is often brought to public attention that there is not one Alevi district governor *(vali)* in Turkey's eighty-two districts. By law, governors are appointed by governments.

When the Turkish Republic was founded in the early 1920s as a nation state, it showed no interest towards the ethnic, cultural and religious diversity inherited from the Ottoman Empire. The new regime did not recognise these cultural, religious and ethnic differences, let alone the existence within the 'new Turkish Society' of social class differences, which were denied until the 1950s and 60s. In the early Republican era, Kemalism largely disregarded the sectarian plurality of Turkish society and, in some cases, even accused Alevism of being an "enemy of the state" (Bulut 1991: 129). Furthermore, it viewed Sunnism as the *par default* religion of the "nation" (Bozarslan 2003: 9).

Until the 1950s, Turkish Alevis used to be concentrated in central Anatolia (Amasya, Çorum, Sivas, Tokat, Çankırı, Yozgat, Kahraman Maraş and Malatya) with additional important pockets throughout the Aegean and Mediterranean coastal regions and in the European part of Turkey. From the 1950s onwards, many left their isolated villages for big cities. Kurdish Alevis were concentrated northwest of the Kurdish settlement zones (Bruniessen 1996: 7–8). During the Ottoman era, population movements generally occurred through forced migration policies, usually applied to various ethnic, religious and cultural minorities. These minorities used to be forcefully settled or resettled across Ottoman lands for all sorts of reasons including demographic, economic, political and military ones (Zurcher 2008). These policies were partially applied in the early years of the Turkish Republic, but were abandoned altogether later on.

The end of World War I signalled a new area for Turkey. Transition to multiparty politics from the single party rule in 1946 and the DP's victory in the elections of May 14, 1950 "constituted a fundamental break in Turkish history" (Keyder 1987: 124).[6] In the 1950s, with the financial backing of the US, the DP government undertook a restructuring program. Due to these policy changes "the first years of the Democratic Party (DP) rule witnessed radical economic and political transformations" (Hale 1981: 86–113, Şenyapılı 1982: 239). Most importantly, the introduction of tractors in agriculture and the increasing mechanisation of agricultural work created a vast surplus of workforce in rural areas, which was left no choice but to abandon the villages in which it was no longer needed and seek employment in thriving urban centres. These changes in the economic sphere triggered a mass migration towards urban areas. In just ten years, between 1950–1960, the urban population grew by 59.1 per cent. This constituted a very rapid rate of urbanisation (Keyder 1987: 120).

6 For a detailed account of this transition period see Gologlu (1982) and Yetkin (1983).

*Rapid Urbanization and Alevi Migration*

Turkey witnessed rapid urbanisation since the 1950s though a much faster acceleration occurred from the 1980s on. Although the term rapid urbanization was initially applied to the phase that started in the 1950s, the rate of urbanization following the restructuring policies of the 1980s greatly surpassed that of the initial period.

The Neoliberal restructuring policies, known as the *24 Ocak Kararları* (1980) (January 24th Decisions)[7] were drawn up by the Demirel government but could not be implemented until after the 1980 military coup, which made it possible to put the January 24th Decisions into practice. In many ways, the 1980s were a turning point for Turkish politics and economy.

The structural adjustment programme, which aimed to replace the closed, interventionist economic model implemented since the 1960s with the neoliberal market economy, had a profound impact on Turkish society.[8] In the 1950s, only 25 per cent of the population lived in the cities whereas the majority, 74.9 per cent, lived in rural areas. Between 1950 and 1990, the annual rate of population growth was 24.4 per thousand. At 43.9 per thousand, the urban growth rate was almost twice this figure for the same period. Reflecting this increase in urban population, the growth rate has been declining in rural areas since the 1950s. In 1960 Turkey's population stood at 27.7 million, of which approximately one-third (32 per cent) lived in the cities and two-thirds (68 per cent) in the rural areas. In 1970, the population reached 35.6 million, of which 38 per cent lived in urban areas and 62 per cent in rural areas (Delibas 2015: 102–110).

In 1980, the population was 44.7 million (44 per cent in urban areas and 56 per cent in rural areas). By the 1990s, the population had increased to 56.4 million with 59 per cent living in urban areas and 41 per cent in rural areas. In 1997 the population had risen to 62.8 million and two-thirds (65 per cent) was urban and one-third (35 per cent) rural. According to the 2011 census, the population had reached 74.7 million and by now nearly three-quarters (76.9 per cent) live in the cities and one-quarter (23.2 per cent) lives in rural areas (Delibas 2015: 102–110). Obviously, this is a phenomenal rate of urbanization with all sorts of downsides. For several reasons, the restructuring policies caused the widespread disruption of the livelihoods of farming communities across Anatolia. What this urbanization and population shift actually tells us is that the Alevi population also migrated to big cities but with one distinction, in that the Alevi

---

7 Also known as *The structural adjustment programme,* it was prepared and announced by the Suleyman Demirel government on January 24, 1980. The program was backed, and in some cases imposed, by the IMF and the World Bank in many countries. It aimed to replace the closed, interventionist economic model with the neoliberal market economy. It had a profound impact on Turkish society. See Boratav (1990: 199–230), Dodd (1990: 101), Ramazanoglu (1985: 220–242).

8 There is a considerable amount of literature on this subject. See Eralp, Tünay and Yeşilada (1993), Boratav (1990), Öniş and Webb (1993: 128–184), Oniş (1997).

community was also more keen to migrate to European countries, as a source of workforce, from the 1960s onwards. As discussed earlier, traditionally Alevi populations lived in remote areas, in the far corners of the country. Rapid urbanization not only made them an easy and visible target of traditional prejudices but their economic backwardness, stemming from their agricultural livelihood, also drove them into the cities by the thousands.

*New Life, New Space: How to Protect Identity in the Urban Jungle*

As already established, historically the Alevis used to be concentrated in central Anatolia; however, from the early 1950s and even more rapidly from 1980 onwards, many left their isolated villages for big cities (Bruinessen 1996: 7). The mass migration that followed the neoliberal policies restructuring in the 1980s had devastating effects on the traditional Alevi identity. In this process, the institutions of *dede* and *talip* (religious leader and follower) lost their foundations. As the Alevis migrated to cities, the historic and vital intuitional tie/relationship between *dede* and *talip* was lost (Okan 2004: 116–117). For centuries, the Alevis had lived side by side in rural areas and the *dede* would perform the religious ceremonies that were of central importance for the Alevi communities. With migration, the one foundation of Alevi institutions dissolved.

Amid fears of losing ties with traditional identity and cultural confusion, Alevi communities attempted to reconfigure and rebuild their identity in order to fit into their new urban settings. Yet, due to the Alevi's diverse cultural, identity and organizational structures it is not yet certain how the Alevi identity will survive. Undoubtedly, as with other special cultures, also the Alevi culture is under the heavy influence of modernisation and needs to rethink itself in a changing world (Pultar and Erman 2005: 308).

The military coup of 1980 was a turning point for Alevi organizations. With the military's intervention, political and civil organizations were closed down and hundreds and hundreds of participants were prosecuted under military courts. Many Alevi organizations were among them too. As political parties and movements were crushed by the military, there was an interim period in which political activity was forbidden. Despite this heavy control, Alevi organizations found new ways to reorganize, sometimes under different names (cultural associations or civil society organizations), which were seen as "harmless". Obviously, compared to the pre-1980 class-based political movements or trade unions, these new kinds of associations and culture/identity politics were not seen as "harmful" or a "threat" to country's interests and unity.

Towards the end of the 1980s, Alevi organisations and associations established Alevi Cultural Centres, various Alevi-Bektashi Federations and *cem* houses where Alevis began to advocate their demands. Thus, the very existence and demands of Alevi communities became visible in wider society. One of the surprising developments that came with rapid urbanization and globalization was the realization of the diversity of Alevism within the Alevi community itself (Okan 2004: 115). This realisation could have hindered the struggle to re-establish the Alevi identity; however, the "wider socialization" caused by rapid urbanization, globalization and the expansion of mass media worked towards converging the diverse Alevi identities. In addition, and more importantly, some historically significant events like the *Madımak Hotel incident* (or *Sivas Massacre*) in Sivas (1993) and the Gazi Neighbourhood (Istanbul) attacks in the early 1990s (both of which targeted Alevis) brought the Alevi communities to the conclusion that despite their diversity, they were viewed as a single group. This fostered the emergence of an Alevi-Bekthasi identity in the new era that is not free of its historical diversity. In addition, the widespread reaction to these attacks, like the reaction to the *Madımak incident,* accelerated the emergence of Alevi organizations. The multiplicity of Alevi organizations and actors still exists, but it is right to say that now there is an umbrella organisation sheltering every diversity.

As put forward at the beginning of this chapter, the main aim here is to discover the objectives, importance and activities of the Alevi organizations that emerged around 1990 in Izmir. Furthermore, this sociological study intends to uncover the importance of Alevi organizations for the survival of the Alevi identity, as well as the roles and functions they play in protecting and reproducing it.

### *Case of Izmir: Alevi Organizations, Functions and Perceptions*

With its four million inhabitants, Izmir is the third largest city in Turkey. It has a long history and is famous for its cultural, religious, ethnic and social diversity. There is no specific data on how many Alevi-Bektashis live in the city, but the apparent secular, liberal, modern, tolerant and relaxed attitude of *Izmirlis* is well known. I do not have a definite number, but from ten years of personal observations I have concluded that Izmir has been one of the most sought-after destinations for migrating Alevis in the last half-century. As a result of the rural population's mass migration, from the early 1980s Alevis migrated in great numbers to the point that they almost deserted their traditional homelands. By the mid-1990s, Alevi-Bekthasi communities began to be visible and became one of the prominent groups in new urban areas.

The Alevi organizations chosen for the fieldwork were located within the boundaries of the Izmir Metropolitan Municipality.[9] In total, ten Alevi organi-

[9] The survey was carried out in Çiğli Pir Sultan Abdal Kültür ve Dayanışma Derneği, (Pir Sultan Abdal Culture and Solidarity Association, Çiğli) (19), Karşıyaka Yamanlar Hacı Bektaş Veli Derneği (Hacı Bektaş Veli Association, Karşıyaka Yamanlar) (19), Aliağa Hacı Bektaş Veli Derneği (Hacı Bektaş Veli Association, Aliağa) (16), Bornova Pir Sultan Abdal Kültür ve Dayanışma Derneği (Pir Sultan Abdal Culture and Solidarity Association, Bornova) (26), Buca Cem Evi (Cem House, Buca) (21), Buca Pir Sultan Abdal Kültür ve Dayanışma Derneği (Pir Sultan Abdal Culture and Solidarity Association, Buca) (18), Konak Limontepe Cem Evi (Cem House, Konak Limon-

zations were visited and two hundred participants were interviewed (78 women and 122 men). While 23 per cent of our informants were born in Izmir, more than three quarters (77 per cent) were not. About two thirds (66.5 per cent) of them are active members of at least one of the Alevi organizations while one third visits them without having a membership. We asked how often they visit such organizations: one quarter of them visit daily, another quarter (22 per cent) once a week, almost a sixth (14 per cent) every other day, 10 per cent on weekends, another third once a month and finally 16 per cent occasionally. How often such organisations are visited is a clear indicator of their importance for the participants.

Do they find these organizations useful for their families? More than nine in ten of our informants (92.5 per cent) stated that they do. These organizations are vital for the preservation and enhancement of their culture. It is essential for them as well as their children to learn their own culture and religious values. These organizations also act as schools to teach skills such as playing the *Bağlama* (a shorter form of the saz [Turkish lute]) for personal development.

When asked how they evaluate their children's attendance at such organisations, more than half (55 per cent) said it is very important that their children attend such organizations, while more than one third said (36 per cent) this is important for them.

To an open-ended question regarding why they wanted their children to attend Alevi organizations, the great majority (181) responded that they wanted their children to attend "to learn about and keep alive Alevi culture and identity" as well as "to develop solidarity and corporation with Alevis" (160). This is in line with our original observations that because of the rapid urbanization process in Turkey, the traditional Alevi communities lost their historic roots and the cultural-religious tie between *dede-talip* (religious leader and follower). Creating a new centre of solidarity and cooperation with other Alevis in the metropolitan cities has become crucial for the new urban Alevi communities. These organisations are also seen as a place "to socialise and develop good communication skills" for more than half (137) of our informants. Finally, Alevi organizations also play the role of an "after-school club" where children learn how to play the *saz* (Turkish lute), *Semah* (ritual dance of Alevis) and so on (63). It is obvious that to most of our informants the Alevi organizations are seen as places where Alevi culture is acquired and kept alive/sustained as well as places where solidarity and cooperation with other Alevi communities is developed. With urbanization, the notion of solidarity and cooperation in Alevi organizations has become increasingly widespread.

---

tepe) (17), Konak Gültepe Hacı Bektaş Veli Derneği (Hacı Bektaş Veli Association, Konak Gültepe) (21), Narlıdere Cem Evi (Cem House, Narlıdere) (18) and Balçova Hacı Bektaş Veli Derneği (Hacı Bektaş Veli Association, Balçova) (16).

In another open-ended question, we asked what the participants thought about the increase in Alevi organisations. About three quarters of my informants (153) replied that these organizations were "endorsing Alevi identity and working for its recognition". Another almost equal number (152) stated that the increase was due to "the need for living and sustaining Alevi culture and its belief system". Around one third (65) of them reminded us of one of the widespread concerns among Alevi communities: namely, that "the government did not show the necessary sensitivity towards Alevis". As to the question of why Alevi communities are setting up their own religious and cultural institutions, 64 respondents quite rightly pointed out that this was due to "the communal and cultural ties lost as a result of urbanization" [which therefore need to be rebuilt through these institutions]. Around a quarter of our respondents (55) stated the reason as being "the need for the Alevi identity", 54 responded with "the desire of having equal rights with the Sunnis", 27 stated that Alevi communities are setting up their own religious and cultural institutions because "today religious, cultural and sectarian identity is at the forefront more than ever" and finally 20 stated "yearning for your hometown and own people" as the reason for the establishment of these institutions.

What emerged from the field data is that the primary aim of Alevi organizations is perceived as keeping Alevi identity alive and promoting an equal coexistence with the Sunni majority. The government's failure to recognise and provide resources for the Alevis and the loss of traditional Alevi ties are further reasons for the continued increase and subsistence of these organisations.

When we asked the participants how they viewed Alevi organizations, two in five (42 per cent) of our informants stated they are "places where Alevis feel cultural and social solidarity", while one in five (21 per cent) stated they are "necessary institutions for Alevi solidarity". When both responses are combined, "the solidarity effect" rises to 63 per cent. One in five (21 per cent) of the informants thinks they are "places in which Alevi identity is learnt and transmitted to the next generations", while the remaining 13 per cent stated they are "places keeping Alevism alive and promoting its existence". In stark contrast to widespread governmental propaganda and the "official" stance, only 2 per cent of respondents stated that they view Alevi organizations as "cultural centres".

The Alevi Opening in 2009 by the government, or more precisely by the ruling AKP (*Adalet ve Kalkınma Partisi:* Justice and Development Party), aimed to "understand and respond" to the Alevi identity claims. They were popularly known as "Alevi opening" (Alevi açılımı). Although several of these workshops have been organised since 2009, they yielded very little in terms of reaching a set of solutions to the cultural, religious and identity problems of the Alevis (Borovali and Boyraz 2015). One of the main problems is the status and nature of Alevi organizations, especially the *Cem Houses*. For the government and the Director of Religious Affairs they are not religious worship places, but cultural centres. Throughout the whole Alevi Opening process the government insisted that *Cem Houses* should not be defined as Alevi religious places whereas all Alevi associations and institutions define them as places of worship.

The answers we received in response to the question, “in your opinion, how significant are Alevi organizations in protecting Alevi identity?” clearly show the central position of Alevi organizations in the quest to rebuild Alevi communities in new urban areas. Around three in five (61.5 per cent) said these organizations are “very important” for the existence and continuity of Alevi identity, while another significant portion (34.5 per cent) of respondents said these organizations are “important” for the existence and continuity of Alevi identity. Almost all (96 per cent) of our informants agree that the Alevi organizations in Izmir, in our case, are of crucial importance both for the existence of the Alevi and to teach younger generations born outside of the traditional rural Alevi communities. This finding further supports our initial observations regarding the functions and perceptions of Alevi organizations in terms of the cultural and identity dynamics of Alevi communities in predominantly Sunni urban areas after 1980. In a related follow-up question on whether these organizations represent Alevi identity correctly or not, an overwhelming number (80 per cent) of our informants replied “yes, they do” (within this, 50 per cent responded “represents correctly’ and 30 per cent “quite correctly”), 14 per cent stated “not quite sure” and the remaining 6 per cent gave various other answers. This question was asked because these organizations are actually new for these communities; as such, it was important to examine how our informants viewed them. From the responses received, it appears that an overwhelming majority of respondents believe in the accuracy of the represented Alevi identity. That said, there is room for doubt since a minority of the informants had mixed feelings about how Alevi identity is represented.

Since our focus was on the functions of the Alevi organizations, in a separate question we asked about their impact on Alevi identity, specifically, whether they helped or hindered the development of Alevi identity; 87 per cent of our informants stated that thanks to these organizations “Alevi identity had become more powerful”, 10 per cent said “neither more powerful nor weaker”, just two people said Alevi identity had been weakened by the Alevi organisations and four did not reply.

When we asked our participants where they learnt about their Alevi culture, three quarters (74 per cent) replied from their families, 14 per cent from various Alevi organizations, around 9.5 per cent from books and journals, 1.5 per cent stated from other sources and only 1 per cent from *dedes*. This data tells us a lot. Since most of our informants were born in rural areas – mostly villages – they were able to learn Alevi culture and rituals within their families, whereas only a small portion learnt Alevism from such organizations. However, when I asked where our respondents’ children had learnt about Alevi culture, the picture began to change. Reflecting the generation gap and the fact that most of the respondents’ children were born in Izmir, whereas only one quarter (23 per cent) of their parents were born there, less than one third (30 per cent) of the children learnt Alevism from their families and one fifth (20 per cent) of our informants' children from Alevi organizations. The rest of our informants (49 per cent) did not have children of their own. These findings evidently indicate that Alevis born in cities tend to learn about Alevi culture from urban-based Alevi organizations, in stark contrast to those born in rural areas where family was the primary source of information.

In a related question, I asked about the changes in the perceptions of Alevi identity over time. I asked my informants whether Alevi identity has become more or less important for them over the last five years. Nearly half (44.5 per cent) of our informants said "Alevi identity has become more important over the past five years", while another third (27 per cent) said "it has become much more important". Compiling the data, nearly three quarters (71 per cent) said it has become more important while 16 per cent said nothing has changed. Alevi identity has lost its importance over the last five years for 12 per cent of our respondents.

One final question regarding the respondents' expectations about the future of Alevi identity was deemed necessary for the data analysis. When we asked how they see the future of Alevi identity, more than half (53 per cent) of our informants stated "it will strengthen and spread", one third (27 per cent) stated "it will continue its existence", 8 per cent said "it will be recognized and expand", 6.5 per cent said "its existence will be endangered due to rapid Sunnification" and the last 5 per cent said "it will lose its value as an identity".

The responses in this regard show that almost nine out of ten (88.5 per cent) participants have positive expectations about the future of Alevi identity while one in ten (11.5 per cent) has negative or pessimistic expectations. The pessimistic outlook shows the initial fears that Alevi communities have probably had for a long time, but with urbanization Alevis faced a cultural and identity crisis (through the loss of traditional community structures, particularly the loss of traditional ties between *dede* and *talip*, the loss of historic roots, the loss of community life, relocation to big cities and so on) that needed to be addressed. The positive outlook on the other hand means that despite the long history of oppression, persecution and the latest challenges faced by the Alevi-Bakthasi communities there is some degree of optimism in the Alevi community. However, it must be said that this optimism did not last long. Attitudes have changed rapidly, particularly since 2010 and 2011 when through an historical referendum the ruling AKP party literally placed total power in the hands of the government. In 2010, the government introduced a constitutional reform package that along with several important changes included the reform of the High Council of Judges and Public Prosecutors, which affects the independence and impartiality of the Turkish judiciary. However, this reform process was a heavy blow to the principle of separation of powers between the judiciary, executive (the government) and parliament. Already dominating the parliament by a crushing majority, the AKP government left no real system of checks and balances, thus establishing a dominant party system in Turkey.

"The AKP government has also held the office of the Presidency since 2007. Once a ceremonial role supposed to be above party politics, the position now has greater political powers" (Waldman and Caliskan 2015). As the current president Recep Tayyip Erdogan has repeatedly declared, unlike previous presidents he will be an active and acting president. He has also declared recently that his election by popular vote has created a de facto situation, like it or not, and the constitution needs to be amended to accommodate this change. Since 2010 the AKP consolidated its full power and became a full-fledged dominant party within Turkish politics in which initial democratic, sensitive approaches and attitudes have changed drastically. For instance, according to Reporters Without Borders, Turkey is the world's leading jailer of journalists and Freedom House now deems Turkey "Not Free". Not only traditional media has been targeted, but also social media, with blanket bans enacted against YouTube and Twitter. Individuals, public figures and private citizens alike, have been arrested and prosecuted because of things they have tweeted or even in some cases retweeted (Waldman and Caliskan 2015).

It is widely acknowledged that under the AKP rule Turkey have been moving rapidly toward an authoritarian state especially since 2010. As a result, the democratic deficit in Turkey is increasing: opposition groups, journalists, intellectuals and writers are intimidated, threatened, prosecuted and in some cases imprisoned for their opinions, writings or criticism of the government. For various reasons, the government's increasingly authoritarian trend fuels fear and widespread anxiety among the Alevi communities across the country.

## Conclusion

Alevi culture and identity has faced several enormous challenges. Moulded by the process of modernization, secularization, urbanization and globalization and by the post-1980s neoliberal restructuring policies that caused mass migration, Alevi communities have lost the traditional roots and close-knit community structures they once had in rural Anatolia. Over the last two decades in particular, culture and identity have emerged as "the key elements of social relations" and this fact has heavily influenced the Alevi communities' struggle to restructure, remodel and reform their religious institutions, rituals and in some circumstances even reinvent parts of their religious institutions and identities to fit and function in this *new time and space,* i. e. urban space. As Harvey (1989: 240) argues, the process of globalization has exacerbated "the time-space compression" that has led to a massive increase in the flow of information and knowledge, thus to increased inter-societal interactions between countries, societies and cultures and a surging rate of social change.

This process, expectedly, gave rise to a crisis of cultural identity, which needed to be renegotiated within and with the "others", and required new strategies and mechanisms to sustain the Alevi identity in the urban setting. Mass migration caused hundreds of years of disruption within the Alevi-Bektashi communities. Inevitably, this process significantly altered and to a great extent destroyed the Alevi way of life and institutions such as *Dedelik* (religious leader), *taliplik* (the follower) *kirvelik,* (kinship) etc., as well as cultural and religious teachings, communities, solidarity networks and sacred cultural heritage. Thus, a variety of new Alevi organisations, institutions and solidarity groups, such as the *hemşehri* (people from the same district) associations and *Cem Evleri* (Cem Houses) began to emerge in all major cities. These are all elements of the formation of a new identity, maintaining one's cultural identity or recreating a new identity within the new urban environment.

My findings show that not only do these organizations seem to have replaced traditional Alevi institutions in urban areas, but are also viewed by the Alevi participants as sufficient, effective and a place where their children can learn about Alevism, Alevi culture and identity. Furthermore, *cem houses* are worship places where religious ceremonies like *cem* are performed, and where the community comes together for all sorts of reasons. They are also seen as a place of socialization, solidarity and unity of Alevi culture.

The fight for the recognition of Alevi culture and identity continues and these newly emerging Alevi organizations have been and continue to be crucial in this process. To this date, the state has been reluctant to recognise the Alevi-Bektashi status. When it came to power, the AKP government with its very liberal and pro-European perspective, looked as though it might solve or at least take steps in solving the identity issues faced by the Alevi-Bektashi community. Instead, it has moved in the opposite direction. The current government has been following ambiguous policies toward Alevis in recent years. Although some high-level conferences have been organized by the government to listen and find solutions for Alevi issues, there have been no tangible results so far. The government's refusal to acknowledge *Cem Houses* as the religious institutions of Alevis persists. In addition, the high level of social and political polarization and the political rhetoric of the Prime Minister and other high-ranking officials have been heightening insecurity in Alevi communities.

The recent developments in the Middle East, the rise of religious, sectarian conflict and its implications on internal politics, have been putting extra pressure on Alevi communities. The Alevi collective memory, shaped by certain political, sociocultural and historical conditions, has often been translated and transferred into today's political, cultural or religious issues and debates. Yet, there is another current issue that fuels fear and anxiety among Turkey's Alevi minority. In this respect, the increasing sectarian violence and escalating threat of war in the Middle East between Sunni and Shia countries are viewed as a threat to Alevi culture, identity and way of life in Turkey too. Since it began in 2011, the vicious war in Syria has been amplifying sectarian sentiments and almost engulfing whole countries into this conflict. Neighbouring countries like Iraq have already been torn apart by sectarian divisions. This historic schism within Islam seems to be generating a new wave of clashes and this development has been seen as threat to close to home also by the Alevi community.

## Bibliography

Ahmad, Feroz (1977): *The Turkish experiment in democracy, 1950–1975*. London: Westview Press for the Royal Institute of International Affairs.

Bahadır, Serap (2008): *AB Üyeliği Sürecinde Kimlik Tartışmaları: İzmir'de Alevi Örgütlenmeleri ve İşlevlerinin Ampirik Bir Analiz* [The Proses Turkey's EU Membership and the Discourse of Identity: Alevi Organizations and their Role in the Process of Construction of Alevi Identity in Turkey]. Aydın: ADÜ, Sosyal Bilimler Enstitüsü, Sosyoloji Anabilim Dalı.

Boratav, Korkut, 1990: Inter-Class and Intra-Class Relations of Distribution under Structural Adjustment: Turkey during the 1980s. In: T. Aricanli and D. Rodrik (eds.): *The Political Economy of Turkey*. London: Macmillan, 199–230.

Borovalı, Murat and Boyraz, Cemil (2015): The Alevi Workshops: An Opening Without an Outcome? In: *Turkish Studies*, 16 (2): 145–160.

Boyle, John Andrew (1972): Turkish and Mongol Shamanism in the Middle Ages. In: *Folklore*, 83 (3): 177–193.

Bozarslan, Hamit (2003): Alevism and the Myths of Research: The Need For a New Research Agenda. In: Paul J. White, and J. Jongerden (eds.): *Turkey's Alevi Enigma*. Leiden, Boston: Brill, 3–17.

Bozkurt, Fuat (1990): *Aleviliğin Toplumsal Boyutları* [The Social Dimensions of Alevism]. Istanbul: Yön Yaynclk.

Bruniessen, Martin van (1996): Kurds, Turks and the Alevi Revival in Turkey. In: *Middle East Report*, 1996/7 (1): 7–10.

Bulut, Faik (1991): *Belgelerle Dersim Raporları* [Reports of Dersim with Documents]. Istanbul: Yön Yayinlari.

Calhoun, Carig (1994): *Social Theory and the Politics of Identity*. Oxford: Blackwell Publishers.

Castells, Manuel (2004): *The Power of Identity: The Information Age: Economy, Society, and Culture*, Vol. II. 2nd Edition with a New Preface. Edition history: Blackwell Publishing Ltd (1e, 1997), Blackwell Publishing Ltd (2e, 2004) [e-book].

Coser, A. Lewis (ed.) (1992): *Maurice Halbwachs on Collective Memory*. Chicago, London: The University of Chicago Press.

Davison, Andrew (1998): *Secularism and Revivalism in Turkey*. New Haven & London: Yale University Press.

Delibas, Kayhan (2015): *The Rise of Political Islam in Turkey: Urban Poverty, Grassroots Activism and Islamic Fundamentalism*. London, New York: I. B. Tauris.

Delibas, Kayhan (2006): The Experience of Secularization in Modern Turkey: Secularization From Above. In: M. Franzmann, C. Gartner and N. Köcek (eds.): *Religiositat in der säkularisierten Welt* [Religiousness in the Secularised World] Leverkusen: Leske + Budrich.

Dodd, D. Clement (1990): *The Crisis of Turkish Democracy.* Consett: The Eothen Press.

Eralp, Atilla, Tünay, M. and B. Yeşilada (eds.) (1993): *The Political and Socioeconomic Transformation of Turkey.* Westport: Praeger Publishers.

Gologlu, Mahmut (1982): *Demokrasiye Geçis, 1946–1950* [Transition into Democracy, 1946–1950]. Istanbul: Kaynak Yayınları.

Hale, William (1981): *The Political And Economic Development of Modern Turkey.* London, Sydney: Croom Helm.

Harvey, David (1989): *The Condition of Postmodernity.* Oxford: Blackwell Publishers.

Keyder, Çağlar (1987): *State and Class in Turkey.* London: Verso.

Kongar, Emre (2000): *21. Yuzyilda Turkiye* [Turkey in the 21st Century]. Istanbul: Remzi Kitapevi.

Livaneli, Zülfü (2001): Excerpts from Lecture Given at Princeton University. Princeton.

Okan, Murat (2004): *Türkiye'de Alevilik* [Alevism in Turkey]. Ankara: Imge Kitapevi.

Olsson, Tord, Ozdalga, Elisabeth and Raudvere, Catharina (1998): *Alevi Identity: Cultural, Religious and Social Perspectives.* Istanbul: Swedish Research Institute.

Öniş, Ziya (1997): The Political Economy of Islamic Resurgence in Turkey: the Rise of the Welfare Party in Perspective. In: *Third World Quarterly*, 18: 743–776.

Öniş, Ziya and Webb, Steven (1993): Turkey: Democratisation and Adjustment from Above. In: S. B. Webb and Steven Haggard (eds.): *Voting for Reform: Democracy, Political Liberalisation and Economic Adjustment.* New York: Oxford University Press, 128–184.

Pultar, Gönül and Erman, Tahire (eds.) (2005): *Türk(iye) Kültürleri* [Cultures of Turk(ey)]. Istanbul: Tetragon Yayınları.

Ramazanoğlu, H. (1985): *Turkey in the World Capitalist System.* Vermont: Gower Publishing Company Ltd.

Savory, Roger (1980): Iran Under the Safavids. Cambridge: Cambridge University Press.

Shapour, Ghasemi (2015): *History of Iran. URL:* http://www.iranchamber.com/history/safavids/safavids.php#sthash.oAEEyykY.dpuf, accessed on May 2, 2015.

Stirling, Paul (1994): *Labour Migration in Turkey: Thirty Five Years of Changes, Humana: Bozkurt Guvenc'e armagan [in Memory of Bozkurt Güvenç],* (eds.) Serpil Altunkent et al. Ankara: Ministry of Culture Press.

Şenyapılı, Tansı (1982): Economic Change and the Gecekondu Family. In: Ç. Kagıtcıbaşı (ed.): *Sex Roles, Family and Community in Turkey*. Bloomington: Indiana University Turkish Studies, 237–248.

Waldman, Simon and Çaliskan, Emre (2015): "Turkey's democratic deficit". Open Democracy, June 5, 2015. URL: https://www.opendemocracy.net/simon-waldman-emre-aliskan/turkey%E2%80%99s-democratic-deficit, accessed on September 12, 2015.

White, J. Paul and Jongerden, Joost (2003): Turkey's Alevi Enigma: A Comprehensive Overview. Leiden: Brill.

Yetkin, Çetin (1983): *Türkiye'de Tek Parti Yönetimi* [Single Party Rule in Turkey]. Ankara: Altın Kitaplar Yayınevi.

Zürcher, Erik-Jan (2008): *The Late Ottoman Empire as Laboratory of Demographic Engineering*. URL: http://www.sissco.it/fileadmin/user_upload/Attivita/Convegni/regionimultilingue/zurcher.pdf, accessed on September 5, 2015.

# Class and Ethnicity in Gender Mainstreaming Projects

## A Case Study of Women's NGOs in Mardin, Turkey

*Nurdan Z. Atalay Güneş*

### Introduction

A growing attention to gender-related issues, especially inequality of treatment, has affected policy formulation at both national and international level. This has led to a growing cooperation among actors for policy formation, mostly via a discourse of "project making". The city of Mardin in southeast Turkey is witnessing sharp gender-based inequalities. Because of this, aside from many small-scale projects, since 2010 Mardin has been home to two large gender mainstreaming projects run by international organizations in cooperation with Turkey: "Empowerment of Women and Women's NGOs in the Least Developed Regions of Turkey" (EWNGOs) and "Women Friendly Cities-2" (WFC-2).

This chapter focuses on the position of various women-focused Non-Governmental Organizations (NGOs) in Mardin toward those projects. Gender inequalities may be analysed with reference to class, ethnicity and religion as well as to geopolitical and socio-demographic regional compositions. These dimensions have an impact on the position of the NGOs toward the project and other partners, especially state agencies. To understand the position of NGO representatives, ethnographic methods, mainly participant observation and unstructured in-depth interviews, were used.

Starting with the question of gender inequalities, I try to conceptualize these inequalities with reference to the intersectionality debate. This debate highlights the main dimension of the mechanisms that produced inequalities among women with special emphasis on contextualizing these dimensions. The main policy tool to reduce these gender inequalities is gender mainstreaming. I analyse gender mainstreaming and its effects on policies regarding women's issues in Turkey with reference to the history of women's organizations in Turkey. In order to contextualize this discussion, Mardin as a research field is described with special emphasis on how gender inequalities are reproduced. After a brief description of these two projects, research findings will be discussed. The position of women's NGO representatives will be understood within this framework.

## Understanding Gender Inequalities

Gender inequalities have become a crucial issue with increasing attention since the 1990s at both national and international level. International and national institutions have different impacts on how gender inequality is understood and how policies dealing with this inequality are formulated. In this chapter, I examine the combined effects of international and national institutions in gender-mainstreaming projects in Mardin and how this institutional setting is understood and interpreted by NGOs as partners as well as by target groups of these projects. In order to understand the role of institutions and their interactions, an overview of the history of these relations is necessary.

With the ratification of CEDAW (Convention on the Elimination of All Forms of Discrimination against Women) in 1981 followed by the Beijing Conference in 1995, gender inequality has become a global issue and a crucial one for international institutions such as the UN, UNDP and the EU. This international recognition and policy-orientation towards gender inequality has contributed to both the legal rearrangement and the empowerment of women's movements at the national level. Before discussing how the international policy climate has affected women's issues in Turkey, it would be useful to review the history of women's movements in Turkey.

Women's movements in Turkey emerged in the last century of the Ottoman Empire (Çakır 1994) and had different ideological emphases: from more secular and republican in the 1940s and 1950s, to more leftist in the 1960s and 1970s and more diversified after the 1990s (Esim and Cindoğlu 1999). During the 1990s, in parallel with the international trend, the institutionalization of the women's movement in Turkey increased (Sayan 2010: 123). This growth trend resulted in the visibility of the feminist movement in the public space and women started to organize and set up NGOs nationwide.

Along with these organizational efforts, the growing awareness of gender issues in the international community led the state to take action at the end of the 1980s in terms of the institutionalization of women's and men's equality (Acuner 2014: 127). In addition to the international environment, the increasing power and visibility of women's organizations resulted in the formation of KSSGM (General Directorate for the Status and Problems of Women) in 1990.[1] Gender visibility policies increased with the legal rearrangement of basic laws, especially after the EU candidacy (Acar and Altunak 2012: 16) and through the endeavours of women's NGOs, especially after the ratification of CEDAW in 1981 (Ertürk 2015).

---

[1] This directorate was incorporated into the Ministry of Family and Social Policy in 2011, a move that feminist organizations in Turkey protested against (see http://www.bianet.org/bianet/kadin/130585-kadin-bakanligi-kaldirildi-kadin-orgutleri-ofkeli).

In parallel with the rise of identity politics, Kurdish and Islamist feminists became more visible and more critical of Turkish feminists "being ethnocentric and exclusionary to other politics" (Diner and Toktaş 2010: 47). Another trend was the dispersion of women's NGOs from big cities to other cities. Yet, their influence on politics and policymaking were still limited during the 1990s (Esim and Cindoğlu 1999). The number of women's NGOs mushroomed throughout the 2000s with an increasing number of projects supported by international and national institutions. Although this "project feminism" is highly criticized (Aksu and Günal 2014: 442) and led women's organizations to become project-based rather than issue-based (Sancar 2011: 92), the projects created collaborative opportunities between different groups of women and consequently to possible conflicts of interest between the different women's organizations (Kümbetoğlu 2014: 177).

This growing visibility and the influence of women's movements have brought women's positions and gender inequalities into discussion. The increase in the number of civic organizations is not limited to women's NGOs but also includes other NGOs. Moreover, there is a growing emphasis on the 'dialogue between NGOs and state bodies' or the "inclusion of these institutions in the decision-making process" (Tekeli 1999). Despite efforts at the discourse level, recent studies (Çaha and Çaha 2012) point up that local participation mechanisms are not inclusive to women notwithstanding all the institutional changes and both international and national pressure for gender equality. As pointed out by Acuner (2014) and also by Gökulu and Furat (2013), this exclusion is partly related to the governmental attitude to implement the policy decided at the top level. Nevertheless, this does not mean that these decisions are implemented in the local context where local authorities and NGOs have to apply these policies. Yet, there is still not enough research on how much these women's NGOs have effectively participated in the policymaking process in Turkey.

Although various fields could be examined to understand gender inequalities, another focus will be on the inequalities within women's NGOs with reference to their positions in gender-mainstreaming projects in Mardin between 2010 and 2015. In order to understand these inequalities, I will address two different discussions related to gender inequalities. The first discussion addresses the question of how to understand gender inequality from an intersectionality perspective. The second discussion is on using gender mainstreaming as a policy tool to contrast gender inequality. By analysing these two different but related discussions, I will try to illustrate the limits of these conceptualizations by applying them to field experiences.

## Intersectionality Debate

Inequality mainly refers to social and economic divisions within society, although its conceptualization has changed over time: from economic and mostly class-centred discussions to more social dimensions, especially to identity-related matters. In particular, the greater emphasis on identity politics in the 1990s questioned how far we could conceptualize group identity as homogeneous by comparing it to the "other" (Barth 1994). Then the question became how to understand the heterogeneity within these identity groups. One answer came from feminist scholars who were trying to understand differences among women through their attempts to develop a gender-equality policy for women with different backgrounds. Disregarding these intragroup differences also means ignoring that identity has been shaped by historical, contextual and contingent differences (Crenshaw 1991).

In order to analyse intertwining social and cultural categories (Knudsen 2006: 61), intersectionality is an accepted way to understand, conceptualize and study social divisions in terms of identity and difference, and inequality or stratification and oppression in the literature (Anthias 1998: 515). Components of identity and difference usually cross over within historical and local contexts (Ferree 2008). From this perspective, what constitutes social inequality is not limited to components of identity like race, ethnicity, gender and age, but also considers how these components intersect within specific times and locations. Such a conceptualization offers the possibility to understand the dynamism behind the interplay of different social structures (Anthias 2001) of gender inequality in various social contexts. Ferree (2009: 14) also reminds us that this dynamism empowers and/or disempowers people in different structural locations.

Empowerment is not only realized through identity dynamics, but also through social policy mechanisms. When we talk about social policies, we mainly refer to national institutions but extended to international or transnational agencies as well (Nash 2014). One of the ways social policy mechanisms are formulated is gender mainstreaming. The next section deals with this concept with reference to how far women's empowerment is successful through this process.

## Gender Mainstreaming

Gender mainstreaming refers to both policy development and to their application for the inclusion of women and women's NGOs in the policymaking process (Çelik and Atabey 2013: 153). Therefore, the main premise of gender mainstreaming is the inclusion of women and women's NGOs in both the policy formation process and policy's application in order to overcome gender inequalities. As it is known from social policy literature, the scope of policymaking is limited to the national framework and lies within the national institutional structure. Compared to this scope, gender mainstreaming is a transnational process with reference to the involvement of diverse actors, including "complex hybridizations" (Walby 2005: 457) with various institutional resources like CEDAW and the UN Human Rights Conference in Vienna in 1993 and institutions like the EU, the UN and UNDP. The areas that gender mainstreaming policies target are employment, gender budgeting and violence against women. To reach equality and overcome the violence against women, these policies require cooperation among various actors from international and national "traditional" policymakers, but also from the groups these policies are going to target, in this case women and women's NGOs as their representatives. Because of this policymaking, there is a stronger emphasis on gender equality and on the necessity of collaboration between different institutions to realize gender mainstreaming.

The main goal of gender mainstreaming, therefore, is to increase women's visibility and empowerment through the participation of both sexes in public and private life and through the inclusion of those who are excluded from both the policymaking and policy application process. Accordingly, it is interpreted as a "process of democratization" (Rai 2003) requiring technical or scientific knowledge or expertise; in other words, political objectives (Walby 2005). However, the question of how much is gender mainstreaming successful is worth thinking about. Verloo (2005) argues that gender mainstreaming is dependent on the political context. In addition, it also depends on the extent to which opportunities mobilize the networks within traditional policymaking bodies and outside of these bodies. Consequently, the same mechanisms do not work in different political contexts. Different scholars (Daly 2005, Walby 2005, Zalewski 2010) also highlight the problematic relation between gender mainstreaming and gender inequality. Gender mainstreaming creates a specific vocabulary for the inclusion of gender without criticizing the concept of gender, which usually includes intersections of different social dimensions as well as power relations. This vocabulary also creates new "gender expertise" that also results in "generating new forms of political practice and alliances" (Walby 2005: 467). Those who do not have this expertise are either not included in these projects or their participation is limited.

Since international and national bodies of government have attempted to reduce gender inequalities and these attempts intersect the interest of women's NGOs, one must understand the social context in terms of how "power relations and conflicts of interest apply within groups as well as between them. At the same time, individuals cannot be considered as abstracted from their specific social positionings" (Yuval-Davis 1997: 22). Accordingly, the following section focuses on the social and economic structure of the city in which these projects are applied.

## Mardin as a Research Field

Discourse on Mardin as a multicultural city of Turkey is gaining both popular and academic attention (Küçük and Atalay 2009). On the one hand, this discourse emphasizes ethnic and religious differences within the city population while on the other it veils class and gender differences (Küçük 2012). In addition, this discourse highlights only one dimension, whereas the rather brighter social dimension blurs the political and military conflict (Öktem 2005) and the social-economic inequalities in Mardin. This section provides an overview of Mardin by trying to understand it as a field in a Bourdieusian sense with reference to whole dimensions. Starting with a more general description of the city, the effects of these socioeconomic variables on gender inequalities in Mardin will be discussed.

Mardin, located in southeast Turkey, is a historical city dating back to the fourth century (Aydın et al. 2001: 8). It neighbours Syria and is very close to the border with Iraq. This geographical position has affected the city's socioeconomic composition throughout its history and continues to affect it. The old town with its unique medieval structure has become a cultural tourism centre, especially over the last decade. In the 2000s, Mardin applied to UNESCO to be included in The World Heritage List.

Mardin's population is 788996 (Turkish Statistical Institute, TSI, 2014[2]) and the majority live in the city centre. Its ethnic composition is Arab, Kurd, Turk and Assyrian, but there is no official information on these groups' exact populations; ethnic information through census has not been collected in Turkey since 1927 (Aydın et al. 2001: 371). The first three groups are in the majority and are members of the same Muslim denomination, while the Assyrian (Christian) population is decreasing. Despite a birth rate above the country's average, there is also a high rate of outward migration compared to the country's average.[3] Limited employment opportunities, a lack of urban facilities and the unstable political environment are among the reasons for this migration pattern.

Urban economy is mainly based on the service sector, like the overall economy in Turkey, closely followed by the agriculture sector (Atalay-Güneş 2012a: 80). Tourism is also increasing thanks to the architectural peculiarity of the old town, which has also been the location of movie and TV serial production over the last decade. Yet, tourism demand is very fragile, especially in case of political instability in the region, and hardly offers stable employment opportunities. The share of industry in the urban economy is limited: mostly agriculture-based small and medium-sized organizations employing high-technology production techniques. Thus, employment opportunities available in the private sector are insufficient and state institutions likewise provide few job opportunities. These few job opportunities are distributed among successful candidates who pass a nationwide general exam open to applicants from all over the country.

The unstable political context during the 1990s due to the armed conflict between the state and the Kurdish Workers' Party (PKK) has also accelerated a socioeconomic downturn in the entire region. In addition to a low level of socioeconomic investment, political liberalization was limited during those years.

---

2 See http://www.turkstat.gov.tr/.

3 See http://www.dika.org.tr/katalog.php?katalog=303.

The unequal socioeconomic development has had many consequences in Mardin, but its effects can be observed in gender inequality: fewer women participate in the labour market and girls receive less schooling than boys do (Atalay-Güneş 2012b). In the last few years, however, there has been a growing trend in girls' participation in the school system. The working-women population is low and only 1 587 women are taxpayers as opposed to 15 443 men. Women's participation in the labour market is very low and, in fact, one of the lowest compared to other provinces. This excludes women from employment opportunities and deepens the discrimination between men and women. Aşık (2012) calculated the women's labour market participation and the lowest level was in the TRC3 NUT2[4] regions including Mardin: 8.6 per cent compared to Turkey's 28.8 per cent overall participation, in 2011.

There is also limited access to health services. As a result, there is still a high mother-infant death ratio. Almost 90 per cent of marriages are between relatives and the issue of child-brides is very common despite increased policy measures and a national campaign against it.[5] The political representation of Mardin's women is increasing in the national assembly where they represent two of the six members from the city; one is from the Justice and Development Party (AKP) and the other was elected as independent and then joined the Peace and Democracy Party (BDP). There is also a co-mayor, a young woman from Mardin's Syriac community.

Although these demographics are important to understand Mardin, it is also important to see how the city compares to other cities in Turkey. The recent study on gender inequality in Turkey by The Economic Research Foundation of Turkey (TEPAV)[6] displayed how inequality has been experienced in Mardin compared to other cities. According to the *Gender Empowerment Index* developed by TEPAV (Demirdirek and Şener 2014), Mardin ranks 66th out of Turkey's 81 provinces. The *Gender Equality Index*, also developed by TEPAV, places Mardin 57th among the other provinces. Therefore, it is possible to argue that the unequal local socioeconomic conditions have contributed more negatively to women's positions.

These differences and the socioeconomic underdevelopment in the southeast part of Turkey were on the political agenda of many governments throughout the republican history. Some promised to redistribute land, but the distribution of land in the region is still unequal compared to other parts of the country. Some

---

[4] Nut2 regions refers to regions organized by State Planning Organization in 2002; TRC3 includes the provinces of Mardin, Siirt, Şırnak and Batman.

[5] Data from author's note taken from the various presentations of the project participants at a meeting held in Mardin on February 24, 2012, for WFC-2.

[6] See http://www.tepav.org.tr.

promised large infrastructural projects, yet one project has been in the making since the 1980s.[7]

The Southeastern Development Project is one of the biggest infrastructure projects of the Republic of Turkey; started in the 1980s, it includes large-scale dams and irrigation projects to increase agricultural production and social development aspects were integrated in the late 1990s. One of the main endeavours was to establish a Multipurpose Social Centre (MSC/ÇATOM) aimed especially at women in the least developed part of the region. The number of NGOs, especially women's NGOs, increased during the 1990s and 2000s. However, women's participation in civil society organizations in Mardin, as in other provinces of southeast Turkey, is low compared to the three big cities: İstanbul, Ankara and İzmir (Yeğen et al. 2010: 108). MSCs also formed NGOs at the end of the 2000s but without turning into full-fledged NGOs. This twofold institutional identity of MSCs was questioned by other NGOs, yet MSCs carry on all kinds of projects in the region, especially these two projects in Mardin alongside the NGOs.

From the perspective of intersectionality, there are different and intersecting sources of identity; namely, gender, ethnicity and class. There are changing relations among these sources, and the emphasis shifts "from class and life-style connotations to ethnic sources" (Küçük 2012: 163) in Mardin. The emphasis on certain locations in intersectionality theory reminds us how these locations produce and reproduce inequalities for certain groups. From this point of view, women have experienced more socioeconomic disadvantages in the city than men have.

## Description of the Projects

In parallel with the growing attention to gender inequality, several projects were put into operation in Mardin after 2000. In this chapter, only two of them will be examined: the *Empowerment of Women and Women's NGOs in the Least Developed Regions of Turkey* (EWNGO) and *Women Friendly Cities-2* (WFC-2). EWNGOs targeted gender equality at the local level by emphasizing partnership between NGOs and public institutions though the development of the Local Equality Action Plan (LEAP).

LEAP makes reference to both international and national legal frameworks. International legal frameworks include UN documents, CEDAW, European Council and EU, which emphasize gender equality at the local level. National references include the constitution, Turkish Civil Law and various laws regulat-

[7] Undertakings to complete this project and to empower the capacities of state institutions through this project are still on the agenda of the current government. See http://www.aljazeera.com.tr/haber/davutoglu-gap-eylem-planini-acikladi.

ing the local administration's reinforcement of the active participation of citizens. In addition to these legal recourses, at the end of the 2000s various legislations pointing to gender mainstreaming were incorporated in order to prevent violence against women.

LEAP is defined as a guideline for gender equality at the local level to reinforce the application of a gender-mainstreaming local administration and to reform women's everyday life experiences. In order to reach these goals, these plans were developed in cooperation with local state agencies and NGOs, especially women's NGOs, via a transparent process. Issues such as education, unemployment, violence, poverty and early marriages were listed as the basic problems of women in Mardin. Among these problems, violence against women and employment were selected and 36 activities were planned in LEAP between 2010 and 2012. Five workshops and four task-force meetings were held during the project. Finally, the LEAP was formulated as a result of these meetings and announced in the meetings attended by project participants, representatives of other NGOs in Mardin and high-level state agencies.

The WFC-2 project aims to create a women-friendly urban environment both by implementing gender-mainstreaming criteria into the planning process and by increasing dialogue among local authorities and women's NGOs and grassroots organizations. This project follows an earlier project called Protecting and Promoting the Human Rights of Women and Girls; six provinces, respectively Adıyaman, Antalya, Bursa, Gaziantep, Mardin, Malatya and Samsun, are included in this phase of the project. The earlier project was implemented in İzmir, Şanlıurfa, Van, Kars, Trabzon and Nevşehir. Partners of this project were the Ministry of Interior, the General Directorate of Local Administration, the United Nations Population Fund (UNFPA), the United Nations Development Fund (UNDP) and the Swedish International Development Coop. Agency (SIDA). The project lasted thirty-six months and ran from April 1, 2011 to April 31, 2014.

The project aimed to increase cooperation between civil society and local administration, i. e. both municipalities and governorates, and to integrate gender-mainstreaming principles into the planning process of local actions. To increase this cooperation, it also aimed to increase the capacity of women's NGOs to advocate gender equality and local services for women. The cooperation should be enlarged to include grassroots organizations at the local level. In Mardin there are no grassroots movements involved in the project. Another target of the project was to increase the level of awareness of gender mainstreaming among both governorates and municipality personnel in planning and providing services.

For the realization of these goals, the Provincial Women's Rights Coordination Committee, Equality Commissions and Equality Units are being represented in the municipality, the office of the governor and in other state institutions. Although the constitutions of these units are under the guarantee of law, in practice their role and effects are quite limited.

State agency partners comprise the Mardin Governorship, Mardin Metropolis Municipality, Provincial Directorate for National Education, Provincial Directorate for Family and Social Policy, Provincial Directorate for Police, Provincial Directorate for Health, Provincial Labour Office, Provincial Office of Mufti, Provincial Directorate of Dormitories, Provincial Directorate of Population and Citizenship, Provincial Office of Social Solidarity, Provincial Office of Gendarmerie, Provincial Directorate for Agriculture, Provincial Office for NGOs, Mardin Artuklu University, Mardin Bar Association and Tigris Development Agency.[8] The representatives of NGOs included the Women's Centre (KAMER), Association for the Prevention of Honour Killings and Evaluation of Women's Potential (TÖRKAD), Mardin Association of Women (MAKİDER), Education and Employment, Mardin Partner Women Cooperation Association (MOKİD), Mardin Branch of Turkish Women Associations (TKB) and four MSCs.

As we discussed, LEAP included only violence and employment issues. WFC-2 added education, health, urban services and local participation of women to this plan. In addition to these changes in the state agencies, the NGO partners of the project are supported by the Civil Society Organization Grant Program, which offered US$ 4 000 for each project. With the exception of the TKB and MSCs, the other NGOs applied for and received these grants within the project's framework.

## Findings

The research was mainly based on two methods, one of which was participatory observation. As faculty members of the Sociology Department at Mardin Artuklu University, a colleague of mine and I were appointed university representatives for these projects from 2010 to 2015. The second method was open-ended and unstructured interviews conducted with representatives of women's NGOs that had joined two projects. Two groups of representatives, MOKİD and TKB, participated only in the second project. I also interviewed only one of the four MSCs. It was not possible to meet with the TKB representative. These interviews were usually held in their office and audio-recorded with the permission of the participants during the spring of 2015. Of the five women, only one was a high school graduate, the others held university degrees and only two had other professional businesses besides working for NGOs. Despite the growing emphasis on Mardin's multi-religiosity, only one interviewee highlighted the multi-religious backgrounds of their volunteers. Women are of either Arabic or Kurdish origin in these NGOs.

As an official participant in these projects, my access to research was easier. I have known representatives of NGOs for years and they thought this kind of research was going to provide a space to state what they could not express dur-

[8] This development agency, founded in 2009, is responsible not only for Mardin, but also for the neighbouring cities of Batman, Siirt and Şırnak.

ing the project meetings. Of course, that was also true for me as a researcher. In addition to participating at these meetings, writing and thinking about the whole process led me to consider questions concerning gender inequality, projects making progress, and how international, national and local dynamics come together within these frameworks. This research also made me and other women reflect on both projects and how they are implemented.

Between 2010 and 2012, we attended the regular meetings organized by project members and brought together all representatives of both state agencies and women's NGOs. A majority of the participants at the project meetings were women with higher educations, usually high school or university graduates employed in state institutions or active representatives of NGOs, in comparison with the rest of the women in Mardin. This called into question who had the power of representation and who had the knowledge to access these projects. As Walby (2005) discussed, these meetings created expertise for all participants. During 2012, the second project started and our meetings doubled. Some of the meetings had overlapping issues, techniques and policy measures, which created a feeling of repetition for the project's participants. Then the previous achievements of LEAP were integrated into WFC-2 just by adding the new dimensions to the LEAP as mentioned above.

Interviewees understood and interpreted these projects very positively. In the first place, these meetings created an opportunity to bring together state officials and representatives of women's NGOs. The aim of the planning agencies of these projects reinforced cooperation and dialogue on gender mainstreaming between state officials and NGOs at the local level. Because of the international legal framework and because they had partnered with these kinds of projects, state officials had to cooperate with NGOs. Members of the NGOs interpreted this as an opportunity. One member stated, "If we arrange some meetings or workshops about issues on gender equality, *they* [italics mine, the reference is here to state officials] do not attend these events. For the sake of the project, they have to attend" (interviewee n. 1).

The effects of the meetings were not limited solely to cooperation among participants as they also created an opportunity for dialogue among these participants. These dialogues could be transformative in terms of gender equality issues as discussed below.

> At the beginning, we did not recognize what LEAP means but then we developed the dialogue with others. I think [it was a] great success. This changed our perspectives on both women rights and equal opportunity. So that has an impact on how organizations understand and interpret the women issues (Interviewee n. 2).

Despite repetitions at the project meetings and the project's long timeframe, the initiatives of cooperation between state officials and women's NGOs created an "accumulated knowledge" as indicated by interviewee n. 2. From the representative's perspectives, this cooperation or "the possibility of cooperation" did not provide room for participation in the policymaking process as indicated by the projects, but it gave them the opportunity to establish a dialogue. One participant said, "If these projects were not implemented, there would be no possibility to bring state institutions with women's NGOs together in Mardin" (interviewee n. 2).

Interviewees knew the differences between these two projects and how these projects could possibly contribute to their positions through the empowerment of their roles as representatives of women in Mardin. Thus, the aim of the empowerment of women's NGO representatives was realized through the projects. Yet, the inequalities of "empowerment" brought by these projects also contributed to the inequalities among women in Mardin. Those involved in the projects already had some accumulated knowledge (Walby 2005) as well as social capital (Bourdieu 1986). This difference was not limited to women since it also affected the NGOs by stipulating which NGOs were eligible to participate and which had sufficient knowledge to access these resources.

Although the city is quite small and these women knew each other in other areas of social life, such as party politics or charity organizations, the projects created a space to develop new collaborations that were clearly defined within the project's framework. However, some interviewees thought both the cooperation between state institutions and women's NGOs as well as room for inclusion of these NGOs in the policymaking process were limited and led to failure.

> I do not know why, but we could not do something together. We tried in Local Agenda 21[9], and we did not succeed, and I do not see any changes these projects have brought into the lives of women in Mardin (Interviewee n. 3).

As mentioned above, these two projects aimed to reform the everyday practices of women in Mardin. Yet, those changes, as interviewee n. 3 indicated, were not observable in the city. Limited participation in policymaking did not bring about the implementation of proposed gender-sensitive policies. When these gender-mainstreaming mechanisms fail, the obstacles to implementation should be studied with reference to both national and specific local conditions. According to the social policy literature, social policy is what is implemented at the street level.

In addition to the problems addressed by interviewee n. 3, there were other criticisms to these projects. One of the main criticisms was directed at the first project, which had no budget for the local women's NGOs within the project framework. The WFC-2 grant program answered these criticisms and created an opportunity to use these funds to fulfil the projects. All NGOs, except

---

[9] Local Agenda 21 or Agenda 21 refers to projects aimed at increasing cooperation among the local groups, NGOs and administration and other partners in order to achieve sustainable development with UNDP. This agenda has been applied since 1997 in various cities in Turkey.

MSCs and TKB, had prepared small grant projects during the WFC-2, which also increased local tensions among NGOs. As mentioned above, the institutional differences among NGOs or the twofold institutional identity of MSCs caused tensions among the NGOs. MSCs were supported by the governors, had more facilities for their target group and did not have access to the grants offered to NGOs. One participant stated, "They are not civil; they are institutions of the governors" (interviewee n. 4). Another participant said,

> MSCs have more resources, money and professional employees. There are scarce resources for other NGOs. In addition, MSCs could reach more women than others. These women are also the target group for other women's NGOs. They use these groups and then they criticize MSCs. I do not really understand (Interviewee n. 3).

The advantages of having resources could have been an obstacle to applying for other grants, a fact mentioned during the interviews by interviewee 1.

The differences among the NGOs were not limited solely to their institutional identity, but also to their approach to women's inequality issues. Despite our respect for their approach, TKB is one of the most criticized NGOs because of their "traditional charity activities". TKB also emphasized their position as a self-sustaining NGO without grants from other institutions. Consequently, access to resources and how these resources should be used creates conflicts of interest among NGOs.

The women's NGO representatives were also quite sceptical about the partners from the state agencies and their involvement in the project, despite the fact that the projects have provided an opportunity for them to work together. Although there is a growing emphasis on gender mainstreaming and on more participatory models for both policy development and policy application at the international and national levels, there are certain obstacles against these inclusionary discourses. As recent studies have shown, in Turkey most of the people think that "politics is men's business" although they have quite a positive attitude towards the increasing participation of women (Kadir Has Univ. 2015). One participant said, "What is the aim of the project? The Foundation of Equality Unit. There is no problem from the side of the NGOs, but the participation from the state agencies is still limited" (interviewee n. 4). In addition to this limited participation, both the state officials and NGOs had to endorse the assignments usually defined within the project framework. One participant pointed out,

> We do sign things that we cannot do because we feel we have to. We got quite bored because of these projects. Usually, they do not really know about the capacity of the associations here. Same trainings for the same people (Interviewee n. 3).

Despite their criticisms, women's NGO representatives were aware of the strength of these projects and that gender-mainstreaming policies have contributed to their empowerment to a limited degree. They tactically used these ways to empower themselves and their NGOs in Mardin. Yet, not all women's NGOs were eligible to access and activate these resources to the same degree. As Walby (2005) pointed out, these projects and gender-mainstreaming policies have created their own professionals with their own specific knowledge that deepens inequalities among women. The city's social and economic inequalities and political instability are a backdrop of the interviews, but interviewees usually avoid talking about these issues openly, though they are quite aware of their "advantage" compared to the rest of women in the city.

## Conclusion

In conclusion, these projects opened a space for women's NGO representatives to be recognized as partners. Women were quite aware of this space and tried to use it for themselves, their organization and their target group, but the inequalities and access to resources were varied among these groups. Thus, these projects unintentionally contributed to the inequalities among women in Mardin. As indicated above, women try to maximize their interest by exploiting the limited opportunities provided via these projects.

Gender inequalities intersect with class and there are multiple ethnicities in Mardin as discussed earlier. One interviewee explained the tension between projects and the current situation in Mardin by stating, "Problems have quite multiplied here and projects only touch a limited part of the problem" (interviewee n. 5). It is easier to talk about a problem without clearly defining it if you are also part of it. The response of representatives of women NGOs in Mardin takes into account the socioeconomic and regional inequalities, but they try to do their best. Although certain dimensions of these projects provide "empowerment" for women's NGO representatives, these projects should be critically assessed.

## Bibliography

Acar, Feride, and Altunok, Gülbanu (2013): The "Politics of Intimate" at the Intersection of Neo-Liberalism and Neo-Conservatism in Contemporary Turkey. In: *Women's Studies International Forum*, 41 (P1): 14–23. URL: http://doi.org/10.1016/j.wsif.2012.10.001.

Acuner, Selma (2014): 90'lı Yıllar ve Resmi Düzeyde Kurumsallaşmanın Doğuş Aşamaları [90s and The Rising Steps of the Institutionalization at the Official Level]. In: A. Bora and A. Günal (eds.): *90'larda Türkiye'de Feminizm* [Feminism in Turkey During 1990s]. (V. Edition). İstanbul: İletişim Yayınları, 125–158.

Anthias, Floya (2001): The Concept of "Social Division" and Theorizing Social Stratification: Looking at Ethnicity and Class. In: *Sociology*, 35 (4): 835–854.

Anthias, Floya (1998): Rethinking Social Divisions: Some Notes towards a Theoretical Framework. In: *Sociological Review*, 46 (3): 505–535.

Aşık, Güneş A. (2012): Türkiye'de Kadınların İşgücüne Katılımı: İstanbul ve Ankara'da Katılım Bingöl ve Tunceli ile Aynı [Women's Participation to Labor Force in Turkey: The participation in both İstanbul and Ankara as same as Bingöl and Tunceli], TEPAV Assessment Note. İstanbul.

Atalay-Güneş, Z. Nurdan (2012a): Theorizing "Trust" in the Economic Field in the Era of Neoliberalism: The Perspectives of Entrepreneurs in Mardin. Unpublished PhD. Diss. Ankara: METU.

Atalay-Güneş, Z. Nurdan (2012b): *KEEP Mardin İl Raporu*. Unpublished Project Report. Mardin.

Aydın, Suavi, Emiroğlu Kudret, Özel Oktay and Ünsal Süha (2001): Mardin: Aşiret - Cemaat - Devlet [Mardin: Tribe, Community and State]. (Second Edition). İstanbul: Türkiye Ekonomik ve Toplumsal Tarih Vakfı.

Barth, Fredrik (1994): Enduring and Emerging Issues in the Analysis of Ethnicity. In: H. Vermeluen and Cora Govers (eds.): *The Anthropology of Ethnicity*. Amsterdam: Het Spinhuis, 11–32.

Bora, Aksu and Günal, Asena (2014): 1980 Sonrası Feminist Hareket [Feminist Movement after 1980s]. In: Suavi Aydın and Yüksel Taşkın: 1960'tan Günümüze Türkiye Tarihi [History of Turkey since 1960 to Today]. İstanbul: İletişim Yayınları, 441–443.

Bourdieu, Pierre (1986): The Forms of Capital. In: G. Richardson (ed.): *Handbook of Theory and Research for the Sociology of Education*, reprinted in N. W. Biggart (ed) (2000): *Readings in Economic Sociology*. Malden, Massachusetts: Blackwell Publishers, 280–291.

Crenshaw, Kimberle (1991): Mapping the Margins: Intersectionality, Identity Politics, and Violence against Women of Color. In: *Stanford Law Review*, 43 (6): 1241–1299. URL: http://doi.org/10.2307/1229039.

Çaha, Ömer and Çaha, Havva (2012): *Yerelde Tango: Kadın Örgütleri ve Yerel Demokrasi (Tango at the Local: Women Organizations and Local Democracy)*. Ankara: Orion Kitabevi.

Çelik, Özge & Atabey, Ertürk, Selin (2013): Toplumsal Cinsiyetin Anaakımlaştırılması ve Toplumsal Cinsiyete Duyarlı Bütçeleme [Gender Mainstreaming and Gender Sensitive Budgeting]. In: *Anadolu Üniversitesi Sosyal Bilimler Dergisi*, 13 (6): 151–166.

Daly, Mary (2005): Gender Mainstreaming in Theory and Practice. In: *Social Politics: International Studies in Gender, State & Society*, 12 (3): 433–450. URL: http://doi.org/10.1093/sp/jxi023.

Demirdirek, Hülya and Şener, Ülker (2014): *81 İl İçin Toplumsal Cinsiyet Eşitliği Karnesi* [Evaluation of Gender Equality for 81 Provinces]. Ankara: TEPAV.

Diner, Çağla and Toktaş, Şule (2010): Waves of Feminism in Turkey: Kemalist, Islamist and Kurdish Women's Movements in an Era of Globalization. In: *Journal of Balkan and Near Eastern Studies*, 12 (1): 41–57. URL: http://doi.org/10.1080/19448950903507388.

Esim, Simel and Cindoğlu, Dilek (1999): Women's Organizations in 1990s Turkey: Predicaments and Prospects. In: *Middle Eastern Studies*, 35 (1): 178–188. URL: http://doi.org/10.1080/00263209908701261.

Ertürk, Yakın (2015): *Sınır Tanımayan Şiddet: Paradigma, Politika ve Pratikteki Yönleriyle Kadına Şiddet Olgusu* [Violence without Borders: Violence towards Women with Dimensions of Paradigm, Politics and Practice]. İstanbul: Metis Yayınları.

Ferree, Myra M. (2009): Inequality, Intersectionality and the Politics of Discourse: Framing Feminist Alliances. In: E. Lombardo, P. Meier, M. Verloo (eds.): *The Discursive Politics of Gender Equality: Stretching, Bending and Policymaking*. London: Routledge, 86–104.

Gökulu, Gökhan and Furat, Mina (2013): "Türkiye"de Kadınla İlgili Kalkınma Politikalarının ve Projelerinin Eleştirel Bir Değerlendirmesi [A Critical Evaluation of Gender Related Development Policy and Projects in Turkey]. In: *Turkish Studies*, 8 (8): 1895–1913.

Kadir Has University (2015): *Türkiye'de Toplumsal Cinsiyet ve Kadın Algısı Araştırması* [Research on Perception of Gender and Women in Turkey]. Project Presentation, URL: http://www.khas.edu.tr/uploads/pdf-doc-vb/news/tckca.pdf, accessed in May 2015.

Knudsen, Susanne V. (2005): Intersectionality? A Theoretical Inspiration in the Analysis of Minority Cultures and Identities in Textbooks. In: *Caught in the Web or Lost in the Textbook*, 61–76. URL: http://doi.org/http://www.caen.iufm.fr/colloque_iartem/pdf/knudsen.pdf, accessed in April 2015.

Küçük, Murat and Atalay-Güneş, Z. Nurdan (2011): Sosyal Bilimlerde Mardin Üzerine Araştırmalar ve Tezler Hakkında Bir İnceleme Denemesi [An Attempt of Examination of Mardin in both Research and Thesis in Social Science]. In: M. Akdağ and F. Aktar (eds.): *VI. Ulusal Sosyoloji Kongresi Bildiri Kitabı*. Ankara: Sosyoloji Derneği 984–1000. URL: http://www.sosyolojidernegi.org.tr/kutuphane/izlec.php?kitap=1&tip=makale&id=31, accessed in April 2015.

Küçük, Murat (2012): *Intersecting Identities: Context and Change in the Case of Mardinian Arabs*. Unpublished M.S. Thesis. Ankara: METU.

Kümbetoğlu, Belkıs (2014): Kadınlara İlişkin Projeler [Projects about Women]. In: A. Bora and Günal A.: *90'larda Türkiye'de Feminizm* [Feminism in Turkey during 1990s] (V. Baskı). İstanbul: İletişim Yayınları, 159–182.

Nash, Kate (2014). Yurttaşlıktan İnsan Haklarına ve Tekrar Geriye [Between Citizenship and Human Rights]. In: A. Durakbaşa, N. A. Şirin Öner ve F. Karapehlivan Şenel: *Yurttaşlığı Yeniden Düşünmek: Sosyoloji, Hukuk ve Siyasal Tartışmalar* [Rethinking Citizenship: Sociology, Law and Political Debates]. İstanbul: İstanbul Bilgi Üniversitesi Yayınları, 23–38.

Öktem, Kerem (2005): Faces of the City: Poetic, Mediagenic and Traumatic Images of a Multi-Cultural City in Southeast Turkey. In: *Cities,* 22 (3): 241–253. DOI: 10.1016/j.cities.2005.03.010.

Rai, Shirin M. (2003): *Mainstreaming Gender, Democratising the State? Institutional Mechanisms for the Advancement of Women*. Manchester: Manchester University Press.

Sancar, Serpil (2011): Türkiye'de Kadın Hareketinin Politiği: Tarihsel Bağlam, Politik Gündem ve Özgünlükler [The Politics of Women Movement in Turkey: Historical Context, Political Agenda and Pecularities]. In: S. Sancar (ed.): *Birkaç Arpa Boyu ... 21.Yüzyıla Girerken Türkiye'de Feminist Çalışmalar* [Few Little Steps ... Feminist Studies in Turkey towards the 21st Century]. İstanbul: Koç Üniversitesi Yayınları, 61–120.

Sayan Cengiz, Feyda (2010): Yeni Sosyal Haraket Olarak Türkiye'de Feminist Hareket: Değerler Değişi mi Alternatif Dinamikler mi? [Feminist Movement as New Social Movement: Change of Values or Alternative Dynamics?]. In: Hülya Durudoğan, Fatoş Göksen, Bertil Emrah Oder, Deniz Yükseker (eds.): *Türkiye'de Toplumsal Cinsiyet Çalışmaları: Eşitsizlikler, Mücadeleler, Kazanımlar* [Gender Studies in Turkey: Inequalities, Struggles and Gains]. İstanbul: Koç Üniversitesi Yayınları, 115–134.

Tekeli, İlhan (1999): Yerel Siyaset ve Demokrasi/Çoğulculuk/Sivil Toplum [Local Politics and Democracy/Plurality/Civil Society]. In: M. Mutman, N. Mert et al.: *Sivil Toplum için "Kent, Yerel Siyaset ve Demokrasi" Seminerleri* [City, Local Politics and Democracy Seminars for Civil Society]. İstanbul: WALD, 195–232.

Yeğen, Mesut, Keyman, E. Fuat, Mehmet A. Çalışkan and Uğraş, Tol (2010): *Türkiye'de Gönüllü Kuruluşlarda Sivil Toplum Kültürü* [Civil Society Culture in Voluntary Organizations in Turkey]. İstanbul: YaDa Vakfı Yayınları.

Zalewski, Marysia (2010): "I Don't even Know what Gender Is": a Discussion of the Connections between Gender, Gender Mainstreaming and Feminist Theory. In: *Review of International Studies*, 36 (01): 3. URL: http://doi.org/10.1017/S0260210509990489.

Verloo, Mieke (2005): Displacement and Empowerment: Reflections on the Concept and Practice of the Council of Europe Approach to Gender Mainstreaming and Gender Equality. In: *Social Politics*, 12 (3): 344–365.

Walby, Slyvia (2005): Introduction: Comparative Gender Mainstreaming in a Global Era. In: *International Feminist Journal of Politics,* 7 (4): 453–470. URL: http://doi.org/10.1080/14616740500284383.

Yuval-Davis, Nural (1997): Women, Citizenship and Difference. In: *Feminist Review,* 57: 4–27.

*Web Sites*

http://www.bianet.org/bianet/kadin/130585-kadin-bakanligi-kaldirildi-kadin-orgutleri-ofkeli, accessed in April, 2015.

http://www.turkstat.gov.tr/, accessed in April, 2015.

http://www.dika.org.tr/katalog.php?katalog=303, accessed in April, 2015.

http://www.tepav.org.tr, accessed in April, 2015.

http://www.aljazeera.com.tr/haber/davutoglu-gap-eylem-planini-acikladi, accessed in June, 2015.

# Controversial Conversions and Intra-Christian Marriages in Pluri-Religious Lebanon

*Benedetta Panchetti*

## Introduction

While Lebanon is truly a kaleidoscope of different religions with its eighteen Christian, Islamic and Jewish confessions officially recognized by law,[1] it is also clear that relationships between these different communities have always encountered various difficulties (Corm 1988: 18).

Problems generally occur in the relationship between Christian churches and Muslim communities as well as in relationships among the various Christian communities. Divergences are noticeable especially in the field of family relationships and, above all, with respect to the institution of marriage. This field, in fact, is deeply influenced by two fundamental principles of the Lebanese legal system: the right granted by Constitution and State law to each officially-recognized religious sect to apply its religious laws to personal affairs concerning its members, and the absolute freedom of faith guaranteed by the same Constitution and State laws to every eighteen-year-old Lebanese citizen. The Lebanese family law system is one of the most significant legacies of the former Ottoman Empire's legal system, based on the so-called "*Millet* system" (Greene 2005); Ottoman subjects were divided into different *Milla* [nation] based on religious affiliation. Each "nation" was headed by an ecclesiastical authority, appointed by the community's members according to specific religious laws, to which the Ottoman Sultan granted jurisdiction over all issues regarding personal relationships between the community's members. An official document called *Firman,* detailing matters subject to the religious authority and to the religious courts' jurisdiction, confirmed this authority to each religious leader. It is necessary to underline that family law has always recognized the competence of religious jurisdiction because it has always been understood that the family represents the core aspect of individual life, a field particularly subject to personal religious

[1] The sects are: six Catholic Churches, five Orthodox Churches, Protestant, Sunni, Shi'a, Druze, Alawite, Ishmaelite and Jewish (divided into three different communities of synagogues). Since 1948, following the founding of Israel and the various Israeli-Arab wars, Jewish presence in Lebanon has declined rapidly, and at present, a very small community is still living in Lebanon. When in 1936 Jews and other religious communities were officially recognized for the first time, Jews represented a large sect in Lebanese society and they still had an important role in 1951, when the State approved the first law on non-Muslim communities after independence.

beliefs. Consequently, the State could not establish a single law for all, given the significant differences in the concept of family between Islamic law and that of the Christian communities (Al-Jamil 2009). Moreover, Lebanon's unique history as a land of welcome and refuge for almost all religious minorities in the Middle East region, explains the presence of such a wide religious pluralism in current Lebanese society.

To this day, therefore, the main difficulties and challenges to inter-religious relations arise from family law and from the coexistence of distinct religious doctrines in the Islamic and Christian communities, and, in the case of the latter, in the Catholic and Orthodox Churches.

This chapter aims to study a specific aspect of inter-Christian relations in Lebanon: since Lebanon lacks legislation governing the celebration of civil marriages and the possibility to get a divorce through the State courts, it seems interesting to focus on the case of Catholic married couples who join Orthodox Churches in order to end their marriage. Data is specifically based on case studies concerning Catholic couples that are considering the possibility of converting to Orthodox Churches, or have already decided to convert, in order to solve their own matrimonial problems. In fact, the Catholic doctrine on marriage, based on the principle of its absolute indissolubility, strictly prohibits divorce as a way to end the union and only allows for an annulment, decreed by ecclesiastical courts, based on a very limited number of reasons that existed prior to the marriage and render the celebration of the union invalid.

A "Declaration of Nullity" issued by ecclesiastical courts does not decree the dissolution of an existing marriage, but rather that consent was never validly exchanged by at least one of the partners due to a failure to meet the requirements to enter into matrimony; thus, effectively, the marriage has never existed (Conde 1996: 519).

Usually Catholic couples decide to convert to Orthodox Churches because those legislations provide the so-called "ecclesiastical divorce" as a way to end a marriage through a sentence handed down directly by Bishops, and also grant divorcees the opportunity to celebrate a second religious marriage.

## Some historical and contemporary difficulties in collecting data on conversions and intra-Christian marriages

Case studies presented in this paper, collected in 2014 in the Beirut and Jounieh areas, have been selected from interviews with Catholic couples facing conversion-related problems, with Catholic ecclesiastical authorities working as judges at Maronite and Melkite ecclesiastical courts and with family law lawyers and family law professors at Saint Joseph University in Beirut and Saint Esprit University of Kaslik (Jounieh).

The interviews were conducted in locations representative of predominantly Christian areas of the country where, in that period of 2014, research activities could be carried out without particular limitations linked to security concerns. It was actually impossible to extend the study to other quarters of the city of Beirut, as in March 2014 the city's stability was again put to the test by a series of terrorist attacks, which came to an end just at the start of this research.

The real identities of the interviewees are always kept anonymous to protect people and religious authorities, as they have requested specifically themselves. Also covered by anonymity are the sources mentioned in studies conducted on the more general subject of marriage in Lebanon, particularly in all those cases in which access to that juridical institution required a change in religious affiliation for at least one of the parties.

In general, any analysis related to juridical-religious themes in Lebanon encounters some unavoidable limitations linked to the safety of the people who agree to be interviewed and explain their own point of view.

Among the most sensitive of these themes are studies on the movement between different communities and religions as the act of conversion shakes the fundamentals of the country's juridical and political system, known as multiconfessionalism because it is based on the citizens' confessional affiliation to one of the eighteen officially recognized communities. These are, therefore, real intermediary bodies between the citizen-believer and the State, since only members of a certain community can accede to certain public offices and the running of the State on the basis of confessional quotas regulating the assignment of all state offices, from the highest levels (Presidency of the Republic, Prime Minister's office and Presidency of Parliament) to local level, including any area of public administration. Consequently, conversion is not merely an act of conscience in Lebanon, but rather an act full of juridical and political consequences because is also affects the exercise of the right to active, but above all passive, voting since the number of parliamentarians is divided in confessional quotas within the equal share of the two large blocks of Christian and Muslim members of parliament (Corm 1998).

Accordingly, data relating to conversions, whether prompted by sincere changes in religious beliefs or stemming from non-religious interests, is particularly sensitive for all religious confessions; in point of fact, during the period of *in loco* research, March-June 2014, it was not possible to obtain any official data on the conversions subject of this study from either the Christian authorities or the Lebanese Ministry of Interior and Municipalities. After all, more generally, there has not been a census of the entire population since 1932 so as to avoid facing up to all the problems inherent in the numbers of the individual religious confessions.

Moreover, as far as the subject of this study is concerned, a further difficulty regards the fact that these conversions from Catholicism to the Orthodox Churches by spouses wishing to end their union must clearly be categorized as conversions not caused by religious motivation, but rather by interest in the juridical institution of ecclesiastical divorce provided for by Orthodox Churches.

Thus, those who choose to change their confessional affiliation are aware they are heading towards defrauding the law, which guarantees and safeguards freedom of conscience, including the freedom to convert, on the assumption that such conversions occur for reasons truly pertaining to conscience.

Finally, it would be a mistake not to highlight that, in general, all themes inherent in marriage law touch on one of the most intimate and private aspects of the spouses' lives, making it difficult for a researcher to penetrate such a personal area that has often become a source of pain and suffering since those who choose to convert to obtain a divorce are, obviously, dealing with the end of the marital union.

For these reasons the interviews were arranged via personal contacts *in loco*, in the university environment, with permission to make contact with people who had already been through the process of conversion and had obtained an ecclesiastical divorce. These people provided their own point of view on the failure of their first union and the reasons why inter-Christian conversion was seen as preferable to submitting grounds for annulment to the competent Catholic court. It was not possible to obtain the point of view of the ex-spouse as well since contacts were made solely via personal links. The contacts were either by telephone or on the university premises, where interviews were carried out with the parties and, in one case, with the family member through whom I had been able to arrange the interview.

The interviews aimed to highlight why the spouses had not opted to take proceedings to the Catholic church court, the Church in which the marriage had been celebrated: i. e. whether the spouses were aware that there were no valid reasons under Catholic ecclesiastical law to grant the annulment *ex tunc* (Latin: "from the outset") of their union; or whether the lengthy Catholic court procedure had made conversion and application to the competent Orthodox bishop for the administrative granting of an ecclesiastical divorce preferable; or, finally, whether there had been other reasons. In both cases, the reasons cited regard the brevity of the marriage union, thus the desire to quickly conclude the judicial process to dissolve the bond on an official level as well. Both marriages, indeed, had lasted just a few years, and in one case, there had been a *de facto* separation caused by the husband going abroad for work. Furthermore, while there had been no children born to one of the couples, there were children from the other marriage who remained with the mother when the father left for work reasons.

The brief period of the marriage and the consequent desire to end it quickly at a juridical level as well, were also two of the most frequent reasons in the cases studied during investigations into the subject that were conducted by international organizations such as Human Rights Watch and published in 2015.

As far as the religious authorities are concerned, it was only possible to interview Catholic presbyters, who provided analysis of trends occurring within their respective communities regarding conversion to the Orthodox Churches, but were unable to provide official data. These authorities also underlined the great difficulty in detecting these conversions, as it is not uncommon for the converted to attend their original Church for many religious activities. This seems much easier to understand in a country where territorial vicinity and sharing of the same city areas by different Christian communities in itself makes the mingling of the faithful from different Churches extremely easy.

The reasons cited by the Orthodox Churches for accepting conversions of Catholic married couples were revealed during interviews with Catholic authorities who, for various reasons, were particularly involved in the ecumenical dialogue and in the juridical area of marriage annulment cases. These authorities, therefore, knew their counterparts in the various Orthodox ecclesiastical hierarchies very well.

Finally, we must consider a historical factor which for centuries has influenced relationships between different Christian communities; the phenomenon of Uniatism[2] and the installation of the Latin Roman Church in the whole Middle-East region (and Lebanon in particular) has hindered peaceful relationships between the Churches for a long time and, at the juridical level, made marriages between members of different communities extremely difficult. Up to the Second Vatican Council (1962–1965), the Catholic Church forbade unions with non-Catholic Christians *sic et simpliciter*, and a similar ban was laid down in the rules of all the Orthodox Churches in Lebanon. This ban was rendered explicit by the obligation to convert on the part of the person who was not an adherent of the doctrine professed by the Church in which the couple intended to marry (Girgis 2004).

Every ecclesiastical authority was therefore very careful that its faithful would not transgress these prohibitions, but exogamy also met strong resistance in the family and social contexts. Marriage between Christians from different Churches was openly opposed by the social groups to which the future spouses belonged, above all where the bride was concerned, since it was she who had to abandon her faith and join her husband's Church, in which the children would then be baptized. From the viewpoint of the bride's community, therefore, exogamic inter-Christian marriage caused a reduction of the number of the faithful in the present because she joined her husband's community and in the future because the children of the union would be brought up in the father's faith. Conversion for marriage purposes was thus historically one of the means to acquire church members, even when it was not accompanied by a sincere, intimate change in religious beliefs on the part of the person who converted.

The obligation to convert had therefore historically been the biggest obstacle in inter-Christian relationships in the country and inter-Christian marriages began to obtain a more favourable legislation and greater social acceptance only after the Second Vatican Council.

Today, in the era following the 15-year-long civil war that polarized the country along the lines of Christians and Muslims, inter-Christian marriages are so

---

2 Uniatism means the union of an Eastern Rite church with the Roman Church in which the Pope's supreme authority is accepted without loss of separate liturgies by local Eastern patriarchs.

widely practiced that the Patriarchs of all the Eastern Churches signed an agreement in 1996 to derogate their respective canonical legislation and make these unions easier, suppressing the obligation on the wife to convert and reducing the bureaucratic process to be completed before such marriages (Girgis 2004).

Nevertheless, ecclesiastical authorities still highlight the requirement that conversions for marriage reasons should not again become an obstacle in relationships between the Churches and a means to acquire a growing number of members.

Finally, this particular viewpoint should include the radical reform of the process of declaration of marriage nullity, introduced by Pope Francis through two *Motu Proprio*[3] [on one's own initiative] promulgated on September 8, 2015 and addressed respectively to the Latin Church [*Mitis et misericors Iesus*] and the Eastern Catholic Churches [*Mitis Iudex Dominus Iesus*]. This legislation, enacted on December 8, 2015, significantly modifies the earlier since it introduces a *Brevior* [shorter] process of marriage annulment aimed specifically at cases in which the nullity is "evident" from conclusive facts and is characterized by quicker proceedings than the ordinary tribunal process and by a reduced cost.

The majority of case studies concern Maronite[4] couples because this Eastern Catholic Church[5] represents the great majority of Lebanese Catholics, but in

---

3 Legal document personally signed by the Pope to signify his special interest in reforming a law.

4 One of the largest Eastern-rite communities of the Catholic Church, it is prominent especially in Lebanon, where it traces its origins. The Church developed after the death of St. Maron, a IV century Syrian hermit who lived in the Oronte area, and it built up its theological doctrine and ecclesiastical structure under St. John Maron, the first Maronite patriarch of Antioch (685–707). Under his leadership, the Maronites confronted the Byzantines, who since the Council of Chalcedon (451) had been persecuting Christians still professing allegiance to the authority of the Pope. During that persecution, the Maronites sought refuge in the mountains of Lebanon and became religiously independent, reaffirming their faith in the Catholic theological doctrine and their unity with the Pope under his authority. For these reasons the Maronite Church is the only Eastern-rite community that has no non-Catholic/Orthodox counterpart. Due to the role played during Lebanese history, the community is commonly identified with Catholicism in Lebanon and it has always played a crucial role in the country's political life. Under the Constitution, the President of the Republic must be a Maronite Catholic (Dib 2011).

5 Communities that some centuries ago established full communion with the Pope recognizing Catholic theology and the Pope as supreme head of the church. Each Eastern Catholic Church is called *sui iuris* and the Pope placed them under a special Code of Canonical laws in 1990 (*Codex Canonum Ecclesiarum Orientalium*, CCEO), recognizing autonomy and specificity in some matters, e. g., each Church has its own marriage rite, independent with respect to other Catholic Churches though all accept the supreme principle of indissolubility. Every Eastern Catholic Church is headed by a Patriarch, who governs it, assisted by the synod of the patriarchal Church, comprising all the bishops of that Church. The Patriarch is elected by that Synod and, once elected,

Lebanon five other Catholic Churches are currently represented and officially recognized by the law: Melkite[6], Syriac-Catholic[7], Armenian Catholic Church[8], Chaldean Catholic Church[9] and the Latin Church. At present, all those Churches, which share the principle of indissolubility of matrimonial ties, are facing this problem related to some of their members who decide to convert.

Among the country's five different Orthodox sects, the law officially distinguishes the Greek Orthodox Church[10], Syriac Orthodox Church[11], Armenian Orthodox or Gregorian Church[12], Assyrian Church[13] and Coptic Orthodox

---

only has to notify the Roman Pontiff of the election, who then grants the *ecclesiastica communio*. The Latin Church's 1983 Code of Canon Law (CIC) uses the term "ritual Church *sui iuris*" (canons 111 and 112) and speaks of "a subject of an Eastern rite" (canon 1015 § 2) (Valognes 1994, Carcione 1998, Farrugia 2000).

6 Also called Greek Catholic Church, it belongs to the Byzantine Rite; after the East-West schism in 1054, some Arab-speaking Greek hierarchs accepted communion with the See of Rome in 1729 (see Descy 1993). The Melkite Church is the second largest Catholic community in Lebanon. It is represented by the Parliament's vice President, who must be a Melkite, according to the National Pact, and by some ministers in all cabinets.

7 It belongs to West Syrian rite; in 1782 the Patriarch of the ancient Orthodox Syriac Church declared himself in full communion with the Pope of Rome and established the Patriarch's see in Beirut (Sélis 1988).

8 After the Armenian Apostolic Church broke off communion from the Pope in the V century, in 1740 the Armenian Patriarch and some bishops restored communion and he became the first Armenian Catholic Church Patriarch confirmed by the Pope. During the Armenian Genocide (1915–1918), a large number of Catholic Armenians scattered among neighboring countries, mainly Lebanon, and the community is currently integrated in social, economic and political Lebanese society (Beledian 1997).

9 It originated from the Assyrian Church of the East, a sect living in ancient Assyria. In 1553, the Patriarch entered communion with the Roman Catholic Church, and nowadays this community is increasing its presence in Lebanon because of persecutions suffered in Iraq during recent decades (Le Coz 1995, Teule 2008).

10 The biggest Orthodox sect in Lebanon, it traces its origins back to the Greek-speaking Byzantine domination period, since the 1054 schism. Greek Orthodox people have always lived in Lebanese territory from that period to the present, playing an important role in political life (Assfalg and Krüger 1991).

11 A distinct church since the schism following the Council of Chalcedon, its history is strictly linked to Middle East territories, its liturgical language is the ancient Syriac and it has always had a large community in Lebanon (Guérillot 2008).

12 It was organized after having refused the Council of Chalcedon theological doctrine. It was a national Church but during and after World War I a great number of Orthodox Armenians took refuge in Lebanon, escaping from Turkish mass killings. At present, it is well represented in political, economic, social and religious life in the country, but it maintains close ties with its language and culture (Beledian 1997, Chaillot 2011).

13 Also known as Nestorian Church, it traces its origin to the Mesopotamia area. Its presence in Lebanon was caused by persecution suffered by Assyrian people in modern Iraq, especially during and after World War I and during massive persecution in 1933.

Church[14]. Each sect is governed by its own canonical law regarding the institution of marriage, the formation of matrimonial consent and its dissolution. According to many senior Catholic figures, due to these differences in Church laws, Catholics usually opt to convert to the Syriac Orthodox and Assyrian Churches.

Before considering case studies on this specific question, it is necessary to examine Lebanon's plural and religious-based family law system to establish why the Lebanese have the right to convert to any sect, but not the right to file for divorce in any State court.

## Lebanon's religious-based "personal status" legislation and the right to convert

Lebanese marriages are only subject to religious laws, and Lebanese civil law grants religious authorities absolute jurisdiction to celebrate marriages according to their traditional legal and ritual ceremonies and to judge family law suits according to their own religious array of laws and regulations. This kind of legal system, known as the "Personal Status Law" system (entry *Statut Personnel* in Messner 2010: 666) and established by article 9 of the 1926 Constitution, is based on some core principles.

Firstly, the guarantee given by the State of the exclusive jurisdiction of religious communities in family law matters regarding their members and, as a result, the absence of a civil legislation applicable to all citizens regardless of their religious affiliation (Messarra 2012). This means that a civil code governing the celebration of civil marriages in Lebanon and granting the right to file for divorce to a State court has never been established in the country, either before or after the Independence era. The second core principle is the guarantee of the freedom of faith, proclaimed by the same article 9 of the Constitution. Under this constitutional guarantee, Lebanese citizens enjoy complete freedom of conversion, which means the freedom to change religious affiliation or not to belong to any sect. Consequently, sects' rights and guarantees must be balanced with individuals' rights and guarantees (Rabbath 1982, Basile 1993).

Under this unique national legal system, conversions decided by married couples have always represented a very specific problem in the Lebanese system of justice, from the French mandate's era[15] to the present, because French governments never managed to obtain the approval of laws introducing the institu-

It is possible to say that this Church is one of the smallest sects in the country (Baumer 2006).

[14] It obtained official recognition as "historical sect" by Parliament in 1999, following the increasing number of Coptic Orthodox people who arrived in the country from Egypt.

[15] It was a League of Nations authorized system of control over the former Ottoman territories including modern Syria, Lebanon, Iraq, Jordan, Israel and Palestine territories. The administration of the region under the French was carried out from 1923 to 1946.

tion of civil marriage or limitations on sects' rights and guarantees due to strong and widespread protests backed by all religious authorities in April 1926 against the French authorities, who approved a rule limiting the jurisdiction of religious personal status judges (Weiss 2010: 110–111).

As a result, the *Arrêté* [rules] approved from 1936 to 1939 during the French mandate merely regulated the official recognition of eighteen different religious sects and the right to change religious affiliation, in the case of married couples and individual single or married citizens (Mahmassani et al. 1970).

It is necessary to point out that those rules still apply to the right of conversion, even if on April 2, 1951 Parliament also approved a new rule on non-Muslim (Christian and Jewish) family laws and the courts' jurisdiction (Gannagé 2001: 41–42, 52–53).

Since the law of 1951 did not repeal the *arrêté* number 60 L.R. 1936, the religious authority that celebrated the marriage maintains jurisdiction to determine the breakdown or dissolution of the bond, even if one of the parties has converted to another faith. If both have converted, however, jurisdiction is granted to the new community.

Article 11 of the 1936 decree number 60 LR[16] concerns the citizen's right to convert and establishes that all 18 year old Lebanese citizens have the right to change their religious affiliation, regardless of religious rules applicable in the sect they belong to. As a result, for example, this *arrêté* entitled the Muslim Lebanese to convert, even if strictly prohibited by Islamic rules.[17]

At the same time, article 23 of this decree prescribed that married people have the right to change religious affiliation but, if the spouses do not agree about the conversion, the marriage remains under the laws of the sect whose authorities celebrated the ceremony. Consequently, in the case of a request to dissolve the union, if a Catholic priest celebrated the marriage then, a Catholic court maintains jurisdiction over issuing a judgment on dissolution of the tie, even if one of the spouses has converted to a non-Catholic Church or to Islam. In this way, the lawmaker intended to protect the principle of certainty of the law and the position of the spouse who did not intend to change faith.

Court of Cassation judgments have usually relied on this article to invalidate any divorce judgment issued by any religious court of a sect different from the one that celebrated the marriage. Due to those kinds of verdicts, regularly upheld by the Lebanese Supreme Court, unilateral conversions to Orthodox Churches

---

[16] This decree recognizes the communities among Lebanese and Syrian territories, calling them "historical sects".

[17] It had great importance in protecting the freedom of the individual because it deprived the religious authorities of the power to prevent acts of conversion, only giving registrars the power to accept the declarations of conversion made in accordance with the prescribed formal requirements. These prescriptions concerned the presence of two witnesses and the presentation of a letter of acceptance from the authority of the new confession.

are rarely confirmed because Supreme Court judgments reaffirm Catholic jurisdiction to pronounce on marriage dissolution.[18]

On the other hand, according to this *Arrêté*, if a couple decide to convert and then decide to end the wedlock, the act of marriage signed under the law of the first sect they belonged to has to be subject to the laws of the new one chosen by the couple. Therefore, the authorities of the new sect obtain jurisdiction to pronounce on the end of the union according to their own rules.

Once again, the lawmaker's aim was to maintain the certainty of the law and the stability of the marriage bond, recognizing that the expression of the will of the family was identified in the couple's decision to submit personal and family life to a new legislation (Basile 1993).

Without the option of a civil law, the Lebanese legal system has reduced the broad spectrum of personal freedoms to the single freedom of conversion from one faith to another, excluding the freedom to not believe. According to several authors, this aspect characterizes the Lebanese legal system as a confessional one (Hadair 2011).

The lack of a civil law gives the Lebanese the opportunity to evaluate different religious personal status laws to find one less rigid in granting a divorce. Thus, this lack of a legal freedom to have no religious affiliation creates the trend towards conversions from Catholicism to Orthodoxy.

Among the matters included in personal status laws, the institution of marriage plays a key role because State law recognizes the confessional competence not only with regard to the celebration and the dissolution of the bond, but also to the determination of property relations between spouses and child custody.

## Differences in Catholic and Orthodox Church marriage doctrines and conversion case studies

A brief analysis of the principal differences between Catholic and Orthodox marriage doctrines allows us to understand some key points, also explained by those couples involved in this kind of conversions.

Above all, people seeking for a way to end their marriage that choose to convert to an Orthodox Church express their willingness to remain under Christian Churches' authority. In fact, as explained below, Lebanese Catholic men could take advantage of a unilateral conversion to a Muslim sect in order to end the matrimonial bond. Indeed, in granting men the right to have more than one wife,

---

[18] Only in case of male unilateral conversion from Catholicism to Islam, even if the Supreme Court invalidates the recognition of divorce issued by the Islamic court, Islamic rules grant men the right to have more than one wife. Consequently, even if the man remains officially married to his first Catholic wife, he has the legitimate right to marry other women, according to Islamic law.

those communities provide the possibility of remaining legally married to the first, Catholic, wife and at the same time to have other marriages.

Those Lebanese who decide to join Orthodox Churches are aware that in case of unilateral conversion the Court of Cassation would reject their conversion and would restore the prior Catholic tie. Consequently, since monogamy is a core legal principle for both Catholic and Orthodox Churches, no Orthodox authority would grant men the right to marry another woman.

Thus, conversions into Orthodox communities are always shared by the couple who usually seek personal status laws that are less strict on matrimonial matters.

Under the Catholic rules, three essential properties define the sacramental marriage: indissolubility, uniqueness and procreation. In fact, under the Catholic doctrine the sacramental nature of marriage sanctioned by Christ prevents any human authority from dissolving a valid bond; the judgment of the competent ecclesiastical tribunal can recognize the nullity *ex tunc* if at the time of the exchange of consent at least one of the parties failed to comply with one or more essential conditions or if it was not free to consent to the marriage. Marriages annulled under the Catholic ecclesiastical courts are considered void *ab initio* [at the beginning], meaning that the marriage was invalid from the beginning in both its religious and civil effects.[19]

As already mentioned, the principal difference between Catholic and Orthodox matrimonial doctrines is the provision for the institution of canonical divorce. Orthodox Churches ground it in the principle of *Oikonomia* [economy], which means the attention to concrete circumstances in people's lives, in order to help in situations in which the marriage has irretrievably failed.

According to this principle, the matrimonial doctrine of these churches includes the possibility of a declaration of divorce by the local Bishop, through which a divorced individual can remarry. The principle of *Oikonomia* provides the opportunity to obtain two canonical divorces, thus to contract three marriages before ecclesiastical authority.

*Oikonomia* has become the Orthodox juridical principle best known to those Catholic couples interested in ending their marriage but saving their Christian affiliation.

Looking at the grounds for canonical divorce admitted by the various Orthodox Churches, the majority of Catholics adhere to the Syriac and Assyrian

---

[19] Grounds for nullity include: simulation of consent by either or both of the contracting parties to one or all of the essential requirements of marriage, deliberate deceit about some personal quality that can objectively and gravely perturb conjugal life, conditional consent, force imposed on a person to obtain their consent, a serious lack of discretion of judgment at consent concerning the essential matrimonial rights and obligations and mental incapacity at consent to take on the essential obligations of marriage (Code of Canon of Latin Church, canons 1101–1103, 1095, 1098; Code of Canon of the Eastern Catholic Church, canon 863).

Churches because their canonical laws grant the largest number of dissolution causes: first of all adultery, but also when one spouse repeatedly enjoins the other to not frequent a ill-reputed place or interact with persons of ill-repute; when the wife spends the night outside the marital home in a place of ill repute; and when the husband after the marriage ceremony discovers his wife was not a virgin.

Interviewees and cases reported by lawyers express the idea that adultery is one of the most frequent causes of conversions from Catholicism: in one case, after few months of marriage, the husband discovered his wife's adultery and together they decided to convert to the Syriac Orthodox Church, knowing that their Catholic court would never have declared the annulment of their marriage. According to this point of view, if Catholic laws gave the right to the betrayed spouse to be liberated from the indissolubility of the bond, the number of conversions from Catholicism would notably decrease.[20]

Moreover, in the opinion of many lawyers, domestic violence is also a cause of conversions: usually if a Catholic woman wishes to sever all ties with her husband, she cannot petition for a Catholic annulment sentence because violence is not grounds for annulment under Catholic rules. According to some nongovernmental organizations that investigated the Lebanese personal status law system, of 14 annulment cases in 2010 referring to "domestic violence" as the motivation, the judge recognized the nullity of the marriage solely in one case (Human Rights Watch: 2015).

It is necessary to underline that in those cases Catholic laws granted the separation of corps, which allows the betrayed woman to leave the family house; consequently, the separation obliges the man to provide economically for the wife and children, even if he looses the possibility to maintain legal custody over them. Moreover, separation of corps could be granted without a time limit, and, according to Catholic authorities, it is a way to stop domestic violence, safeguarding women and children and breaking up every conjugal contact, moreover maintaining the sacramental value of marriage.[21] This could be considered a sufficient way to protect betrayed women from their husbands, according also to the new law on domestic violence approved by Parliament one year ago.

A third cause of Catholic conversions is criticism of the excessively long court procedures, usually lasting more than one year. In contrast, an Orthodox Bishop's ecclesiastical divorce sentences are quicker, giving the chance to remarry and start a new life in a short time. This problem was reported by some informants (lawyers and university professors), though from the ecclesiastical authorities' point of view it is justified by the need to interview the spouses, at least three witnesses and, if necessary, hear a psychologist or a doctor as an ex-

---

[20] Personal communication from a Lebanese Catholic Bishop, May 2014.

[21] Personal communication from a judge at a Catholic Court, March 2014, Beirut.

pert witness.[22] Moreover, Catholic procedure grants the right to appeal, which, according to ecclesiastical authorities, is an essential guarantee in order to be sure about marriage annulment, whereas the spouses view it as a hindrance to ending the bond and starting a new marriage.

Some Catholic couples declared that, in the case of short-lived unions, they would simply like to forget their "mistake" and have the chance to marry again soon.[23] On the other hand, Catholics sometimes petition for an annulment sentence when the spouse has left the family home years ago. As reported by ecclesiastical authorities and nongovernmental agencies, at times men who go to work abroad decide to form a new family there while the first wife, in order to avoid the husband's conversion to Islam, agrees to convert to an Orthodox Church and file for divorce under the clause referring to a spouse's long absence from the family home (Human Rights Watch: 2015).

Of course, all these justifications are not actually linked to a genuine religious desire to embrace an Orthodox faith; this is why they have important consequences both for civil law and in the relations between Catholic and Orthodox Churches.

Regarding civil consequences, informants generally agree in defining these conversions as truly "fraudulent", because when an act of conversion is formally entered in civil registers people have to declare their sincere affiliation to the new faith.

A crucial point in case is a judgment issued in 1955 by the Lebanese Court of Cassation, the authority called upon to settle conflicts between the jurisdictions of various religious courts. The Court voided the divorce judgment issued by a Greek Orthodox Bishop in the case of a couple that converted from the Maronite Church just five days before submitting a petition for divorce to the Greek Orthodox authority. The Court underlined that any conversion stemming from nonreligious motivations was a fraud.

Informants largely agree with this point of view, stating that the Court of Cassation should have persevered with those kinds of sentences in order to ensure the citizens' full and sincere respect of civil law. However, it is necessary to underline that, after that sentence, the Court stopped rejecting those kinds of conversions. According to Melkite authorities, the trend is increasing year by year and the Court could not reject the growing number of conversions.

Due to the difficulties in obtaining official information from registrars about this kind of conversion, it was only possible to obtain some information from

---

[22] Personal communication from a judge at a Catholic Court, March 2014, Beirut.

[23] Personal communication from a Maronite woman in Beirut, May 2014.

the Baabda[24] civil register: over the last twenty-five years, about fifty Catholic couples convert to Syriac Orthodoxy each year and forty to the Assyrian one.[25]

Regarding the Orthodox authorities, even if it was not possible to interview them directly, family law experts and lawyers reported that the official ecclesiastical standing usually points to the freedom to convert and to the impossibility of knowing the intimate reasons of couples that ask to join Orthodox communities.

Catholic authorities, on the other hand, generally underline that those conversions create serious obstacles to ecumenical dialogue, explaining that non-genuine conversion is a serious sin under Church doctrine and that Orthodox authorities endorsing these procedures respect neither civil nor religious laws. The latter, in fact, accentuate the rifts between the Christian communities and encourage people to belong to a Church not as a religious choice linked to sincere religious feelings, but merely as a means to obtain personal advantages at the juridical level. For this reason, in December 2013 the Maronite Patriarch, Bechara Butrous Rai, denounced this trend. This was the clearest and strongest stance ever taken against this trend by the highest Catholic authority in Lebanon. As reported in the press, Patriarch Rai, addressing a delegation of judges from religious courts visiting him, stated "Every lawyer who helps a married couple to convert in order to divorce them is banned from representing cases in religious courts" (Mroueh 2013).

The strategy chosen by Maronite authorities is addressed specifically to lawyers because every single Church has the right to create a register of lawyers admitted to its own religious courts. Therefore, if any lawyer does not respect Catholic rules relating to sincere conversion, ecclesiastical authorities have the right to ban their access to Catholic courts.

This strong stance of the Catholic ecclesiastical authorities is undoubtedly motivated by the desire to preserve the authentic reasons of personal faith that should guide any conversion and to prevent that such a serious act full of consequences at the religious level may be used to obtain personal or family advantages. The religious authorities also underline the significant differences between the Catholic doctrine and the Orthodox theological doctrines, although still within the Christian sphere.

However, this trend in the ecclesiastical hierarchies appears to contrast with the position expressed by the faithful at the centre of these conversions.

This increasing practice of shifting from one Church to another, indeed, appears to portray a rather "lay" use of Christian religious persuasion, which seems to be reflected in the phenomenon of a more general secularization of the Lebanese Christian communities. This phenomenon can also be seen in the increasing number of Catholic and Orthodox Christians who choose to celebrate

---

[24] Capital town of Baabda district in Mount Lebanon governorate, it has a mainly Maronite population of 500000. As of 2005 elections, Baabda has six seats allocated in the Parliament: three Maronites, one Shi'a Muslim and one Druze.

[25] Personal communication from a Catholic ecclesiastical authority.

their weddings abroad as civil ceremonies, as laid down by Article 25 of the *Arrêté*, which only authorizes citizens of the Christian faith to enter into civil marriages abroad.[26]

Furthermore, key informants point out that a growing number of couples feel that they cannot, in conscience, adhere completely to the Catholic doctrine of marriage; therefore, while they formally enter into a religious marriage and refuse the option of a civil wedding abroad, they are ready to find any lawful way out if the marriage fails.

Personal religious beliefs thus become a secondary factor so that in cases where the regulations of the Catholic Church, in which the marriage was contracted, conflict with personal and family life choices, conversion within the Christian Churches is seen as the solution that allows people to safeguard their new life choices and their Christian identity alike. By converting and obtaining an ecclesiastical divorce, the parties have the possibility of creating new, but still Christian, families.

Remaining in the Christian faith, therefore, is the second crucial element in choosing to convert in a society and state structure whose main dividing line of confessional belonging still lies between "Christian communities" and "Muslim communities".

This is why these changes in inter-Christian religious affiliation should also be read as evidence of the couples' desire to maintain their Christian identity and create a new family while remaining within the faith. Indeed, as is evident in some interviews carried out in the country and in numerous studies, a couples' decision to join the Assyrian Church is mainly motivated by the greater ease in obtaining an ecclesiastical divorce according to the rules of that Church.

It should not be forgotten that the constitutionally guaranteed freedom of conversion also allows inter-religious movement, i. e. from Christianity to Islam (and vice-versa). In this context it should be noted that, while there is no official data, there are cases of inter-religious conversions originating from matrimonial problems: of these, the most complex ones relate to the husband's unilateral conversion. Indeed, in addition to gaining the right to contract up to three further unions without divorcing the first Catholic wife, the husband can validly end this first marriage via the unilateral act of repudiation. In this case, the act is considered valid by the husband's new community but has no juridical relevance in the law of the Catholic community that had celebrated the marriage.

These cases open up wide-ranging problems regarding inheritance, when the heirs of the husband who has converted are his wives of different religious con-

[26] These unions remain subject to the body of legislation of the countries in which they are celebrated, even if the parties decide to proceed before the Lebanese civil judge to end them.

fessions, married before and after his conversion, because difference in religion is an impediment to the recognition of the status of heir.[27]

Furthermore, since the father's conversion tacitly implies the conversion of children who are minors, this event also significantly modifies the awarding of custody of the offspring: it should only be remembered that the law in force for the Muslim communities awards custody to the Muslim spouse.

These conversions, therefore, create strong tensions between communities and represent even more serious challenges to the multi-confessional system than the inter-Christian ones. They occur in a society in which relationships between Christians and Muslims still feel the effects of fifteen years of fierce civil war and in a political system still structured on the basis of prevalently confession-based political parties, which are incapable of fully implementing the removal of the confessional quota system for access to public office and public administration, as provided for by the reform of Article 95 of the Constitution established by the Taif Agreement in 1990.

It will be particularly interesting to assess how the institution of the so-called "shorter process" provided for in the very recent *Motu Proprio* promulgated by Pope Francis on September 8, 2015 will affect the cases of inter-Christian conversions in the light of the acceleration of the marriage annulment process that it is intended to guarantee. This streamlining could become a valid alternative to conversion to the Orthodox Churches for couples whose marriage is "manifestly null".

## Conclusion

According to people involved in this kind of conversion, it is necessary to underline that almost all of them agree that if civil divorce had been allowed under Lebanese civil law nobody would have considered the option of shifting from Catholicism to Orthodoxy.[28]

This is why even though the great majority of Catholic authorities strongly disagrees with any proposal regarding the introduction of civil marriage and di-

[27] The Court of Cassation (March 13, 2001), as competent Court in cases of conflicts of competence between different religious tribunals, has had to pronounce on cases of inheritance contested by families of different religions originating from marriages contracted by a man who had converted from a Christian Church to a Muslim community. The Court has always recognized that both families enjoyed the status of heirs, as the unilateral conversion of one spouse does not imply the dissolution of the first bond contracted according to the rules of the Christian confession they belonged to. Those verdicts have significantly affected the debate between the experts on the subject.

[28] Personal communication from two Maronite and Melkite couples who joined the Syriac Orthodox Church, in Beirut, May 2014. See also Human Rights Watch, 2015: 50–65. On civil marriages, see also Karam 2006.

vorce into the Lebanese legal system, a few of them, like Father George Massouh, do agree, and justify their point of view by explaining that civil marriage would solve the problem of false conversions entirely.[29] In his opinion, in fact, if only genuinely faithful Catholic chose religious marriage, they would accept the Catholic doctrine entirely and, in case of a request for annulment, they would wait for one.

It is possible to state that this kind of conversion is one of the most significant consequences of the lack of real State control over the ancient Lebanese personal status laws system. Therefore, if Parliament should ratify a law on civil marriage perhaps people would stop resorting to this practice of "non-religious conversions". This leads us to highlight that this problem is only one facet of a more significant one relating to State control over the family law system. At the moment, this represents one of the more complex challenges in Lebanon's political life because it is related to the relationship between civil and religious powers and to the profound role that religious affiliation has always played as the core personal identity in the great majority of Lebanese society, and above all among Lebanese politicians in Lebanon's history both past and present.

Nevertheless, one can fully understand the complexities inherent in Parliament's approval of legislation on the civil form of marriage just by considering the clear-cut refusal expressed towards the argument, since the time of the mandate, by the authorities of all the Muslim communities officially recognized by Lebanese law.

Indeed, State control of family law conflicts with Koranic rules, which include this branch of law among those directly governed by God.

As evidence of this, the law that guarantees Lebanese citizens the freedom to enter into civil marriages abroad is specifically limited to Christians.

At present, therefore, the opposition expressed by the various religious authorities, albeit in different forms, and the objective use of religious affiliation in the political-legislative sphere by the parties and members of parliament combine to make approval of a law on the subject particularly unlikely.

If at the State law level we cannot perceive developments that could solve the entire issue, including the problem of false inter-Christian conversions, the most significant new developments would then appear to be concentrated at the level of Catholic canonical law. It will be particularly interesting to see if and to what extent the modifications introduced by the *Motu Proprio* promulgated by Pope Francis on September 8, 2015 will be able to stem the conversions to the Orthodox Churches.

---

[29] In 2013, the Director of the Center for Christian-Muslim Studies at the University of Balamand told the press that after their civil marriage a faithful couple could get married in church (http://www.thefreelibrary.com/Rai+denounces+conversion+for+divorce,+but+Catholics+afforded+few...a0353536413).

Bibliography

Al-Jamil, Mikhael (2009): *Statuto personale della "gente del libro" e autorità patriarcale nella città islamica. Studio storico-giuridico sul "berat" concesso al Patriarca dei siro-cattolici Pietro Jarwé.* Rome: Serafica.

Arroba, Conde and Manuel, Jesus (1996): *Diritto processuale canonico.* Rome: EDURCLA.

Assfalg, Julius and Krüger, Paul (1991): *Petit dictionnaire de l'Orient chrétien.* Turnhout: Brepols.

Basile, Basile (1993): *Statut personnel et compétence judiciaire des communautés confessionnelles au Liban: étude juridique comparée.* Kaslik: Université Saint-Esprit.

Baumer, Christoph (2006): *The Church of the East, an Illustrated History of Assyrian Christianity.* London, New York: I. B. Tauris.

Beledian, Krikor (1997): *Les Arméniens.* Turnhout: Brepols.

Carcione, Filippo (1998): *Le Chiese d'oriente. Identità, patrimonio e quadro storico generale.* Cinisello Balsamo: San Paolo.

Chaillot, Christine (2011): *Vie et spiritualité des Églises orthodoxes orientales des traditions syriaque, arménienne, copte et éthiopienne.* Paris: Le Cerf.

Corm, Georges (1998): *Histoire du pluralisme religieux dans le bassin méditerranéen.* Paris: Geuthner.

Descy, Serge (1993): *The Melkite Church: an Historical and Ecclesiological Approach.* Boston: Sophia Press.

Dib, Pierre (2001): *Histoire des Maronites: L'église maronite du XVI^e^ siècle à nos jours,* Vol. 3. Beirut: Librairie Orientale.

Farrugia, Edward (2000): *Dizionario enciclopedico dell'oriente cristiano.* Roma: Pontificio Istituto Orientale.

Gannagé, Pierre (2001): *Le pluralisme des statuts personnels dans les états multicommunautaires – Droit libanais et droits proche-orientaux.* Beirut: Presses de l'Université Saint-Joseph.

Girgis, Raimondo (2004): *I Matrimoni misti nelle situazioni particolari delle Chiese Patriarcali Cattoliche.* Beirut: Dar el Machreq.

Greene, Molly (2005): *Minorities in the Ottoman Empire.* Princeton: Marcus Weiner.

Guérillot, Claude (2008): *L'Église d'Antioche Syriaque Orthodoxe. Une Église martyre.* Paris: Véga.

Karam, Karam (2006): *Le mouvement civil au Liban.* Paris, Aix-en-Provence: Karthala-IREMAM.

Hadair, Wafaa (2011): *La dimension religieuse dans le mariage au Liban*. PhD Thesis, Université Montpellier I, Faculté de Droit et Science Politique – Université Libanaise Ecole Doctorale de Droit et des Sciences Politiques, Administratives et Economiques.

Human Rights Watch Dossier (2015): *Unequal and Unprotected: Women's Rights Under Lebanese Personal Status Laws.* URL: https://www.hrw.org/

report/2015/01/19/unequal-and-unprotected/womens-rights-under-lebanese-personal-status-laws, accessed on 17.12.2015.

Le Coz, Raymond (1995): *Histoire de l'Église d'Orient (Chrétiens d'Irak, d'Iran et de Turquie)*. Paris: Cerf.

Mahmassani, Maher et al. (1970): *Statut personnel: textes en vigueur au Liban*. Beirut: Sirey.

Messarra, Antoine (2012): *Théorie juridiques des régime parlementaires mixtes*. Beirut: Librairie Orientale.

Messner, Francis (2010): *Dictionnaire de droit des religions*. Paris: CNRS.

Mroueh, Wassim (2013, December 21): *Rai Denounces Conversion for Divorce, but Catholics Afforded Few Choices*. In: The Daily Star. URL: http://www.dailystar.com.lb/ accessed on 17.12.2015.

Rabbath, Edmond (1982): *La Constitution libanaise: origines, textes et commentaires*. Beirut: Publications de l'Université libanaise.

Sélis, Claude (1988): *Les Syriens orthodoxes et catholiques*. Turnhout: Brepols.

Teule, Herman (2008): *Les Assyro-Chaldéens. Chrétiens d'Irak, d'Iran et de Turquie*. Turnhout: Brepols.

Valognes, J. Pierre (1994): *Vie et mort des Chrétiens d'Orient*. Mesnl-sur-l'Estrée, Paris: Fayard.

Weiss, Max (2010): *In the Shadow of Sectarianism*. Harvard: Harvard University Press.

# Epilogue: Illusions of Universal Modernity and Delusions of Global Secularization

*Christian Giordano*

This volume, though its title may not point it up explicitly, centres on religious identities that evidently can be cloaked in ethnic discourses. On this point, the natural question is why has religion become such a crucial issue not just in the geographical area examined in this volume: a place where religions, thus also identities, have been known to coexist for several centuries and even more often clash.

We need to ask ourselves, therefore, why religion, contrary to the opinions and predictions of distinguished social scientists, has returned peremptorily to the centre of the global stage. Accordingly, the case studies presented in this volume offer far more than an interesting albeit abstruse and nowadays unusual ethnographic collection. Beyond theoretic conjectures on the obsolescence of religions, these case studies provide empirically verified evidence of what may be defined as the significance and perhaps even the resurgence of religiosity in today's world.

Consequently, we need to pinpoint the misjudgement or, better yet, the lack of perception of most part of the social sciences that have focused on the Euro-American Occident and its evolution in modernity. This teleological process guides Western societies along the path to modernity as the ultimate goal or, better yet, the final stage of a more or less rigid evolutional development.

The evolutionist conception of the world is widely known to be an outcome of Enlightenment, which originated in the second half of the 18th century in western Europe (especially in France, Great Britain and partially in Germany, Italy and even in the most Catholic Spain) as well as the United States though to a lesser degree (consider personalities such as Benjamin Franklin and Thomas Jefferson). This optimistic and in a way millenarianist vision of social development envisaged a final goal for all societies, which would later become known as the stage of modernity.

According to this conception of universal development, clearly not all societies have the same development modalities and pace, thus some societies are more advanced than others are. Nevertheless, eventually all societies will reach the final goal because this urge for development is inherent to human nature as well as induced by societies and nations reckoned more culturally and socially developed. We need only mention France's notorious and by now utterly discredited *mission civilisatrice* as a colonialist power in the countries it controlled, especially in Africa. Rejected towards the end of the Algerian War even by a conservative politician such as Charles de Gaulle, the *mission civilisatrice* was a political and cultural strategy aimed at spreading and imposing the *founding* values, the *sacred* ideals and finally the *good* practices of the French Revolution and its Jacobinism on the colonized societies, such as Lebanon and Syria as well. However, the export of these Western values cannot be ascribed to France alone since Great Britain, Germany and Italy (during its relatively brief period of colonial domination) and ultimately even the United States have resorted to very similar strategies. On this point, consider George W. Bush's renowned *spread out democracy* in the Middle East, which has triggered so many of the current humanitarian and sociopolitical crises.

In this epilogue we will not discuss whether these conceptions stemming directly from Enlightenment and Jacobinism have been domination strategies pure and simple as well as convenient ones; it is such a given that any further discussion seems redundant. Moreover, it would lead us far away from our intent; namely, to uncover the illusion of universalizing, thus also of exporting modernity at a global level.

That said, we will discuss the other components that characterize Western modernity as a universal paradigm since we also need to ask ourselves whether there may be several or, better yet, multiple modernities, thus culturally-related and specific ones as Israeli sociologist Shmuel N. Eisenstadt rightly upholds (Eisenstadt 2002).

Consequently, we first need to underscore that it would be illusory to believe that modernity is universal and that all societies hanker for that final goal proposed by nineteenth-century theorists of evolutionism, albeit it is still and always lurking in Western culture's collective subconscious. Skimming through most newspapers articles, even renowned and authoritative ones, be it a highbrow political analysis or the local news we are bound to come across stereotypes created by Auguste Comte, Herbert Spencer etc.

In practice, nearly all social sciences, but especially sociology and political sciences, have been beguiled by the Enlightenment-derived evolutionism. This was plausible in the context of the 19$^{th}$ century, at the highpoint of the Occident's power and credibility. One can even make sense of the post-WW II evolutionist optimism when the so-called *Theories of Modernization* (Lerner etc.) were devised. These overly optimistic and superficial theories envisioned a rapid change that would lead those societies deemed underdeveloped of the then *Third World* to socioeconomic and political conditions conceivably on a par with those of the empowered Occident or at least to similar or comparable conditions.

Despite the obvious nonfulfillment of the *Theories of Modernization,* this rather overconfident but illusory optimism still reverberates affecting specific theoretic conceptions regarding present-day globalization processes. We need only mention the book *The End of History* (Fukuyama 1992) and several other similar texts published by respected reviews and newspapers, such as *The National Interest* (Summer 1989), *The Wall Street Journal* (October 5, 2001 and June 6, 2014) *The Guardian* (April 4, 2007) and *The Washington Post* (August 6, 2006 and August 24, 2008), in which Francis Fukuyama, after the fall of the Berlin wall and the dissolution of the Soviet Union, enthuses over a bright globalized future, thus a sort of happy ending of Western modernity at a global level. The oddity is that Fukuyama, with some success too, continues to spread his theoretic vision.

These succinct observations already point to this scenario's deceptiveness since the universalism inherent to the above-mentioned theories works on the assumption of a permanent equality amongst human beings. Nobody challenges the fact that regardless of race and gender all individuals are equal; still, we need to bear in mind that individuals live in highly different societies and cultures. Society and culture are not an irremovable straitjacket imposed on mankind. Every society, however, has its specific historical capital that represents the core of what German historian Reinhart Koselleck defined as a group's *space of experience* (Koselleck 1979). In turn, this collective *space of experience* influences, though does not determine, the *horizon of expectation* (Koselleck 1979). In specific societies, the *horizon of expectation* mirrors the *space of experience,* whereas in others the *horizon of expectation* is conceived as an alternative, i.e. as something substantially different from the *space of experience.*

In the first case, the *horizon of expectation*, i. e. the interpretation and construction of the present as well as plans for the future, is a more or less accurate though never identical reproduction of the *space of experience.* In some ways, the present and the future are a rational and not fatalistic reaffirmation of the past. In the second case, the *horizon of expectation* is constructed in alternative to the *space of experience.* In the first case, because of negative past experiences this type of society tends to be rationally sceptic about radical changes, which may turn out to be catastrophic. In the second case, instead, societies aim to bring about even radical changes to their internal social, economic and political relations because they want to achieve a new order, different from the one inherent to their *space of experience.*

These few observations already highlight that a sociological and anthropological universalism is a pipe dream because at a global level some societies will be more open to changes, even radical ones, whereas others will be more reluctant to give up their past as well as their traditions. We ought to underscore that both types of societies have a specific rationality. Therefore, the distinction between modern societies open to change and closed societies, i. e. traditional and conservative ones, which underpins the *theories of modernization,* is nonsensical. Thanks to Koselleck's (1979) theoretic approach, various forms of rationality can be envisaged, one of these being modernization, which presupposes a specific type of rationality along with several others. Thus, a sociological and anthropological analysis requires a reasonable comparative relativism that should not be compounded with sweeping contentions of ethical relativism.

There is yet another important dimension inherent to the concept of unilinear evolution, progress, modernization and its final goal, i. e. modernity.

We are referring to the notion of laïcité, famously an ideological cornerstone of the French Revolution and to this day one of the fundamental characteristics of the French republican State and of other national political entities strictly or loosely based on the French model.

Broadly speaking, laïcité is the affirmation of a group, a nation or a society's independence from any religious conditioning; moreover, it presupposes a specific culture that believes in the positive qualities inherent to each individual, hence where individualism is intrinsically a positive value. Human beings have the power to self-determine themselves, thus to better themselves in keeping with the enlightenment principles of freedom, respect, tolerance, brotherhood and more in general of progress. Consequently, this is an optimistic and positive vision of mankind, seen as capable of being constructive and of shaping its own destiny.

The important aspect, especially with reference to this book's general theme, is that by the principle of laïcité human beings deem they no longer need to limit their individual freedom in accordance with a creed's teachings. However, there is also a more radical version of laïcité, often known as secularism as in the French State. Accordingly, secularism at a state level aims to exclude from the public sphere, not least from the public debate, any religion-related issue especially if endorsed by official representatives of religious confessions deemed backward if not indeed anti-state.

Yet, laïcité is not achieved instantly as it is the outcome of a definitely ineluctable process, but one that can be very long in the making. This evolution is often known as secularization: a process by which religions, along with their institutions and their corresponding ethical and moral codes, lose their significance, hence their political influence as well. Secularization does not imply a denial of religion's influential role, but rather a relativist approach to its role in the unavoidable sociopolitical and mental process linked to evolution and progress.

Secularization has unquestionably been regarded as a cornerstone of the process known as modernization, especially by sociology, political science and philosophy as well. In fact, according to these outlooks secularization frees mankind from obsolete representations such as *sin, redemption, deliverance, paradise, hell, apocalypse* etc. Therefore, secularization is an epoch-making social and cultural change grounded in values deemed universal such as freedom, equality and solidarity, thus it paves the way to a political framework based on democracy, common good and psychophysical well-being. Consequently, secularization is a fundamental phenomenon that ensures the passage to a stage of humanity to which mankind naturally aspires.

According to Max Weber, secularization is above all *Entzauberung der Welt,* i.e. *disenchantment of the world* (Weber 1919). By this, he expressed the idea that secularization goes hand in hand with having confidence or, better yet, faith in the soundness and effectiveness of technical means and rational assessments rather than in magical-religious practices. Therefore, this is firstly a process of intellectualization and rationalization of knowledge. Always a sceptic however, Weber regarded the *disenchantment of the world,* along with its accompanying secularization process that called into question several magical-religious tenets, as a very specific development associated with Western societies, namely those few Euro-American nations that came in touch with the Enlightenment. As mentioned above, this involves a small number of societies located in the European continent's west plus the United States.

Another very important point is that Weber, unlike the Enlightenment thinkers, the theorists of modernization and the more radical universalists, did not believe in a process of *disenchantment of the world,* i. e. a worldwide diffusion of secularization. I need to stress that Weber viewed the *disenchantment of the world* and secularization more from a relativist stance, i. e. as very limited phenomena both socially and geographically, thus not a generalizable one. This approach, in my view a sceptical one, strengthens the Weberian argumentation, thus sidesteps the glib universalistic generalizations critiqued above.

Max Weber, however, did not foresee, and probably it was impossible to foresee at the time, that the *disenchantment of the world* actually emerged only in some rather circumscribed sectors of exact science. In everyday life, it has surfaced only occasionally. In present-day's alleged postmodernity or late modernity, the structures of collective thought and unitary action strategies are no longer present; everything is rather fragmented, fluid, volatile and contradictory (Bauman 2000). For the time being, there are no single and definitive certainties as the ones dictated by the metaphysics of the past or by the previously mentioned classic modernization theories.

Secularization, therefore, has remained an unfinished torso, whereas religion in the Western world, from which it should have disappeared or at least play a subordinate role, is nonetheless a fundamental component of society and of collective identities. Given the current variety of options available, perhaps it would be better to speak of religion in its plural form.

After reading this volume's chapters, I realized the importance of religion in the various societies examined by the authors even though not all deal specifically with religious themes. This may lead to view these human collectivities as traditional or, worse still, less advanced, whereas we should assume the opposite; namely, that these societies antedate the Western ones, thus they have a far more insightful and ingrained social knowledge and social wisdom. Accordingly, to avoid by now hackneyed or utterly flawed analytical schemes that would play up the theme of the social and cultural backwardness of the region this book focuses on, my intent was to reverse this perspective. Therefore, I aimed to show that ultimately what goes by the name of civilized Occident, a rough approximation at best to be taken with a generous pinch of salt, is not that distinctive and specific despite modernization processes that should have showcased its supremacy.

## Bibliography

Bauman, Zygmunt (2000): *Liquid Modernity.* Cambridge: Polity Press.

Eisenstadt, Shmuel N. (ed.) (2002): *Multiple Modernities*. New Brunswick: Transaction Press.

Fukuyama, Francis (1992): *Trust. The Social Virtues and the Creation of Prosperity*. New York: Free Press Paperbacks.

Koselleck, Reinhart (1979): *Vergangene Zukunft. Zur Semantik geschichtlicher Zeiten* [Future Past. On the Semantic of Historical Time]. Frankfurt am Main: Suhrkamp Verlag.

Weber, Max (1919): Wissenschaft als Beruf [Science as a Vocation]. In: Max Weber (ed.): Vier Vorträge vor dem Freistudentischen Bund. München, Leipzig: Duncker & Humblot.

# Authors

**Tamar Antadze** is a PhD student at Ivane Javakhishvili Tbilisi State University, Georgia, and invited lecturer at Tbilisi State Medical University where she teaches Medical Anthropology. She is program manager at the NGO "Center for Civil Integration and Interethnic relations" where she works on integration and education of ethnic minorities. Her research focuses on the integration processes of ethnic minorities (Ninotsminda region, Georgia), education, health and inequality of ethno-religious minorities, and cross-border relationships.

**Zehra Nurdan Atalay Güneş** is Assistant Professor at Mardin Artuklu University, Turkey, since 2013. She holds a PhD in Sociology from the Middle East Technical University, Ankara, Turkey, and previously worked as research assistant (Middle East Technical University until 2002 and Mardin Artuklu University until 2012). She teaches Methodology, Academic Writing, Contemporary Sociological Theories and Economic Sociology at both undergraduate and graduate levels. Her research interest includes qualitative methodology and financial sociology (financial citizenship practices in Turkey).

**Kayhan Delibaş** is Professor of Sociology and Head of the Department of Sociology at the Adnan Menderes University, Turkey. He is Honorary Research Associate at the University of Kent, UK and part-time Lecturer at the Izmir University of Economics, Turkey. He earned his PhD in Sociology from the University of Kent. His area of research involves political sociology (Islamic movements, political parties and participation, grassroots activism, theories of secularization), identity, religion and citizenship in Turkey and the Middle East as well as risk society, trust and rumours.

**Christian Giordano** is Professor of Social Anthropology at the University of Fribourg, Switzerland. He holds a PhD in Sociology (University of Heidelberg, Germany) and a doctorate honoris causa awarded by the University of Timisoara, Romania. He is Permanent Guest Professor at the universities of Bucharest, Murcia, Bydgoszcz, Sains Malaysia and Kaunas, and Guest Lecturer at Humboldt University, Berlin, Russian State University of Humanities, Moscow, and University of Malaya, Kuala Lumpur. He has conducted fieldwork in political and urban anthropology in Southeast Europe (Bulgaria, Romania), Southeast Asia (Malaysia, Singapore) and in the Mediterranean societies (Italy, Greece, Spain).

**Rozeta Gujejiani** holds a PhD in History and is Associate Professor at Ivane Javakhishvili Tbilisi State University, Georgia. She is Head of the Ethnology Department at St Andrew, University of the Patriarchate of Georgia and consultant at Tbilisi National Museum. She lectures at undergraduate, masters and doctoral levels. Her research interests are Georgian culture and historical ethnology, Svaneti traditional culture, anthropology of religion, traditional culture of Georgians of Turkey and contemporary ethnocultural and sociocultural processes.

**Arsen Hakobyan** holds a PhD in Cultural Anthropology (Institute of Archaeology and Ethnography, Yerevan, Armenia). He is research fellow at the Institute of Archaeology and Ethnography, National Academy of Sciences of Armenia and visiting lecturer at the Yerevan State University. He is presently participating in international projects such as the Academic Swiss Caucasus Net and DAAD. He teaches Ethnic, Religious and Linguistic Minorities and Religions in the Caucasus. His research interests are diasporas and refugee studies, political and ethnic violence, ethno-linguistic and ethno-religious minorities.

**Ketevan Khutsishvili** is Professor of Anthropology at Ivane Javakhishvili Tbilisi State University, Institute of Ethnology at the Faculty of Humanities, Georgia. She holds a PhD in Historical Sciences, with a specialization in Ethnology and Anthropology. She has conducted fieldwork in the Caucasus and the Anatolian peninsula. Her fields of interests are ethno-cultural processes in the Caucasus, religious issues, ethnic identity and relations, Internally Displaced People studies.

**Marcello Mollica** holds a PhD in Social Science (KUL, Leuven, Belgium) and a European Doctorate in Conflict Resolution (Deusto, Bilbao, Spain). He was pre-doc Marie Curie at Ulster University, UK, post-doc IUF Marie Curie at the University of Kent, UK, and is presently visiting staff member at the University of Fribourg, Switzerland and Rita Levi Montalcini Fellow at the University of Pisa, Italy, where he teaches Cultural Anthropology and Divided Societies and Conflict. His research interests are religious and political violence, ethno-religious minorities and political mobilization.

**Benedetta Panchetti** is a visiting researcher at the University of Fribourg, Switzerland and a fellow of the Catholic University Centre in Rome. She holds a PhD in Law, Market and Person at the Ca' Foscari University and the Fondazione Generale Studium Marcianum in Venice, Italy. She was a visiting PhD student at Saint Joseph University of Beirut, Lebanon, in 2014. Her main research interests are religious minorities, personal status laws, law and religion, interreligious marriages and religious conflicts.